THE ENCYCLOPEDIA OF
STARS & PLANETS

THE ENCYCLOPEDIA OF
STARS & PLANETS

A. RÜKL

IVY LEAF

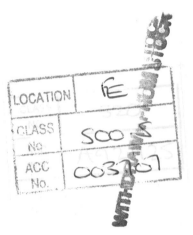
Translated by Olga and Ivan Kuthan
Graphic design and illustrations by A. Rükl
Designed and produced by Aventinum for
The Hamlyn Publishing Group Limited

Originally published in 1988 by
the Hamlyn Publishing Group Limited
under the title
The Hamlyn Encyclopedia of Stars and Planets

This edition published in 1992 by
Ivy Leaf
Michelin House
81 Fulham Road
London SW3 6RB

This edition produced exclusively for Bookmart Limited

ISBN 0 86363 027 8

Printed in Czechoslovakia
3/99/59/51-02

Contents

Introduction

Scattered throughout the immense expanse of the Universe are untold numbers of celestial objects. They are a vast distance from the Earth and therefore cannot, as a rule, be observed directly, but are only detectable by photographic means. Their variety and colour often evoke awe and wonder, as well as the strong emotions that we feel each time we are confronted by the beauty of nature.

The purpose of this illustrated atlas is to present the reader with a representative selection of the objects in the Solar System and the Universe of stars and galaxies — objects that are typical, important, of great interest, or of great beauty. One and the same object may completely change its appearance when observed in various regions of the electromagnetic spectrum. In this book, apart from a few exceptions, celestial objects are presented in their basic likeness — i. e. as they appear in visible light.

All the illustrations are drawn by hand, and they often represent a synthesis of several photographs of a particular object, made by various instruments and with various exposure times. The drawings are based on photographs made by large telescopes at the world's leading observatories, and by spaceprobes. This is probably the first publication where exact illustrations drawn by hand are used throughout in place of the usual photographs. In many instances the pictures have thus become more comprehensible, they are graphically all of a kind, and it has been possible to emphasize minute details. For scientific purposes, of course, nothing can replace an original photographic record.

The main body of the book consists of illustrations accompanied by a brief text. It is addressed to a wide range of amateur astronomers. For beginners who have no previous knowledge of astronomy there are short introductory and closing sections, and a glossary of astronomical terms. Suggestions for further reading are provided for those interested in learning more about the Universe and astronomy as a whole.

A large part of the book consists of maps of the planets and their satellites, star charts, and constellation charts, where the locations of the objects illustrated are marked. Readers will become familiar with the appearance and location of celestial objects, and also with some of the terms used in astronomy, which will help them in reading more specialized books. A number of subjects for amateur observation are also suggested, because nothing can be as valuable and satisfying as personal observation, even if only a small telescope is available for use.

There is a great difference, of course, between a picture representing a celestial object and what it looks like through an amateur's telescope. What makes the observed object of interest, however, is not only what we can see but also, to a great extent, what we know about it. It is that which transforms faintly luminous points of light and barely visible clouds into what they truly are — fascinating celestial objects of untold beauty and size with dramatic evolutionary histories, which raise thought-provoking questions. And it is the process of finding out, discovering and learning, that is the great adventure — an adventure that never ends.

The author himself would not have been able to prepare this book without the help of many experts, astronomers as well as illustrators, who provided him with invaluable advice and pictorial material. Without their friendly help he would have been unable to overcome the material and technical problems of drawing with an air-brush, which is indispensable for the exact and realistic depiction of celestial objects. The author is deeply indebted for their assistance to Dr. Merton E. Davies of Santa Monica, California, the leading specialist in the mapping of bodies in the Solar System; Dr. Robert McMillan and Gloria McMillan of Tucson, Arizona; Hugh D. Moore of Del Mar, California; Hermann Mucke, Director of the Vienna Planetarium, Austria; and Dr. Thomas W. Rackham of Jodrell Bank, England.

He is also indebted to Dr. Pavel Andrle and Ing. Pavel Příhoda for reading the manuscript and making valuable suggestions, and to Mrs. Helena Holovská, who gave the finishing touches to the manuscript. He also extends his thanks to Dr. Zdeněk Horský; the library of the Astronomical Institute of the Czechoslovak Academy of Sciences; and the library of the Museum of Czech Literature in Prague, whose kind cooperation made it possible to enhance the pictorial section with period illustrations from past centuries. Acknowledgements are also due to the editors of the Aventinum Publishing House, who prepared the book for publication, and last but not least, the author extends his thanks to his wife for her patience and support.

Objects in the Solar System

In the vast reaches of space that surround us, which objects are nearby and which are far away? What is the structure of the Universe and what is Earth's place in that structure? Even in the days when Man had no knowledge whatsoever of that realm, he was able to distinguish three types of celestial objects: the Sun, the Moon, and the stars. More systematic observation of the night sky led to the discovery of yet another type of object. Five bright stars were observed to move in a strange manner—compared with the fixed position of the other stars—as if they were wandering. The five were Mercury, Venus, Mars, Jupiter and Saturn. Later it was found out that deciphering the complex movements of these five wandering stars — planets — held the key to learning the Earth's true place in the Universe. The Earth is also a planet revolving round the Sun. Only recently in the history of astronomy has Man acquired a more or less complete picture of the Solar System. It consists of one star, nine planets, and a vast number of smaller (and even minute) objects. Only the Sun is self-luminous. All the other objects are cold and shine by the reflected light of the Sun.

The major part of the system's mass is concentrated in the Sun, which is a rich source of radiation as well as the light and heat necessary for life on Earth. It is difficult to imagine that the Sun is just an ordinary star, similar to the countless other faint stars that are barely visible in the heavens. The real nature of stars is concealed by their vast distances, which are so great that it takes their light, travelling at a speed of 300,000 kilometres per second, years, centuries, and even longer, to reach us. From the Sun, it takes light a mere 8.5 minutes to reach the Earth, 5.5 hours to reach the farthermost planet, Pluto, and 4.3 years to reach the nearest neighbouring star, Alpha Centauri. If we could fly to one of the nearest stars and looked from there back towards the Sun the situation would be reversed: from afar, the Sun would appear like a tiny star and our efforts to locate the Earth and the other planets would prove to be fruitless. To date (1990) the efforts of astronomers to prove the existence of planets near other stars (or suns) have been equally without success. Even though we believe that other suns have planets revolving around them (and proof of this will not be long in coming) we only have reliable details for one planetary system: our own home in the Universe.

The planets revolve around the Sun in orbits that are nearly circular ellipses, which are situated in almost the same plane. They are divided into two basic groups: terrestrial planets (from Mercury to Mars) and Jovian or major planets (from Jupiter to Neptune). The outermost planet, Pluto, does not fit into either of these groups: it is more like the large satellites of the major planets. The basic data on the planets are given in the table on p. 221.

The terrestrial planets have high densities, and predominantly consist of rocks, metals and minute quantities of volatile substances, surrounded by a meagre atmosphere. In spite of this basic resemblance, there are profound differences in the physical conditions on the surface of the terrestrial planets and the reason for this apparently is not just their distance from the source of energy — the Sun. The present natural environment on each planet is the result of lengthy action by internal and external forces. The more we learn about the planets, the more clearly we realize how fragile and sensitive the natural environment is on our planet, the Earth, and what a rare and precious thing life is in the inhospitable realm of the Universe.

The major planets have much greater masses and are larger than the terrestrial planets. Their mean density is close to the density of water and their chemical composition is more like that of the Sun than the Earth. They are gaseous giants, consisting predominantly of hydrogen and helium with small quantities of methane and other compounds, and they all have extensive atmospheres. The solid core, composed of rocky material, is relatively small. The major planets are surrounded by large families of satellites and complex systems of rings.

The table on pages 221—22 contains the basic information on the satellites of the various planets. Six of them have a diameter of more than 3,000 km. Among their number are some very exotic worlds, such as Jupiter's satellite, Io, with its extraordinarily violent volcanic activity and Saturn's largest satellite, Titan, with its nitrogen-methane seas. The small mean density of most of the satellites indicates the presence of a large amount of water in the form of ice. As in the case of our Moon, the rotation of the other satellites is captured, which means that one hemisphere of the satellite remains permanently turned towards its planet, the other hemisphere being permanently turned away from the planet.

The least massive inhabitants of the Solar System are comets, asteroids, and meteoric bodies. A closer look at these is presented on page 92. Of the lot, comets have always enjoyed extraordinary attention, particularly the brightest ones with long tails. The interest of scientists, however, is focused on the far less striking nuclei of comets, which may contain samples of unaltered material, remaining from the time when the Solar System was formed.

When and how did the Solar System come into being? Its cradle was a large cloud of interstellar dust and gas that collapsed due to its own gravitation and certain external forces. Gradually, it developed into a rotating disc, with the bulk of the mass concentrated in the centre. Further contraction of the central condensation then gave rise to the star known as the Sun. It attained its full brightness when the temperature and pressure in its interior reached the values needed to 'ignite' thermonuclear reactions within the core, which convert fuel — hydrogen — into helium. The planets, their satellites and other objects formed from the remaining parts of the proto-planetary disc through the gradual aggregation of dust and gaseous material. This took place 4.6 thousand million (4.6×10^9) years ago. The ensuing evolutionary phase was marked by countless collisions, and the bombardment of the surfaces of the planets and smaller bodies by the remaining material. This period of intense bombardment was accompanied by the formation of impact craters which exist to this day, for instance on Mercury, the Moon, and many other bodies.

Objects in Deep Space

ELECTROMAGNETIC RADIATION, above all in its visible range — light — is almost our only source of information about objects in the Deep Space. Light consists of a range of spectral colours and is characterized by its wavelength λ (lambda). This is given here in nanometres: 1 nm = 10^{-9} m = 1 thousand-millionth of a metre. The continuous spectrum of visible radiation (Fig. 1) extends from the violet ($\lambda \sim 300$ nm) through blue, yellow, orange to deep red ($\lambda \sim 700$ nm). Some objects do not emit a continuous spectrum but radiate only in certain, very narrowly limited, colours or spectral lines.

Our vision is not sufficiently sensitive to register shades of colour in most astronomical objects. Apart from a few exceptions, we see the distant Universe more or less in black and white. A far more objective and precise view is provided by pictures obtained through large telescopes or by modern, electronic methods of recording and processing images. For scientific purposes, the object under investigation is generally depicted separately in various colours—see, for example, the pictures of the Ring Nebula on page 179. The lovely colour pictures of nebulae, galaxies and other objects that we admire in popular books and magazines are intended mainly for the general public.

Equally important for a full knowledge of a celestial object is its invisible radiation. Besides light, the Earth's atmosphere allows only parts of the range of infrared and radio radiation to reach the surface of the Earth. Nowadays, however, celestial objects may be observed over the entire range of the electromagnetic spectrum by means of special instruments on artificial satellites. In addition to classical optical astronomy, the Universe is also studied by radio, infrared, ultraviolet, X-ray, and gamma-ray astronomy. The recordings made by invisible radiation detectors can then be processed as required to give pictures in arbitrary colours expressing, for instance, the distribution and intensity of radiation. An example of this is the 'radio picture' of the centre of the Galaxy on page 192.

STARS are very hot bodies of plasma, usually spheroidal in shape. Their masses are much greater than those of planets and they have their own thermonuclear sources of energy in their interiors. The Sun, which is an average star, is often used as a unit of measurement for comparing the diameter, mass, luminosity, and other characteristics of stars.

The stars appear in the sky as points of light of different brightness. This brightness is expressed in apparent stellar magnitudes (m). The faintest stars visible with the naked eye are about sixth magnitude ($+6.0^m$), while the brightest stars are approximately magnitude zero (0.0^m), and Sirius even has a magnitude of -1.4^m. To compare the luminosity of stars objectively, their apparent magnitudes are used to claculate their absolute magnitude (M), which is the magnitude they would have at a standard distance of 10 parsecs (32.6 light-years). For this calculation it is, of course, necessary to know the star's distance.

The distance of a star is determined most exactly by trigonometry by using its parallax, which is the angle between lines from the star to two fixed points of observation (for example, two opposite points on the Earth's orbit around the Sun). This method, however, fails at distances greater than about 300 light-years, because then the stellar parallaxes are immeasurably small. For this reason astronomy also uses the inverse method: if it is possible to determine the absolute stellar magnitude M, then the star's distance can be calculated from the difference between M and m (M—m). M can be determined, for instance, from the temperature-luminosity diagram in which the star is placed according to its spectral type (Fig. 2). Such indirectly derived distances cannot be precise, of course, and may differ from actual distances by as much as 30 per cent or more. There are, of course, also differences — often quite perturbing to the layman — between distances given for one and the same object by various sources. Nevertheless, the success in drawing a reasonably reliable picture of the relative positions of objects in space must be seen as a great triumph for astronomy.

Of key importance in learning more about the stars, their properties and evolution, is the temperature-luminosity diagram, which is closely linked to the classification of stars into various spectral types. Both these terms are of fundamental importance in astronomy and are explained in simplified form on page 10 (Fig. 2) and page 104.

Stars are formed by the gravitational concentration of clouds of interstellar dust and gas. A star begins to shine brightly following the 'ignition' of the hydrogen in its core

Fig. 1 —Continuous Spectrum

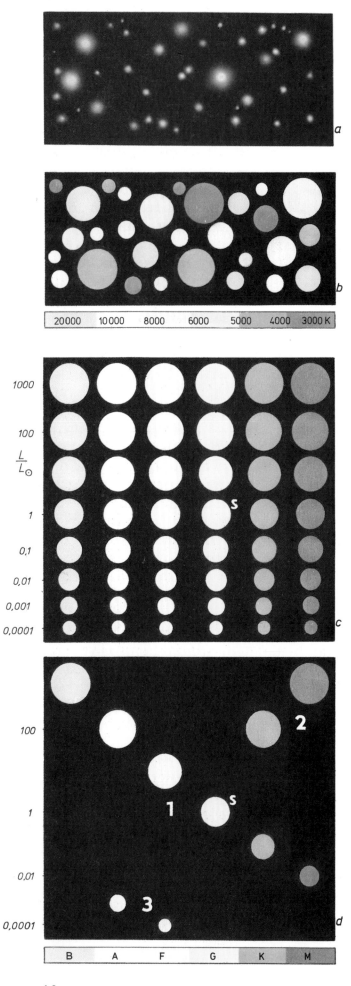

Fig. 2 — Temperature-Luminosity Diagram

To the terrestrial observer the stars in the sky appear to be of varying brightness (a). This is due not only to the differences in their luminosity but also to the marked differences in their distances. The colour of stars depends on their temperature: the hottest stars are generally blue and the coolest are red.

For the purpose of comparing the luminosity of stars, they are depicted as discs of various sizes (b); the greater the luminosity, the larger the disc. This indicates that a star with larger surface area is more luminous than a smaller, equally hot star. The temperature of stars is denoted by the colour of the disc. The spectrum of a star corresponds to its temperature; stars are accordingly divided into spectral classes. The illustration shows only the main classes B, A, F, G, K, and M; in actual fact stellar temperature diminshes continuously, with no sharply defined boundary between one spectral class and the next.

Let us now sort the chaotic mixture of stellar discs according to their size (luminosity, L) and colour (temperature), arranging discs of the same colour in one column. We shall sort all the stars in the sky in this manner, including the Sun (S), whose luminosity will be taken as the unit of measurement ($L_\odot = 1$); the surface temperature of the Sun is 6,000 K.

What will be the outcome of sorting the stars in this way? One might expect that with the enormous number of stars in the heavens there would be a complete range of disc sizes (luminosity) for every colour, as shown in the accompanying illustration (c). Such, however, is not the case! No matter how great a number of stars we sort, their discs always exhibit a tendency to cluster in certain parts of the diagram, leaving the remainder empty (d). The overwhelming majority of stars, including the Sun (S), fall along the so-called *Main Sequence* (1), running diagonally as a continuous band from the top left to bottom right. Other important groups of stars are the *giants and supergiants* (2) and the *white dwarfs* (3). These descriptions are truly apt, for a star must be a real 'giant', because while having the same temperature as a 'dwarf', a red giant, for example, may have a luminosity a million times greater.

Although the above method is very simplified, we have derived a form of the extremely important temperature-luminosity diagram (see also page 104).

(in a thermonuclear reaction). It then enters the Main Sequence in the temperature-luminosity diagram where it passes most of its life. The fate of stars is determined at the very beginning of their existence — by their initial mass. The more massive the star, the more rapidly the hydrogen is burned, the higher the temperature and luminosity, and the sooner the hydrogen fuel is exhausted, when the star leaves the Main Sequence to become a giant or supergiant for a time. The star changes over to a more complex nuclear reaction. The final stage of a star's evolution commences when the nuclear fuel is consumed. Radiation from the star's interior no longer provides any resistance, so gravitational contraction takes over, resulting in a rapid collapse, which is sometimes accompanied by an explosion and the scattering of part of the stellar material into space. Depending on the mass of the collapsing star, continued gravitational contraction may cause it to develop into a 'white dwarf' or a neutron star. In the case of an extremely massive star it turns into a 'black hole'. Some examples of such exotic objects with extremely high densities may be found in the pictorial section.

DOUBLE STARS AND MULTIPLE STARS are simply systems of stars that are orbiting around a common centre of gravity. If the components of a double star can be resolved with a telescope it is a *visual double*. If the components are so close to each other that they cannot be resolved with a telescope and the presence of a second component is only revealed in the spectrum, then it is a *spectroscopic double*. Particularly important are *eclipsing binaries* where the two components regularly eclipse one another; this is shown by periodic variations in brightness. From observations of double stars it is possible to determine the mass, dimensions and other characteristics of their components.

Double stars rank among the most popular objects for observation by amateurs. Particularly attractive are doubles in which the two components have strikingly different colours. The pictorial section of this book includes many examples of the apparent orbits of double stars in which the relative positions of the components change rapidly. The components of double stars and multiple stars are designated by the letters A, B, C, etc. in order of diminishing brightness. In the diagrams the brightest component, A, is considered to be fixed, and positions for selected dates are marked on the apparently elliptical orbit of component B.

VARIABLE STARS are ones whose brightness varies at regular or irregular intervals for physical reasons, i. e. because of changes in their diameters and surface temperatures. The most common are pulsating variables, of which there are several types. Best known, perhaps, are the *cepheids*, so called after the star δ Cephei, a typical example of this group. The cepheids have sometimes been called the lighthouses of the Universe. The period of their variation in brightness is related to their absolute stellar magnitude M and, as we know, the difference between M and m depends on the object's distance (see also page 206).

The signature of each variable star is its light-curve — the diagram showing the course of changes in its brightness in relation to time. In the pictorial section there are many examples of light-curves, particularly those of variable stars with striking variations in brightness that can be readily observed.

Extraordinarily marked changes in brightness are caused by explosive processes that occur in stars' final evolutionary stages. Such stars are called novae and supernovae according to the nature of the outburst.

STAR CLUSTERS are systems of stars of common origin and common evolution, bound together by the force of gravity. *Open clusters* contain several tens, hundreds or even thousands of stars, and their true diameter is generally between 5 and 50 light-years. There are more than 1,000 such clusters known near the plane of the Milky Way. They are relatively young objects. *Globular clusters* are concentrations of stars that are regular and spherical in shape. They contain hundreds of thousands, to millions of stars that are fewer in number towards the outside, but which show a marked increase in concentration towards the centre of the cluster. The true diameters of globular clusters are between 50 and 300 light-years. There are more than 120 such clusters known which together from part of the galactic halo. These are the oldest objects in the Galaxy. In the schematic view of the Galaxy (Fig. 3), they are depicted as orange dots.

NEBULAE are objects in interstellar space, and consist of gas (chiefly hydrogen) or dust. In the vicinity of hot stars that emit intense ultraviolet radiation, gaseous clouds are ionized and appear as glowing *emission nebulae* or H II regions. They radiate strongly, and chiefly in the red region of the spectrum. Dust clouds, on the other hand, scatter the light of nearby stars (even those that are cool) and we see them as *reflection nebulae*. Blue is often the predominant colour in the light scattered by the dust particles.

Nebulae generally contain both gas and dust, and therefore emission and reflection nebulae are often found together. The full beauty of their fantastic shapes and delicate coloration appear in their photographs.

They rank among the most beautiful objects in the Universe.

If the clouds of interstellar matter are farther away from stars they are not luminous. Dust clouds absorb the light of more distant stars and form *dark nebulae*, visible chiefly against the background of the rich fields of stars in the Milky Way.

Planetary nebulae are formed round certain types of stars nearing the end of their lives that shed the outer layers of their stellar atmosphere. Viewed through the telescope they generally look like a small disc that resembles a planet—hence the name. The central stars of these nebulae are extremely hot: 30,000 K to 150,000 K. They emit intense ultraviolet radiation, which in turn causes the extremely thin gas of the nebula to emit visible radiation.

THE GALAXY (also often known as the Milky Way) is a stellar system of which our Sun is just one member. We can imagine it as a huge stellar island. It occupies a spherical region of space but most of the stars are concentrated in a flattened disc that is thicker in the centre (Fig. 3). The central, bulging part of the disc has a diameter of approximately 15,000 light-years; the diameter of the whole disc is about 90,000

Fig. 3 —A diagrammatic representation of our Galaxy

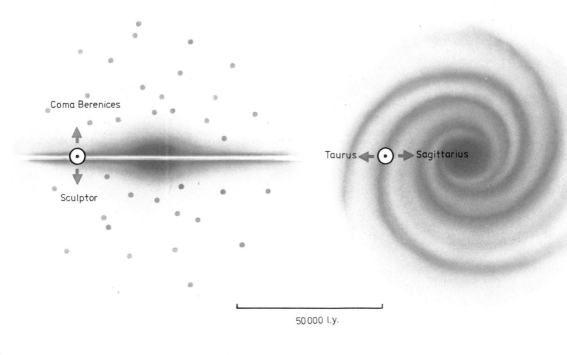

50 000 l.y.

light-years. The disc has a spiral structure. Near the plane of the disc (the galactic plane) clouds of interstellar dust and gas are concentrated. The Sun ($\odot$) is some 30,000 light-years from the centre of our Galaxy, which is located in the direction of the constellation of Sagittarius (the Archer).

As we look out in the galactic plane countless nearby stars appear to form the silvery belt of the Milky Way in the sky. Outside the plane of the Galaxy there are 'galactic windows' through which it is possible to get a glimpse of intergalactic space, and of the world of galaxies.

The disc is surrounded by a spherical halo, 100,000 light-years in diameter, consisting of old stars and globular clusters. Since 1973 it has been suspected that there is still another, external part of the Galaxy called the corona, at least 400,000 light-years in diameter (not shown in Fig. 3). The corona is very thin and as yet we know nothing about its composition. It is detected by its gravitational effect on the rotation of the Galaxy. Including the corona, the Galaxy probably has a mass of more than one million million (10^{12}) Suns.

STELLAR SYSTEMS known as *galaxies* are the basic building blocks of the Universe. Some of them resemble our Galaxy, others differ markedly in mass as well as structure. Galaxies are divided according to their appearance into the following types: elliptical galaxies (E), spiral galaxies (S), and barred spirals (SB) (Fig. 4). Elliptical galaxies are shaped like ellipsoids without distinct boundaries. Spiral galaxies are divided into sub-types a, b, c, according to the openness of the arms and the diminishing size of the nucleus. In a barred spiral, the spiral arms begin at opposite ends of a flattened, rectangular central bar. Types S0 and SB0 possess characteristics of both elliptical and spiral galaxies but without a developed spiral structure. Galaxies of irregular shape are designated by the letters Irr. Besides the foregoing, which is Hubble's classification, other, more detailed classifications of galaxies are also used.

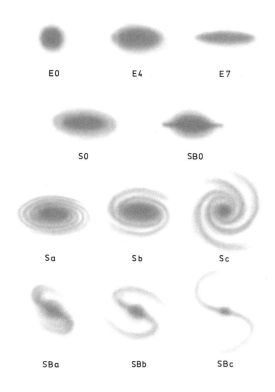

Fig. 4 — Hubble's Classification of Galaxies

Only the brightest galaxies can be observed with small telescopes, and then generally only as vague hazy clouds. Large telescopes, however, bring these fascinating objects close enough so that, at least in the nearest ones, we are able to distinguish individual stars, star clusters and nebulae. In colour photographs, the spiral arms are a bluish colour due to the radiation emitted by the young hot stars formed in the arms. The yellow to red colour of the central parts of galaxies testifies to the presence of older stars.

Galaxies congregate into other systems of various sizes: *groups* numbering up to several tens of members, or *clusters* with hundreds or thousands of members. There are also even higher systems, known as *superclusters*. Our Galaxy is a member of the so-called Local Group which contains about 25 galaxies.

We are part of an expanding Universe. The distances between galaxies are continually increasing—the greater the distance, the faster the rate. This fact is used to determine the distances of galaxies.

Astronomical maps

MAPS OF OBJECTS IN THE SOLAR SYSTEM are nowadays primarily derived from photographs made by space probes. Some of the planets and their satellites have, as yet, only been partially mapped. Apart from the Earth, the most completely mapped objects to date are the Moon and Mars. The coordinate systems on planets and satellites are similar to that used on Earth: from observations of the object's rotation the locations of the equator and of the poles are determined, thus defining the system of parallels of latitude and meridians of longitude, one of the latter being selected as the prime meridian. For purposes of mapping, the surface of a smooth reference sphere is generally substituted for the irregular surface of the object and this reference sphere is then laid out on the plane surface of a map by standard cartographic methods. This naturally results in distortion of the shapes or of the relative dimensions of the formations depicted. Maps of the Moon intended for the terrestrial observer, where the Moon is depicted as it is seen from the Earth, are a special case. Here, the marginal parts of the lunar disc are greatly distorted and circular craters appear as narrow ellipses.

The nomenclature used on the maps of planets and satellites dates its development from the 17th century. Until the beginning of the 20th century it was common practice for every cartographer to name the mapped formations as he wished. Since the 1930s, the final authority in all matters pertaining to the mapping of objects in the Solar System is the International Astronomical Union (IAU), which has already accepted more than 3,500 names on 20 planetary and satellite bodies. It can be expected that by the end of the 20th century this number will have greatly increased. Apart from proper names (of persons, mythological beings, and the like) the nomenclature of surface formations is consistently taken from Latin (see page 225).

The pictorial section of this book also includes schematic maps of all the Solar System bodies that have been mapped to date. They show the main characteristic surface formations, together with their names. In all the maps North is at the top.

The STAR CHARTS in this book are of two kinds. Six general location charts, marked A to F, depict the whole celestial sphere, covering both northern and southern skies. Also marked on these charts are the boundaries of all 88 constellations and their international Latin names. All the star charts are drawn with the system of coordinates valid for epoch 2000.0 (see the glossary of terms on page 224). The coordinate grids marked on the charts are useful both for orientation and for giving an idea of true angular dimensions in the sky. The hour-circles ('celestial meridians'), drawn here at intervals of 1 hour in right ascension, are analogous to geographical meridians of longitude. The circles of declination, drawn at 10° intervals in declination, are analogous to geographical parallels of latitude.

Following each of the general charts A—F is a series of more detailed constellation charts where the positions of the celestial objects illustrated are indicated. The legend to these charts appears on page 106. Bright stars are designated by either their traditional proper names or by letters of the Greek alphabet (introduced by Bayer in 1603). The Greek letter is given with the genitive of the Latin name of the constellation concerned, e. g. α Lyrae. Brighter stars are also commonly designated by Flamsteed numbers, e. g. 61 Cygni. There are also other systems for the designation of stars, mainly according to their numbers in various catalogues. Variable stars are generally designated by capital Roman letters, e. g. VV Cephei.

Bright star clusters, nebulae, and galaxies that can be seen with small telescopes are frequently known, particularly among amateurs, by the numbers under which they are listed in Messier's catalogue. In 1784 the French astronomer Messier made a catalogue of 104 objects, to which several were added later. They are designated by the letter M followed by the number under which the object is listed in the catalogue, e. g. M 42 — the Orion Nebula. Some of the best-known and most beautiful clusters, nebulae and galaxies have proper names of their own (Trifid, Sombrero, Lagoon, and the like). Otherwise these objects are generally designated by the numbers under which they are listed in the New General Catalogue of Nebulae and Clusters of Stars (NGC, 1888) or its supplement, the Index Catalogue (IC). The star charts in this book serve to give an indication of the positions of the objects illustrated and for locating the brightest ones. Amateur astronomers who want to locate fainter objects with their telescopes require a more detailed star atlas.

Pictorial section

Locating the required part of the pictorial section is assisted by the astronomical symbols and abbreviations given in the margin on the left-hand pages. A key to the symbols is given below. The abbreviations of the names of constellations are explained on page 215.

The top of each two-page spread in the pictorial section carries a supplementary period illustration. The colour depictions of the constellation figures on pages 106 to 202 are reproduced from an astronomical codex which probably originated in Italy about the 14th century and which is housed in the library of the Czech Museum of Literature at Strahov in Prague. Some of the colour illustrations are from Cellarius's astronomical atlas *Harmonia macrocosmica* (Brussels, 1763). The majority of the period engravings are from the writings of Peter Apianus, dating from the first half of the 16th century.

Classic drawings of celestial objects from the 17th to 19th century, and illustrations from astronomical literature that are more than a hundred years old document the beginnings of visual observation with telescopes which opened the way to our present knowledge of the Universe.

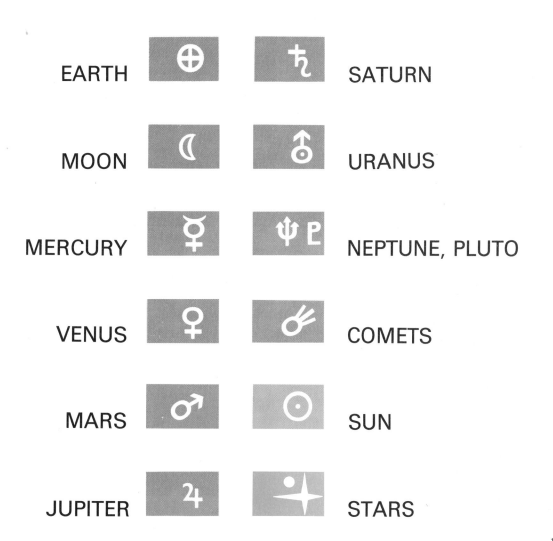

EARTH	⊕	♄ SATURN
MOON	☾	⛢ URANUS
MERCURY	☿	♆ ♇ NEPTUNE, PLUTO
VENUS	♀	☄ COMETS
MARS	♂	☉ SUN
JUPITER	♃	✦ STARS

Earth

The Earth revolves around the Sun. Cellarius, *Harmonia macrocosmica*, 1763.

We look at the planet Earth from outer space and admire its beauty. Beneath the bluish haze of the atmosphere, in between lacy white clouds, we observe the vast blue expanse of the world's oceans and the brownish hues of the continents with dark green areas covered with vegetation. In a thin layer near the surface of the Earth, water, the atmosphere and the warming rays of the Sun together produce suitable conditions for the development and maintenance of life. Our planet is the only place in the Universe where life is known to exist. Looking at the Earth from afar, we realize how fragile and vulnerable is this home of ours, surrounded by the vast, inhospitable, lifeless environment of outer space. Even though we may gaze with awe and delight at the much larger actors on the infinitely varied stage of the Universe, we always turn back to the gem called Earth with increasing wonder and admiration.

The planet Earth, like every celestial body, is an organic part of the surrounding Universe,

bound to it by gravitational and magnetic fields, energy exchange, and other ties. This should be kept in mind when we observe distant celestial objects; our eyes show us only surface relationships.

The bottom picture shows the Earth's magnetosphere, the region surrounding the planet in which the Earth's magnetic field is dominant. This region is distorted into the shape of an elongated teardrop by the solar wind of charged particles coming from the Sun (yellow arrows from the left). The solar wind meets the Earth's magnetic field in a shock wave (1); beyond this is the boundary of the magnetic field, known as the magnetopause (2). The belts of energetic radiation (3), regions of danger for the crews of space ships, are coloured red. Periods of increased solar activity (p. 94) are often accompanied by changes in the magnetosphere, giving rise to such phenomena as magnetic storms and aurorae.

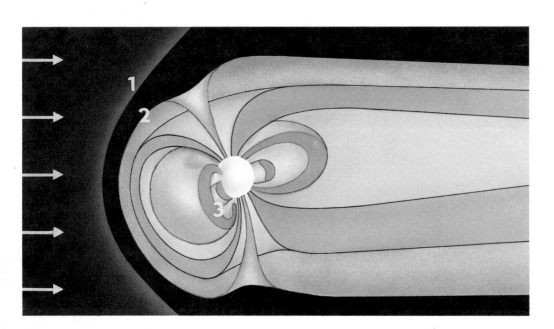

The Moon

Viewed from the Earth

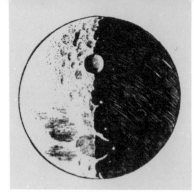

One of the first telescopic observations of the Moon. G. Galilei, 1610.

Earth's eternal companion, the Moon, is the brightest, most striking, and most easily observed celestial object after the Sun. Even with the unaided eye we can observe the continual changes in its appearance; the phases that are displayed by the Moon over a period of 29.5 days — from New Moon through first quarter, Full Moon and last quarter to the next New Moon, when the Moon disappears in the Sun's glow. At the same time we will notice that the dark areas on the lunar disc—called seas (maria in Latin)—remain practically in the same place the whole time. The Moon always presents the same face to the Earth, having captured rotation—the Moon rotates on its axis in exactly the same period as it revolves round the Earth. This agreement is not accidental but is the result of mutual gravitational effects in the Earth-Moon system. Most of the satellites of the planets in the Solar System behave in a similar manner.

On the opposite page is a small general map of the near side of the Moon. It contains the names of the main lunar seas and certain large craters and mountain ranges which are useful for initial orientation. Note also the officially approved marking of the points of the compass and the way in which positions on the Moon are determined with the aid of *selenographic coordinates*. These are the same as on the Earth: selenographic latitude is analogous to geographic latitude and selenographic longitude is analogous to geographic longitude.

The near side of the Moon is divided into four equal parts — quadrants, more detailed maps of which may be found on pages 23-29. The Moon's surface is depicted on the map as if illuminated by the Sun from the east (from the right in the pictures) and as if the Sun were just above the horizon at every point on the Moon. In reality, of course, this can never be the case. The Sun illuminates only part of the lunar surface at this low angle (depending on the phase of the Moon) and the lunar surface must be observed accordingly.

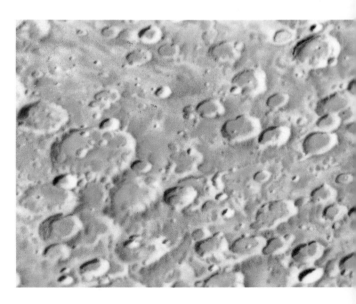

Crater fields near the southeastern limb of the Moon, two days after Full Moon. The terminator — the dividing line between day and night on the Moon — is on the right-hand limb. Near the terminator, where the Sun is setting, the shadows are long and the surface formations stand out distinctly. Farther away from the terminator (at left) shadows disappear and craters and other forms of relief fade into the background.

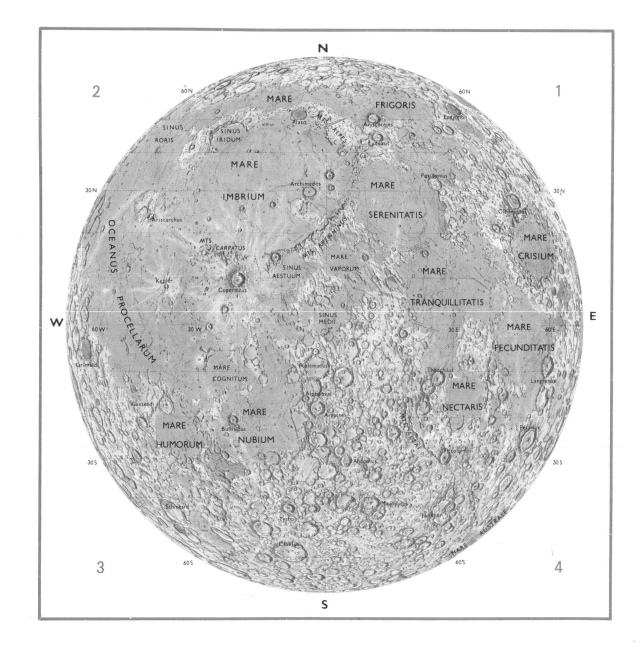

N

60 N   60 N

MARE   FRIGORIS
SINUS   Aristoteles   Endymion
RORIS   SINUS   Plato   MTS ALPES
           IRIDUM   Eudoxus
30 N   MARE   Posidonius   Cleomedes   30 N
           IMBRIUM   Archimedes   MARE
                                  SERENITATIS   MARE
Aristarchus   CRISIUM
           MTS   MTS APENNINUS
           CARPATUS   MARE   MARE
OCEANUS   Kepler   SINUS   VAPORUM   TRANQUILLITATIS
           Copernicus AESTUUM

W   60 W   30 W   SINUS   30 E   E
PROCELLARUM   MEDII   MARE
                                 0°   FECUNDITATIS   60 E
Grimaldi   Ptolemaeus   Theophilus
           MARE   Langrenus
           COGNITUM   Alphonsus   MARE
Gassendi   Arzachel   NECTARIS
           MARE   Bullialdus   Petavius
           HUMORUM   MARE   Abulfeda   MTS ALTAI
30 S   NUBIUM   Piccolomini   30 S
           Schickard   Maurolycus
                       Tycho   Janssen   MARE AUSTRALE
                       Clavius
60 S   60 S

S

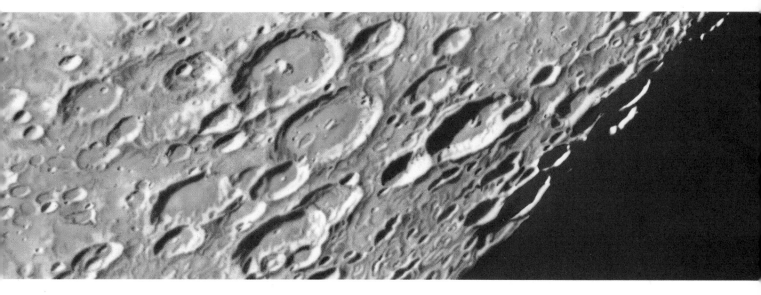

The Moon

Surface formations

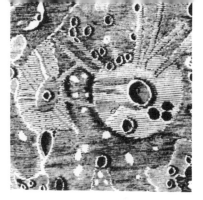

Detail from a map of the Moon.
Cherubin d'Orleans,
Dioptrique oculairé, 1671.

Two types of surface can be readily distinguished on the Moon, even without a telescope — the light-coloured 'continents' and the dark-coloured 'seas'. A closer look reveals that the 'continents' are mountainous in character and pockmarked with an enormous number of craters, ranging from small holes to large ring mountains and walled plains 100—300 km in diameter. The 'seas', on the other hand, are like flat plains with local undulations in the form of low mountain ranges and solidified lava flows. The light and dark hues on the surface of the Moon are caused primarily by the different chemical compositions of the continental rocks and of mare material (which is mostly basalt), as revealed by analyses of the rock samples brought back to Earth from the Moon.

The Moon acquired most of its surface markings from the impacts of countless meteoritic bodies. On the near side of the Moon these left behind over 300,000 craters with diameters of more than 1 km.

The black, contrasting shadows may readily give rise to the mistaken impression that the craters are deep holes with steep walls. In reality they are relatively shallow formations with gentle slopes. This is also shown by the profile of the crater Eratosthenes (bottom). The depth of this crater is merely a sixteenth of its diameter.

A section through the crater Eratosthenes.

The Sun rises above the crater Eratosthenes at the southwestern tip of the lunar Apennines. The inside of the crater is still immersed in shadow.

Sixteen hours after the Sun has risen the central peak of the crater is illuminated. The crater measures 58 km in diameter and is 3,570 metres deep.

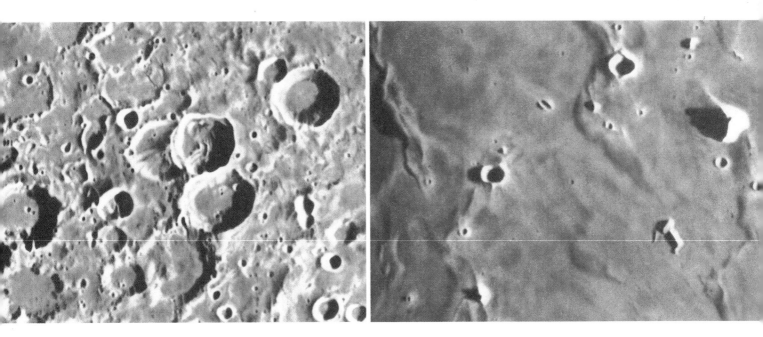

Close-up of a lunar 'continent'. This field of craters is located about 200 km west of the Altai Scarp (4th quadrant, map on p. 29). The prominent crater Geber (top right) measures 46 km in diameter and is 3,510 metres deep.

Detail of the Moon's Mare Imbrium and Mt Piton (at right), 2,250 metres high. The Sun is very low, close to the horizon, so even small mare ridges, resembling prominent veins and raised only several tens of metres above the surrounding surface, may be observed.

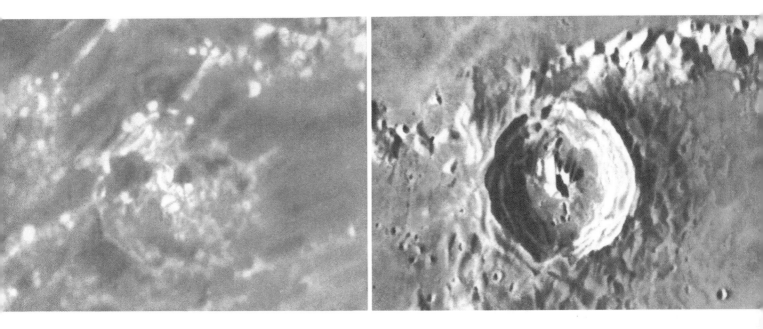

At the period of Full Moon, the Sun is high above Eratosthenes, the shadows have vanished and the huge crater is practically unrecognizable.

One and a half days before the Sun sets. The entire floor of the crater is still illuminated, but the terraces on the western wall are plunging into shadow.

The Moon

Map of the near side of the Moon — 1st quadrant

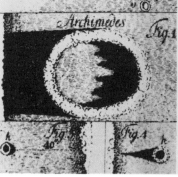

The Crater Archimedes.
J. H. Schröter,
Selenotopographische Fragmente, 1791

Conspicuous in the northeastern quadrant are the large 'seas', Mare Serenitatits, Mare Tranquillitatis and the oval Mare Crisium, easily visible even without a telescope.

East of the Alps there are two large mountain rings: Aristoteles (diameter 87 km) and Eudoxus (67 km).

The craters Hercules (67 km) and Atlas (87 km) on the eastern edge of Mare Frigoris make a striking pair. North of these is the large crater Endymion (125 km) with a huge wall and a dark, flat floor, covered with lava.

A typical walled plain, Posidonius (diameter 100 km, height of wall 2,300 m) is located on the northeastern edge of Mare Serenitatis. The region of the small crater Cauchy in Mare Tranquillitatis is interesting to observe with a telescope. Here one can see long rilles and faults (Rupes Cauchy), easily visible near the terminator (where the Sun rises or sets).

On the limb of the Moon's near side there are three small seas that partly extend onto the far side: Mare Humboldtianum, Mare Marginis and Mare Smythii. The visibility of marginal details is influenced by the Moon's librations, or the apparent oscillation of the Moon's disc relative to the Earth. These librations make it possible to see parts of the far side beyond the 90° meridians.

The black triangles on the map mark the places where the American lunar probes Ranger (R), Surveyor (S), Apollo (A) and the Soviet probe Luna (L) landed. Mare Tranquillitatis is where Man, represented by Neil Armstrong and Edwin Aldrin of the Apollo 11 mission, first set foot on the Moon on 20 July 1969. Round longitude 60° E is where the probes Luna 16, 20 and 24 landed to take rock samples from the Moon's surface (in the years 1970—1976). Near the southeastern edge of Mare Serenitatis is where the last Apollo mission (A 17) landed on 11 December 1972, and farther north, in the crater Le Monnier, is where the mobile laboratory Lunokhod 2, transported to the Moon on 15 January 1973 by the Luna 21 probe, carried out its automatic exploration of the surface.

The lunar Alps (Montes Alpes) on the northeastern edge of Mare Imbrium reach heights of 1,800 to 2,400 m. The highest peak is 3,600 m above the level of this waterless 'sea'. The mountain range is divided by a 130-km-long valley (Vallis Alpes). The long, pointed shadows of the mountains are caused by the low altitude of the rising Sun. In reality the slopes of the lunar mountains are not at all steep.

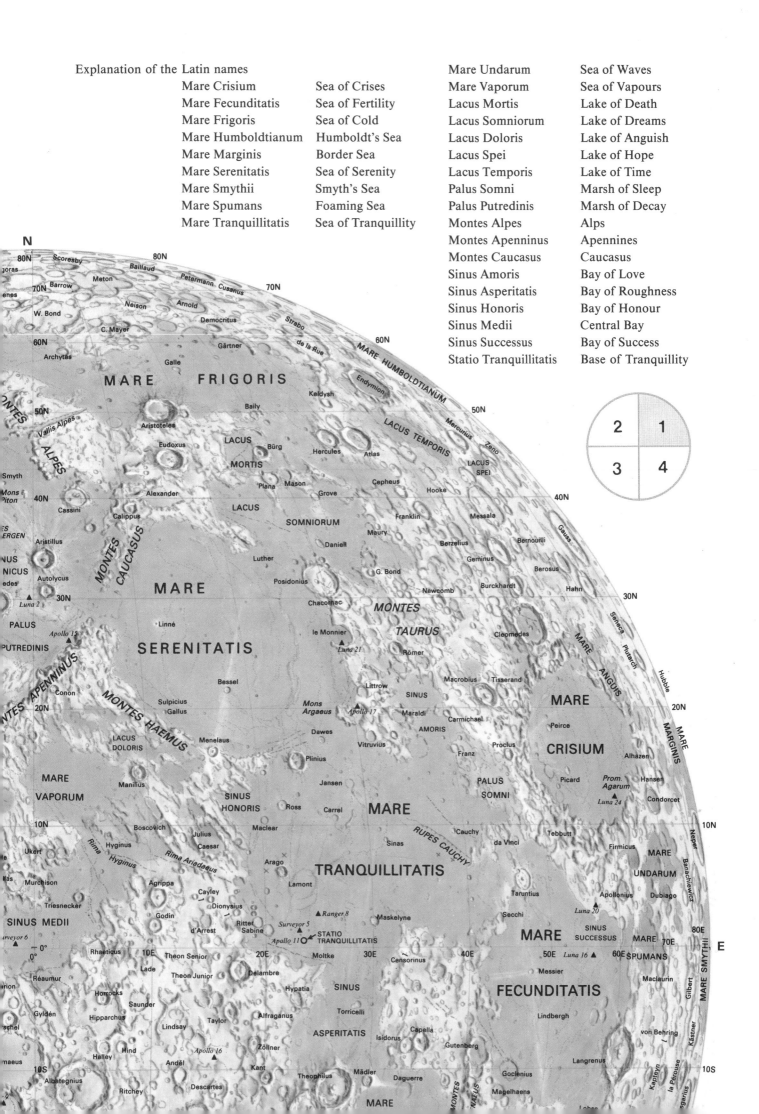

Explanation of the Latin names

Mare Crisium	Sea of Crises
Mare Fecunditatis	Sea of Fertility
Mare Frigoris	Sea of Cold
Mare Humboldtianum	Humboldt's Sea
Mare Marginis	Border Sea
Mare Serenitatis	Sea of Serenity
Mare Smythii	Smyth's Sea
Mare Spumans	Foaming Sea
Mare Tranquillitatis	Sea of Tranquillity
Mare Undarum	Sea of Waves
Mare Vaporum	Sea of Vapours
Lacus Mortis	Lake of Death
Lacus Somniorum	Lake of Dreams
Lacus Doloris	Lake of Anguish
Lacus Spei	Lake of Hope
Lacus Temporis	Lake of Time
Palus Somni	Marsh of Sleep
Palus Putredinis	Marsh of Decay
Montes Alpes	Alps
Montes Apenninus	Apennines
Montes Caucasus	Caucasus
Sinus Amoris	Bay of Love
Sinus Asperitatis	Bay of Roughness
Sinus Honoris	Bay of Honour
Sinus Medii	Central Bay
Sinus Successus	Bay of Success
Statio Tranquillitatis	Base of Tranquillity

The Moon

Map of the near side of the Moon — 2nd quadrant

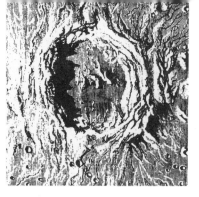

The Crater Copernicus.
Drawing by James Nasmyth,
2nd half of the 19th century.

The period of intense bombardment of the Moon ended about four thousand million years ago with several huge impacts that formed the basins of the future seas. This was followed by a period of vast flows of lava that filled the mare basins and disrupted their surrounding ramparts. That is also how Mare Imbrium was formed some three and a half thousand million years ago—at one time it was a gigantic crater 1,250 km in diameter. What is left are the remnants of the wall in the form of a chain of mountain ranges rimming the basin: the Alps, the Caucasus, the Apennines and the Carpathians. Sinus Iridum is another remnant of what was once a large crater, measuring 260 km in diameter, which is now partly filled with lava.

Dark mare basalts likewise fill the floor of the walled plain Plato (diameter 100 km) and the crater Archimedes (diameter 83 km, depth 2,150 m).

At full Moon the bright systems of rays that spread outwards from the craters Copernicus, Kepler and Aristarchus are clearly visible on the surface of Mare Imbrium and the neighbouring Oceanus Procellarum. These rays consist of material ejected during the formation of these craters. Near Aristarchus (diameter 45 km) lies the sinuous valley Vallis Schröteri, 200 km long and about 1,000 m deep; it is easily visible even with a small telescope.

The crosses (x) on the map mark what are called lunar domes — formations shaped like low rounded mounds with a circular outline 10 — 20 km in diameter, but only several hundred metres high. They are visible only close to the terminator with a larger telescope and are to be found chiefly near longitude 30° W, west of the crater Copernicus.

Between the craters Archimedes and Autolycus is the spot where Earth's first messenger to reach the Moon — the Soviet probe Luna 2 — landed on 13th September 1959. The western shore of Oceanus Procellarum is the site of the first successful soft landing on the Moon (Luna 9, 3 February 1966). The foot of the lunar Apennines is where the Apollo 15 mission, the first to be equipped with a lunar rover, set down (30 July 1971). South of Sinus Iridum is where the first mobile laboratory, Lunokhod 1 (transported there by the Luna 17 craft on 17th November 1970) automatically explored the surface.

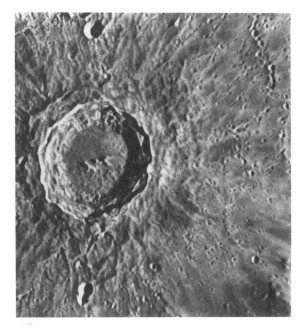

The ring-mountain forming the crater Copernicus is perhaps the best known such formation on the Moon. It measures 93 km in diameter and is up to 3,760 m deep. The walls are terraced and the floor relatively flat with a group of central peaks up to 1,200 m high. The ridge of the ramparts rises 900 m above the surrounding landscape. In other words, the floor is below the level of the surrounding terrain, and this is true of all lunar craters. Copernicus was probably formed by an impact one thousand million years ago.

Explanation of the Latin names

Mare Frigoris	Sea of Cold
Mare Imbrium	Sea of Rains
Mare Insularum	Sea of Islands
Oceanus Procellarum	Ocean of Storms
Sinus Aestuum	Bay of Billows
Sinus Iridum	Bay of Rainbows
Sinus Medii	Central Bay
Sinus Roris	Bay of Dew
Sinus Lunicus	Lunik Bay
Palus Putredinis	Bay of Putrefaction
Montes Alpes	Alps
Montes Apenninus	Apennines
Montes Carpatus	Carpathians
Montes Jura	Jura Mountains
Montes Spitzbergen	Spitzbergen Mountains

The Moon

Map of the near side of the Moon — 3rd quadrant

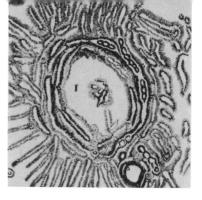

The Crater Bullialdus.
Detail from a map of the Moon
by J. Schmidt, 1878.

The large Oceanus Procellarum extends into the southwestern quadrant and links up with the dark areas of Mare Cognitum, Mare Nubium and the circular basin Mare Humorum.

On the edge of the last sea named lies the lovely walled plain of Gassendi (diameter 110 km, depth 1,860 m), which together with the smaller crater on the northern rampart resembles a ring set with a precious stone. A distinctive feature in Mare Nubium is the crater Bullialdus (59 km/3,510 m) and on the eastern edge of this sea the best known of the lunar scarps — Rupes Recta — can be seen. When the Sun is just above the horizon this scarp casts a striking shadow — a straight black line visible even with a small telescope. Its length is 96 km, the height is 240 to 300 m, and the gradient of the slope is about 7° (1 in 9). In other words it is not a steep slope as was once believed.

The formations Ptolemaeus, Alphonsus (118 km/2,730 m) and Arzachel (97 km/3,610 m) are very distinctive and useful for location. The whole southern hemisphere of the near side of the Moon is dominated by the crater Tycho (85 km/4,850 m), the centre of the largest system of bright rays which extend to distances of thousands of kilometres. It is a relatively young formation, formed by an impact about 300 million years ago.

Clavius (225 km), Schickard (227 km) and, on the southwestern limb, Bailly (303 km), are three of the largest walled plains on the Moon. Adjoining Schickard is the remarkable crater Wargentin (84 km) filled almost to the rim with lava.

The name Mare Cognitum (Known Sea) is a reminder of the first detailed photographs of the lunar surface (with information about features down to a size of 50 cm) transmitted by the TV cameras on the Ranger 7 probe, which landed here on 31st July 1964. Also located in this quadrant are the landing sites of the first (S 1) and last (S 7) probes of the Surveyor programme, which carried out detailed examinations of the properties of the lunar surface in 1966—1969 prior to Man's first landing on the Moon.

The crater Ptolemaeus is a typical example of the walled plains on the Moon. It is 153 km in diameter and the height of the rim is up to 2,400 m above the level of the relatively flat floor, filled with dark 'mare' material. The floor is not really flat, of course, but has the same curvature as the general lunar surface. To an observer standing in the centre of Ptolemaeus practically the whole of the wall would thus be hidden from view below the horizon, and he would hardly have any idea that he was standing inside a crater.

OCEANUS PROCELLARUM

Cardanus
Galilaei
Marius
Milichius
Copernicus
Eratosthenes
SINUS AESTUUM
VAPO

10N
Kepler
Hortensius
Fauth
Stadius
Bode
Ukert
10N

Luna 9 ▲
Reiner
Maestlin
Encke
Kunowsky
Reinhold
MARE INSULARUM
Gambart
Pellas
Murchison
Schröter
Triesn

Cavalerius
Hevelius
Hedin
Olbers

Damoiseau

Riccioli
Grimaldi

W 80W 70W 60W 50W 40W 30W 20W 10W

Surveyor 1 ▲
Flamsteed
Lansberg
Surveyor 3
Apollo 12 ▲
Apollo 14 ▲
Turner
Mösting
Mösting A
Réaumur
SINUS MED
Surveyor 6 ▲
0°
0°

Flammarion
Lalande
Fra Mauro
Herschel
Gyldén

Euclides
MONTES RIPHAEUS
MARE
Bonpland
Parry
Palisa
Ptolemaeus

10S
Sirsalis
Hansteen
Letronne
Billy
Kuiper
Ranger 7 ▲
Guericke
COGNITUM
Davy
Ranger 9 ▲
Albate
10S

Rocca
LACUS AUTUMNI
Darney
Alphonsus

Crüger
Fontana
Gassendi
Zupus
Opelt
Lubiniezky
MARE
Lassell
Alpetragius
Arzachel

MONTES ROOK
Darwin
(MARE ORIENTALE)
MONTES CORDILLERA

Agatharchiedes
Prom. Taenarium
Bullialdus
Nicollet
Birt
RUPES RECTA
Thebit
la Caille

20S
Mersenius
MARE HUMORUM
König
NUBIUM
Purbach
We
20S

Henry
Liebig
Hippalus
Kies
Regiomontanus

Byrgius
Cavendish
Prom. Kelvin
Campanus
Mercator
Hesiodus
Deslandres

Vieta
Doppelmayer
Pitatus
Hell
Walter

30S
Fourier
Vitello
PALUS EPIDEMIARUM
Wurzelbauer
Gauricus
Ball
Lexell
30S

Ramsden
Capuanus
Cichus
Heinsius
Sasserides
Orontius
Miller

LACUS EXCELLENTIAE
LACUS TIMORIS
Surveyor 7 ▲
Nasireddin

Lacroix
Hainzel
Wilhelm
Pictet
Saussure

40S
Drebbel
Mee
Tycho
40S

Lagrange
Piazzi
Longomontanus
Maginus

Vallis Bouvard
Baade
Schickard
Wilhelm

50S
Inghirami
Wargentin
Phocylides
Schiller
Bayer
Rost
Porter
Deluc
50S

Pingré
Segner
Clavius

60S
Zucchius
Bettinus
Kircher
Scheiner
Blancanus
Cysatus
Zac
60S

Bailly
Wilson
Klaproth
Casatus
Moretus
Curtius

70S
70S

80S
80S

S

Explanation of Latin names

Mare Cognitum	Known Sea
Mare Humorum	Sea of Moisture
Mare Insularum	Sea of Islands
Mare Nubium	Sea of Clouds
Mare Orientale	Eastern Sea
Lacus Excellentiae	Lake of Excellence
Lacus Timoris	Lake of Fear
Oceanus Procellarum	Ocean of Storms
Palus Epidemiarum	Marsh of Epidemics
Montes Cordillera	Cordilleras
Montes Riphaeus	Riphaean Mountains
Rupes Recta	Straight Wall

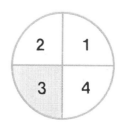

27

The Moon

Map of the near side of the Moon — 4th quadrant

Detail from a map of the Moon by Riccioli. Cellarius, 1763.

The largest cratered areas on the near side of the Moon are located in this southeastern quadrant. The lunar surface here is literally saturated with craters; in many places we can see how younger craters encroach and cover the older formations. A detailed picture of part of this crater-filled region is shown on p. 19.

The small, circular Mare Nectaris fills the central part of the large basin formed here by a great impact more than 4 thousand million years ago. The Altai Scarp — Rupes Altai — is a remnant of the outer wall of this basin. The formation of the lunar basins was accompanied by the formation of whole systems of faults, clefts and valleys, which fanned out like rays in all directions from the centre of the basin. The crater chain Vallis Rheita, pointing towards Mare Nectaris, is apparently of such an origin. Much better preserved is the system of faults around the basin of Mare Orientale, which lies on the western limb between the near and far sides of the Moon (see the map folloving overleaf).

The craters Theophilus, Cyrillus and Catharina form a striking trio. Theophilus boasts impressive dimensions: it is 100 km in diameter and 4,400 m deep; the central mountain chain is up to 2,000 m high and the ridge rises 1,200 m above the surrounding landscape. Equally striking are the large craters Langrenus (diameter 132 km) and Petavius (177 km) with extremely rugged walls.

An interesting detail is the pair of small craters named Messier in Mare Fecunditatis. From the more westerly of the two, designated Messier A, two narrow bright rays extend westward.

On the southeastern limb of the Moon one can see part of Mare Australe, which extends onto the far side of the Moon: it is nearly circular, with a diameter of approximately 900 km. Closer to the equator, on the limb of the Moon, is the small Mare Smythii, which likewise extends onto the far side.

The region of the crater Descartes, approximately 300 km west of Theophilus, is where the Apollo 16 mission landed on 21st April 1972.

Lunar rilles and clefts near the craters Triesnecker (large crater at bottom) and Hyginus (small crater in the centre of the upper rille). Under oblique illumination close to the terminator these formations, several tens of kilometres long, resemble bottomless canyons and abysses. In actual fact they are very shallow valleys only hundreds of metres deep, with rounded edges and slopes that are not at all steep.

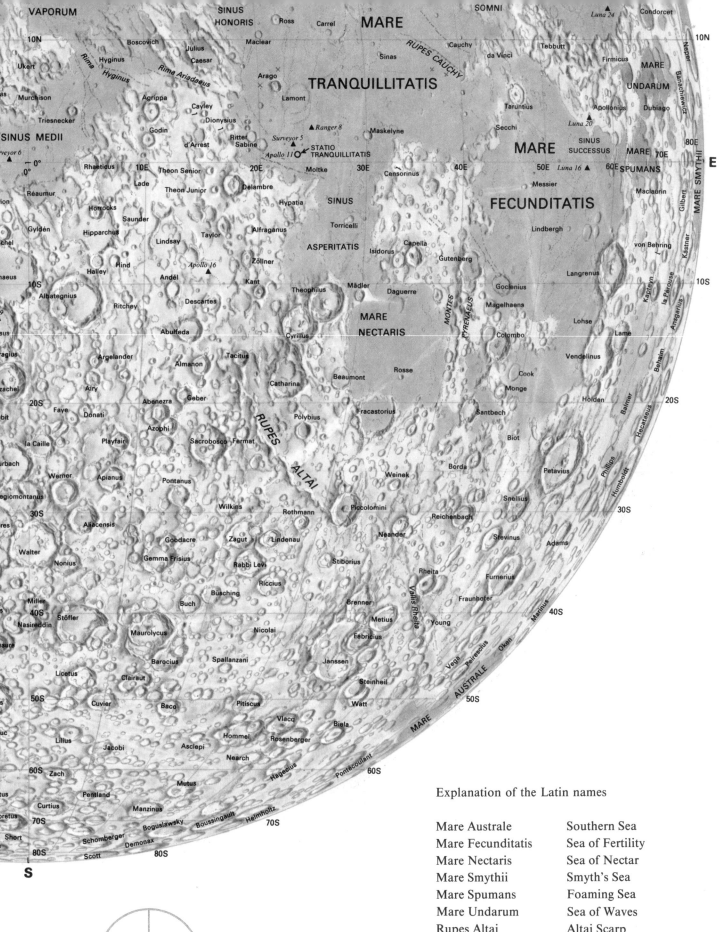

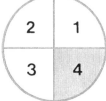

The Moon

General map of the whole Moon

Detail from a map
of the Moon by Riccioli.
Cellarius, 1763.

In the years 1959—1967 almost the whole surface of the Moon, including the far side, was mapped with the aid of space probes. To date all that remains unmapped is about 1 per cent of the lunar surface near the South Pole.

Comparison of the near and far sides of the Moon reveals marked differences in the proportion of 'seas' and 'continents'. On the far side there are several small seas: Mare Moscoviense (Moscow Sea), Mare Ingenii (Sea of Ingenuity), Mare Orientale (Eastern Sea) and part of Mare Australe, Mare Marginis and Mare Smythii, extending beyond longitude 90° E. We cannot be certain about the reasons for these differences between the near and far sides of the Moon.

One of the most striking formations on the far side is the Mare Orientale basin, whose outer wall — the Cordillera mountain range — may be observed occasionally on the western limb of the near side of the Moon. An important object is the crater Tsiolkovski, filled with very dark mare material.

Near side of the Moon

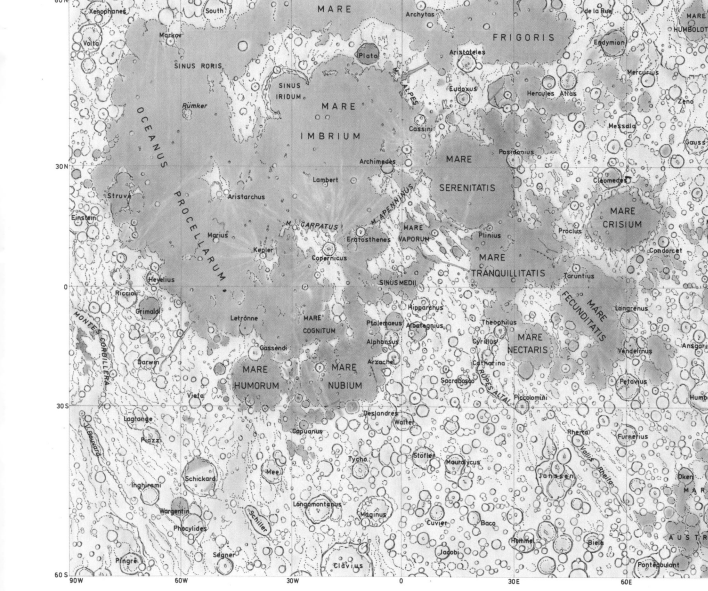

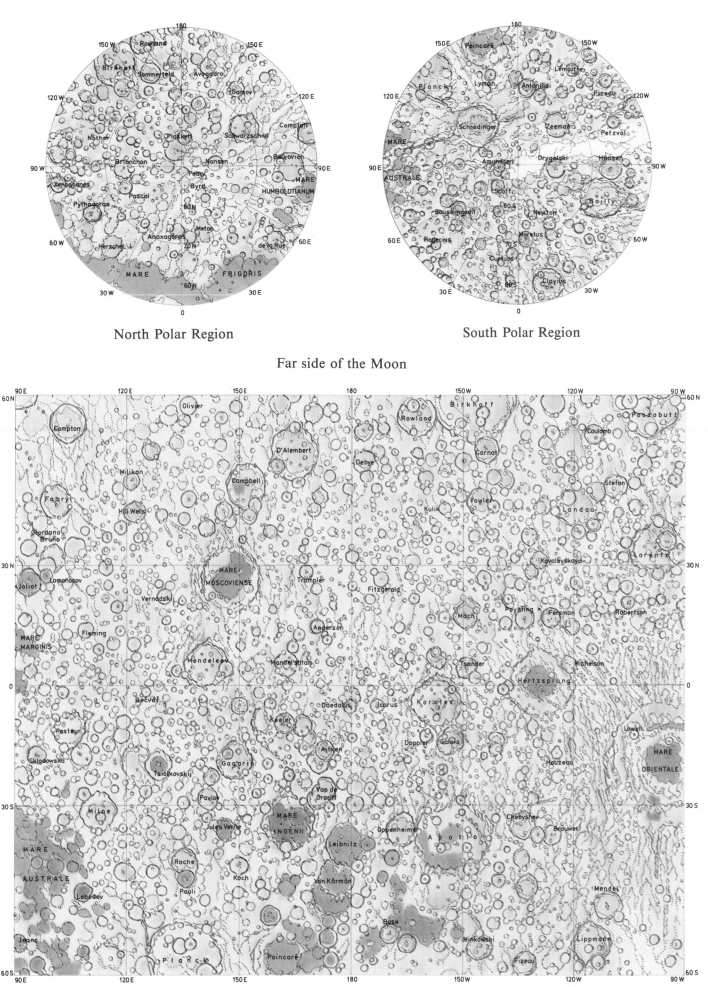

North Polar Region

South Polar Region

Far side of the Moon

31

Mercury

Maps of Mercury

Mercury according to J. H. Schröter's observations, 1800.

Astronomical observations from the Earth of the planet closest to the Sun do not reveal much. Mercury is always close to the Sun in the sky and can only be observed with a telescope during the day or, briefly, at twilight, through the turbulent lower layers of the atmosphere. At best one can see only vague light and dark spots—albedo formations.

Until 1965 not even the period of Mercury's rotation was known. It was found that the period of rotation (58.6 days) is synchronized with the orbital period (88 days) in which Mercury revolves round the Sun; in two orbits the planet rotates three times round its axis. The temperature on the surface of Mercury fluctuates between day and night from 427°C to −173°C. Such large fluctuations — the largest of all the planets — are increased by the marked eccentricity of Mercury's orbit, i.e. by great differences in its distance from the Sun (from 46 to 70 million km). At the same time it is interesting to note that because of its synchronized rotation, at perihelion (i. e. when it is 46 million km from the Sun) the same points on Mercury are always turned towards the Sun. These are either the zero or the 180th meridian, where the so-called 'poles of heat' are located.

Most of the current knowledge about Mercury was obtained with the aid of the interplanetary probe Mariner 10, which flew past the planet three times in the years 1974—75. Because the conditions of illumination of Mercury by the Sun were identical in all three instances, it was only possible to map and explore one half of the planet's surface, as shown by the map on the adjacent page.

Photographs from Mariner 10 (with details of features down to a size of about 100 m!) revealed that Mercury's surface is very like that of the Moon. It too is densely pockmarked with craters. However, there is nothing precisely similar to the lunar seas found here. There are also large numbers of small craters with bright rays. It appears that the differences in albedo observed from the Earth are generally caused by bright rays systems, because the differences between the albedo of the 'continents' and 'seas' on Mercury are nowhere near as pronounced as on the Moon.

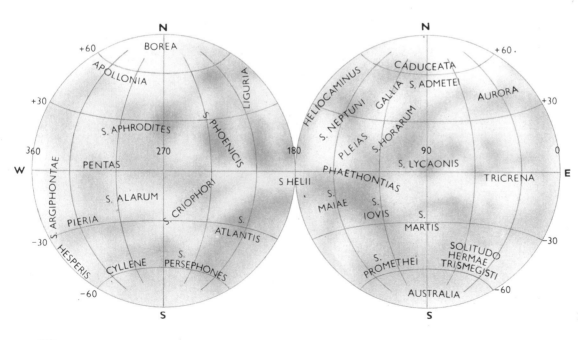

A map of albedo formations visible on Mercury from the Earth. Instead of 'seas' the dark spots on Mercury are called Solitudo, or Desert (S. on the map). The hemisphere of Mercury photographed by Mariner 10 is marked in yellow.

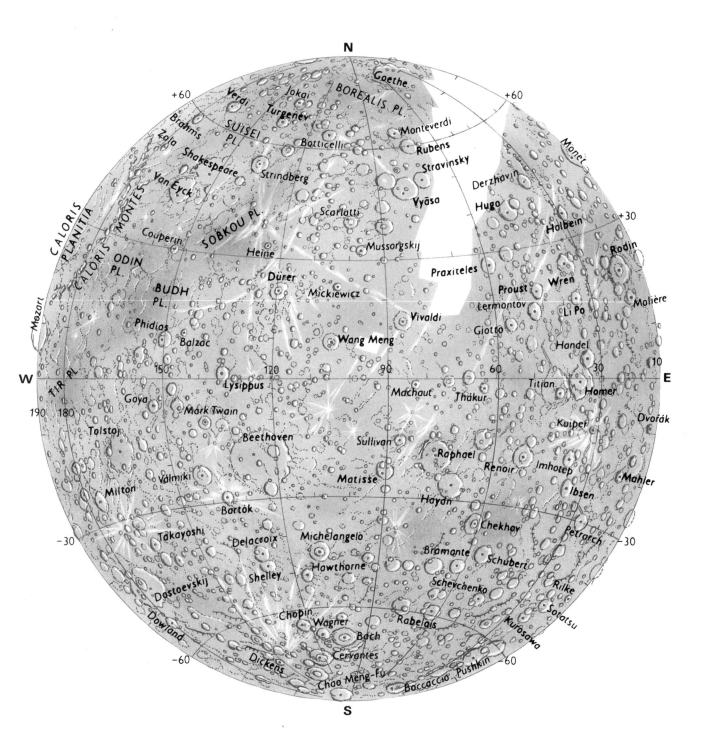

The craters on Mercury are named after prominent authors, poets, painters and composers from various countries of the world. The one exception is the bright crater Kuiper, named after the American astronomer Gerard Kuiper, who played an important role in the preparation for the mapping of Mercury by Mariner 10, and who died before the probe completed its mission. Plains (Planitiae) bear the names for Mercury in various languages, and the names of gods of bygone cultures who were analogous to Mercury of the Romans (e. g. Tir, Budh, Odin, Suisei). The faults on Mercury are named after famous oceanographic research ships, such as Discovery, Astrolabe, Vostok, and the like.

33

Mercury

Surface formations

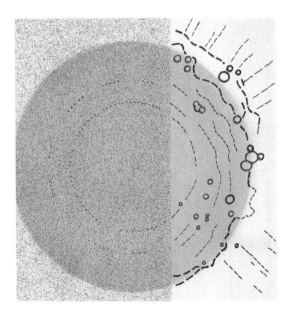

Venus
after Denning's observations
on 5th and 6th November 1882.

The resemblance between the cratered areas on Mercury and on the Moon is so striking that even experts sometimes hesitate in examining detailed photographs over whether they belong to the one or the other. There are, of course, also significant differences between the two, such as, for instance, the absence of large dark 'seas' on Mercury. There is a very substantial difference in the interior structure of Mercury and the Moon: the mean density of Mercury is approximately 60 per cent higher than that of the Moon. This means that in all probability Mercury has an exceptionally large iron core.

It is obvious that the evolution of Mercury differed from that of the Moon, even though some of the stages were similar. This was particularly the case during the period of intense bombardment that gave rise to the bodies in the Solar System, and was the origin of the large number of impact craters. The ensuing volcanic activity, accompanied by lava flows, then led to the formation of plains that somewhat resemble the lunar seas.

An extremely important event in Mercury's history was the huge impact that gave rise to the Caloris Planitia basin which measures 1,300 km in diameter. This formation, with numerous concentric walls and faults, greatly resembles the Mare Orientale basin on the Moon (see map on p. 31). The material ejected by the impact shaped the older cratered terrain out to a distance of 1,000 km from the surrounding mountain wall, and seismic waves caused a 'Mercuryquake', the results of which may be observed on the opposite side of the planet in the form of the so-called chaotic terrain.

A unique feature on Mercury, one that is unknown on the Moon, is the system of remarkable scarps 500 to 1,000 m high, and hundreds of kilometres long. One example of such a formation is the Discovery Scarp (Rupes), depicted at right. The tectonic processes that resulted in the formation of such an extensive system of scarps on a global scale were probably caused by movements of the crust during cooling or heating of the planet's interior. The planet's crust may also have been disrupted during the slowing of Mercury's originally faster rotation, down to its present value by the Sun's gravitational effects.

Only part of the Caloris Planitia basin is known and its entire shape — concealed on the night side of the planet during Mariner 10's flybys — can only be a matter of rough conjecture. The name 'Plain of Heat' is apt, because this site is located close to a 'pole of heat' (see p. 32) where the temperature at noon reaches its maximum, 427°C.

Below:
Rupes Discovery (Discovery Scarp) more
than 400 km long and 500 to 1,000 m high.
The scarp intersects two older craters.

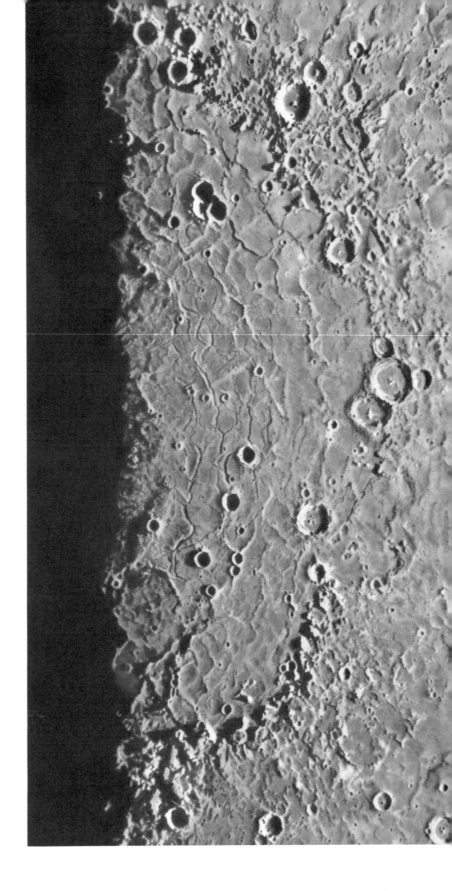

Above:
Part of the huge Caloris Planitia basin from
a photograph made by Mariner 10. Individual peaks in the mountain wall encircling the
basin reach heights of 1,000 m. The interior
of the basin is furrowed with numerous concentric faults, rilles and low ridges.

35

Venus

The atmosphere of Venus

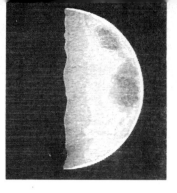

Drawing of Venus,
Folaché, 1883.

Of all the planets Venus is most like the Earth in size, mass, mean density, and amount of energy received from the Sun. It is, however, the least-known of the terrestrial planets. It is surrounded by a dense atmosphere, filled with impenetrable clouds that obscure the planet's surface. It is therefore no wonder that as late as the fifties scientists still considered it possible for life forms to exist on Venus. More recent explorations, however, revealed fundamental differences: Venus has a very dense atmosphere, about a hundred times denser than that of the Earth, which consists of 97 per cent carbon dioxide, CO_2. The planet's surface is rocky, without water (the atmosphere contains only several tenths of one per cent of water vapour), and very hot — with a temperature of more than 450° C during both day and night. The pressure on the planet's surface is 90 times greater than the atmospheric pressure on the surface of the Earth.

From the Earth or from a spaceprobe one can observe the uppermost cloud layer, the top of which is 70 km above the surface of Venus. Above this, up to a height of 90 km, there is a haze of ice crystals that makes observation in visible light very difficult. That is why Venus appears only as a white disc without any distinguishable details when viewed through a telescope. The upper haze is transparent to ultraviolet radiation, however, and it is possible to observe the dark and light clouds in the highest cloud layer, which extends from 70 km to 56.5 km above the surface of the planet. In the four pictures on the opposite page, based on ultraviolet photographs made by the Pioneer Venus Orbiter, one can observe the changes and movements of the cloud formations — in other words, the atmospheric circulation — and also the general rotation of the atmosphere, which rotates round the planet's axis once in 4—5 days. The clouds on Venus primarily consist of sulphuric acid, H_2SO_4, with some other materials, and can be said to resemble Earth's hazes and smog. Their vast extent — there are three layers from 45.5 to 70 km above the surface — is responsible for the apaqueness of the atmosphere in visible light. On the surface of Venus, however, visibility is about 3 km and the illumination of the landscape is about the same as on the Earth on a very cloudy day.

The phases of Venus as they appear when viewed from Earth. The apparent diameter of Venus changes markedly in accordance with the planet's distance from Earth. Similar phases are also exhibited by the planet Mercury.

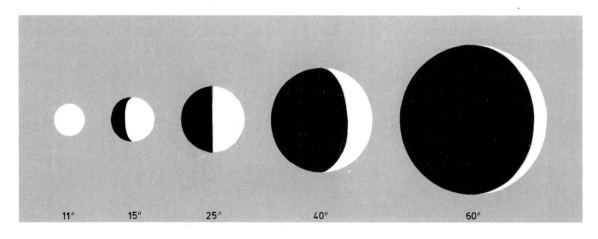

11"   15"   25"   40"   60"

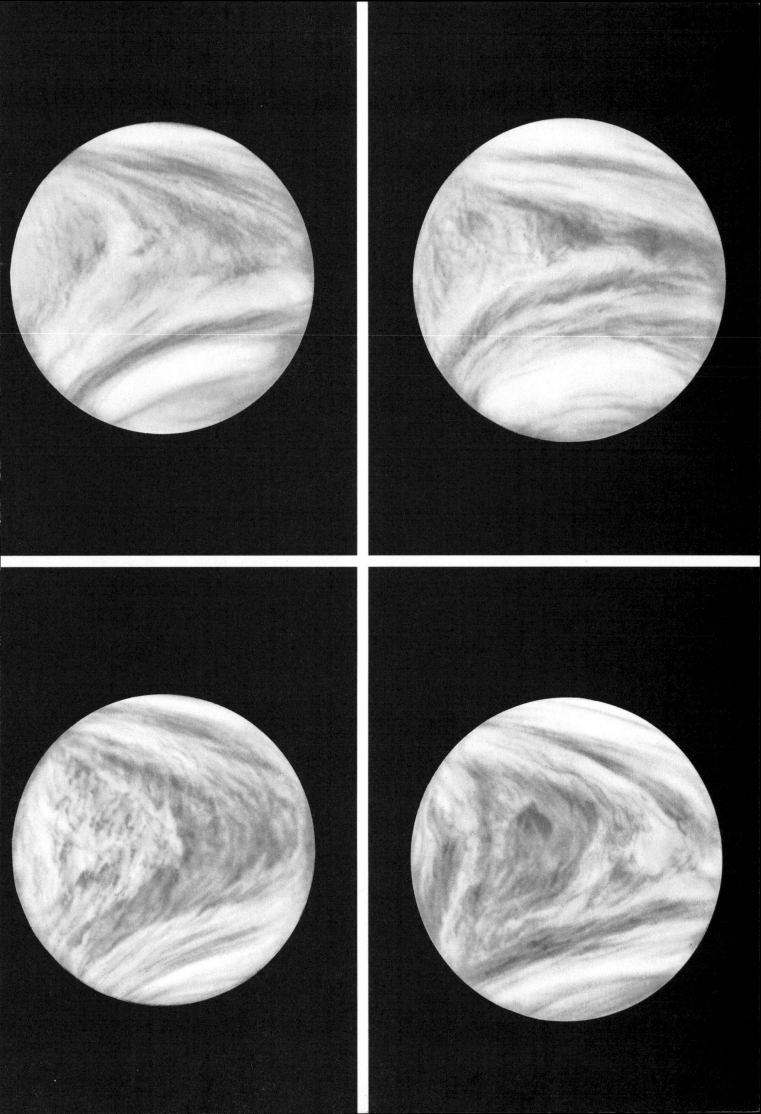

Venus

The surface of Venus

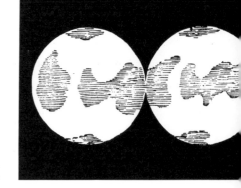

Hypothetical seas on Venus.
Bianchini, 1710.

The impenetrable atmosphere on Venus is not an obstacle to radar, which makes it possible to explore the planet's surface from a vast distance, to distinguish its features, measure the height of its mountains and the depth of its valleys. Certain parts of the planet's surface may be examined with large terrestrial radars, but it was not until the early 1980s that radar on the orbiting spaceprobe Pioneer Venus Orbiter provided the first global map of Venus.

A simplified version of this map (right) gives us a general idea of elevations on Venus. The difference between the lowest and highest point is immense — more than 13 km! Nevertheless, the surface of Venus is much 'smoother' than the surface of the Earth. Great relative elevations, from 1.5 km to 10.6 km (above the officially adopted mean radius of 6,051.5 km), are found on only 8 per cent of the planet's surface; these are highlands resembling terrestrial continents. The highest of the highlands is Aphrodite Terra, measuring 3,200 by 9,800 km. The highest point on Venus is Maxwell Montes (10.6 km), rising from the 'continent' of Ishtar Terra. This general picture of Venus is very approximate; the size of the smallest features shown here is more than 100 km.

More detailed radar exploration from the Earth and from the space probes Venera 15 and 16 show, for instance, shield volcanoes (both Theia Mons and Rheia Mons have calderas), about 150 large craters 4—350 km in diameter, canyons, and the like. Igneous rocks — basalts — predominate on Venus. In photographs made by probes that landed on the surface (Veneras 9, 10, 13, 14) one can see numerous sharp-edged rocks. This indicates that Venus is geologically active and that surface features are still being formed. Global mapping of Venus by the space probe Magellan with details down to 120 m will help throw light on the geological evolution of the planet.

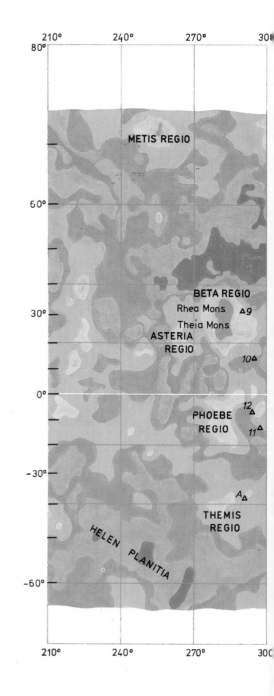

On the general map of Venus the height contours are marked in various colours. Because there is no water on the planet that would allow heights to be determinated above sea level, this role is filled by the surface of an imaginary sphere, with the same centre as Venus, and having a radius of 6,051 km.

Small triangles mark the spots where the landing modules of spaceprobes sent to Venus up to 1985 reached the planet's surface. 1 to 14 are the numbers of the respective Soviet Venera probes, V 1 and V 2 are for Vega 1 and Vega 2 probes. Let-ters A, C, D, E and F designate the five probes dropped by the American Pioneer Venus 2 mission in 1978. Landing places of the modules Vega 1 and Vega 2 (1985), and the first course of their balloon probes, used here for the first time in the exploration of Venus's surface, are also marked.

The first successfull transmission of measurements from the surface of Venus was made by Venera 7 on 15th December 1970. Photographs of the planet's surface were transmitted to Earth by Veneras 9, 10, 13 and 14.

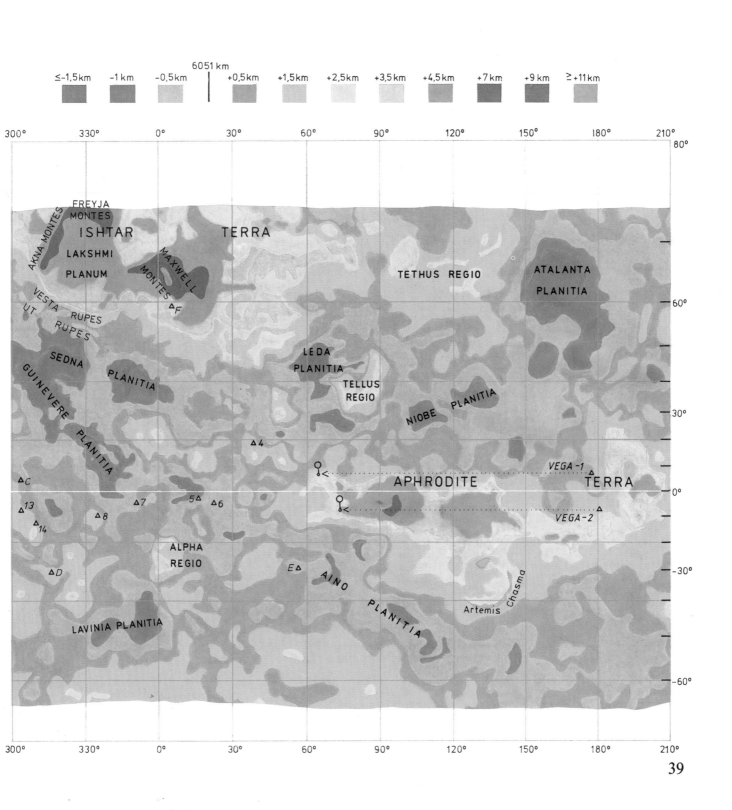

Mars

Albedo formations

Mars according to R. Hooke's observations, 12 March 1666.

Of all the planets, Mars most resembles the Earth, even though the resemblance is often a very faint one. Mars is half the size of the Earth; its diameter being just over half as large. Day on Mars is approximately the same length as on Earth. It has alternating seasons but these are twice as long as those on Earth. The temperature on Mars is reasonable, sometimes rising even above the freezing point, though the average daily temperatures are close to $-30\,^{\circ}C$. The atmosphere on Mars is sparse, composed of 95 per cent CO_2, 2 per cent nitrogen, 1—2 per cent argon, plus other trace gases, including oxygen and water vapour. Until recently, all this, together with observed changes on the planet, inspired great hopes that there was life on Mars — though no longer in the form of Martians, but at least in the form of micro-organisms.

Because of the transparent atmosphere, the planet's surface may be observed directly, unless momentarily obscured by dust storms, clouds, or atmospheric haze. The surface formations that can be observed through the telescope are divided into three basic types, differing by their albedo (the reflecting power of the surface) and colouring: reddish orange areas called 'continents' or 'deserts', dark grey or otherwise coloured spots called 'seas', 'lakes', etc., and last of all the dazzling white polar caps (top right). Unlike the 'seas' of the Moon, however, the dark areas on Mars vary in size and albedo, as well as colour, according to the season of the year, in particular after dust storms. The size of the polar caps likewise depends on the season. The caps may be observed even with a small telescope, and the same is true of the darkest formations, such as Syrtis Major, Mare Acidalium, Mare Sirenum, and others. Exploration of Mars by spaceprobes has revealed that the 'seas' and other albedo formations do not usually correspond to the planet's surface relief, but may spread over high and low areas alike.

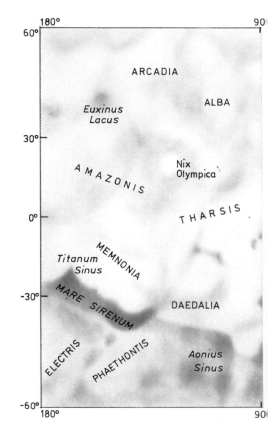

A general map of the main albedo formations on Mars

Shown on the map are relatively stable features with their traditional Latin names, as approved by the International Astronomical Union. These names are a combination of old geographical names from maps of Europe, Asia and Africa, and also mythological names. The following are the designations used to denote the dark areas: mare—sea, lacus—lake, sinus—bay, palus—marsh, fretum—strait. The areographic longitude on Mars (*areo* is derived from Ares, the Greek counterpart of the Roman god, Mars) is analogous to geographic longitude. It is expressed in degrees from 0° to 360° measured westward from the zero meridian. North is at the top of the map.

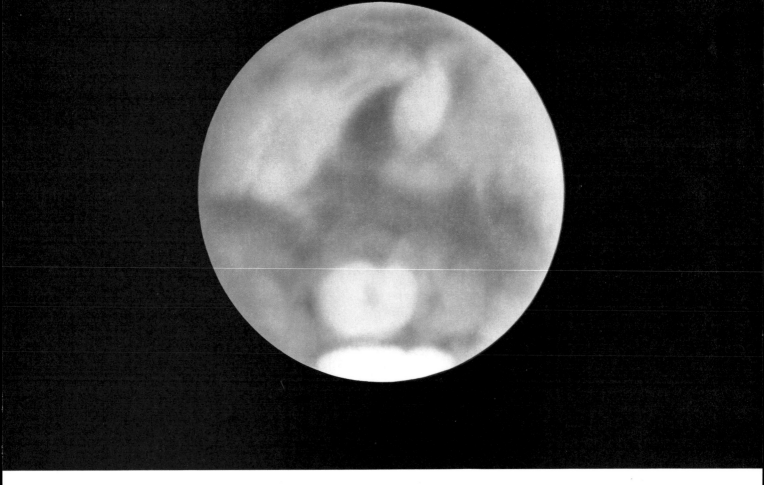

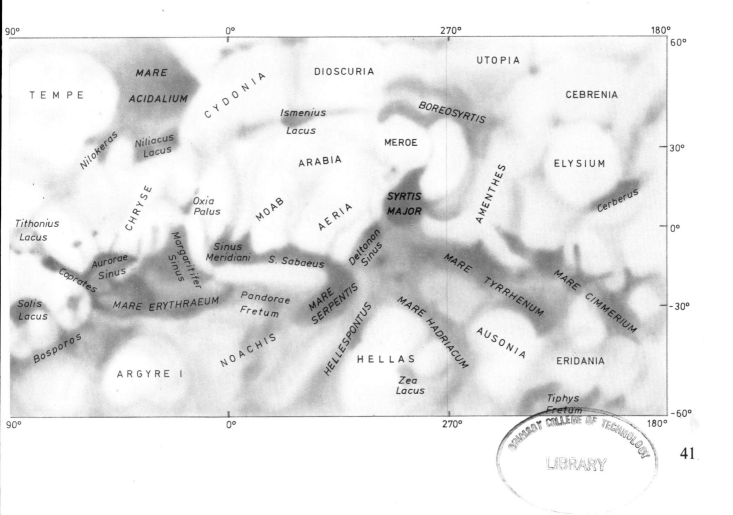

Mars

Topographic map of the eastern hemisphere. Changes on Mars

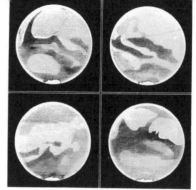

Mars according to observations in 1877.

The exploration of Mars by spaceprobes in the seventies led to more detailed mapping of the planet. Close-up views revealed that the albedo formations, i. e. the dark and light areas on Mars, do not correspond to specific types of surface, as is the case, for instance, on the Moon. The general maps of Mars on pages 43 and 45 likewise show that 'seas', for example, cover crater fields and plains, often irregardless of the boundaries of the morphological formations. For that reason the nomenclature used on topographic maps is different from that used on albedo maps. Albedo formations are subject to variation (picture at bottom).

A large part of the southern hemisphere and a smaller part of the northern are heavily pockmarked with craters, like the continents on the Moon. This large cratered area is geologically the oldest, and perhaps dates from the period of heavy bombardment (see p. 8). The large basin Hellas Planitia, 1,500 km in diameter and 6 km deep, and the smaller basin Argyre in the western hemisphere are obviously of impact origin.

These basins, however, are not filled with lava as are the basins of the lunar seas.

The northern hemisphere is mostly flat, particularly the northernmost part named Vastitas Borealis — Vast Northern Plain. There are far fewer craters here and the predominant type are 'splash' craters (p. 48). Two huge shield volcanoes — Elysium Mons and Hecates Tholus — rise above the Elysium Planitia plain. About 200 km from the crater Mie is the region where Viking Lander 2 landed on 3rd September, 1976, finding it to be a desert strewn with stones and covered with dust.

In the region of the most prominent albedo formation of all, Syrtis Major, there are no unusual surface formations, merely a long, gradual slope with numerous variable dark bands (picture at bottom right).

The craters on Mars are named, like those on the Moon, after prominent scientists and technologists as well as travellers and artists. Small craters, shown on detailed maps, are named after towns and villages on Earth.

Left: Seasonal changes in the landscape of Pandorae Fretum (marked with an arrow). In early spring the landscape is a light colour (left), then it begins to turn dark and in summer resembles a broad dark band. Changes like this are caused chiefly by the wind, which shifts the dust material from one place to another. If, for instance, light-coloured dust is blown away from a dark surface the landscape becomes darker.

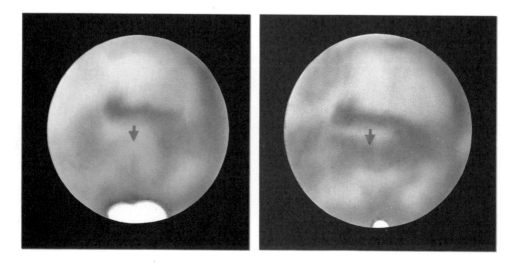

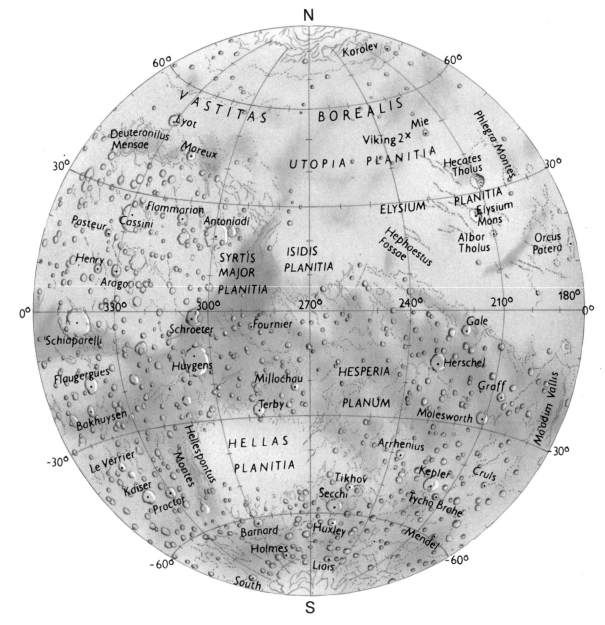

Clouds similar to those on Earth are formed in Mars' atmosphere. The picture shows the cloud cover produced by a depression about 600 km in diameter. The clouds are 6 to 7 km above the surface of the planet. (Based on observations made by Viking Orbiter 1.)

Following a dust storm we see bands of dark ground from which the wind has removed a layer of light-coloured dust. (Detail from the eastern edge of Syrtis Major, about 250 km across. Based on material obtained by Mariner 9.)

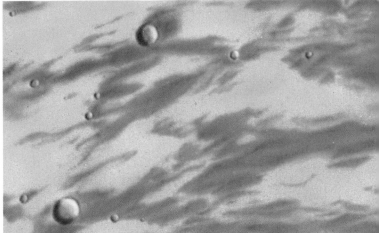

Mars

A topographic map of the western hemisphere. The polar caps

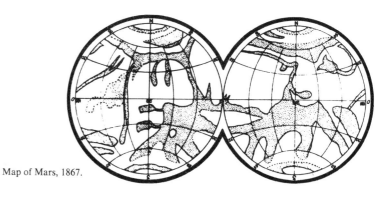

Map of Mars, 1867.

Close to the equator in Mars' western hemisphere there are two extraordinarily interesting regions, the largest of their kind in the Solar System: the Tharsis volcanic region and the Valles Marineris complex of canyons.

Tharsis is the largest volcanic region on Mars and in the long-distant past vast quantities of lava erupted from the interior of the planet, flowing over thousands of square kilometres of the surface and forming a cover of increasing thickness. It gradually built up a circular region as much as 10 km high and which recent measurements have shown to have a radius of more than 1,000 km. Rising above this regional bulge, by a height of about 20 km, are the peaks of the Tharsis Montes range: Arsia Mons, Pavonis Mons and Ascraeus Mons. These are shield volcanoes whose cones were formed, layer by layer, by the eruption of fluid lava that solidified to give features like Hawaiian volcanoes. The craters (calderas) of these volcanoes measure tens of kilometres in diameter and the solidified lava flows can be observed extending for hundreds of kilometres. The largest giant of the Tharsis region is Olympus Mons, described in greater detail on p. 48.

The great loading of Mars' crust by the Tharsis massif evidently led to extensive tectonic changes, to the formation of complex systems of fissures, rilles and faults in the planet's crust. The largest formation of tectonic origin is the Valles Marineris complex of canyons, named after the orbiting spacecraft Mariner 9, which in the years 1971—72 mapped the entire planet in detail for the first time. The formation extends eastward some 4,500 km from the centre of the Tharsis range in the form of rows of parallel, steep walled canyons up to 200 km across (for a more detailed description and picture see p. 46).

The region of Chryse Planitia is where Viking Lander 1 touched down on 20th July, 1976. The probe's cameras revealed a stony desert with small sand dunes. Biological analyses of soil samples did not reveal any traces of life.

The meanings of the Latin names shown on maps of Mars are as follows: *planitia* — plain, *vallis* (plural *valles*) — valley, *mons* — mountain, *tholus* — dome-shaped hill, *mensa* — table mountain, *patera* — depression, irregular crater, *fossa* — shallow trench, *chasma* — canyon.

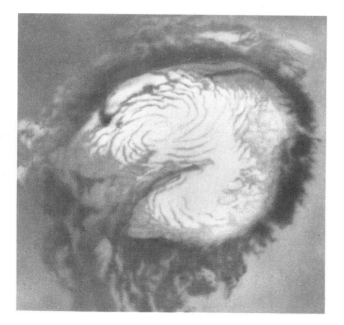

Left:
Melting of the north polar cap during the period of late spring in the northern hemisphere (after photographs by Mariner 9). Winds blowing out from the pole carry light-coloured dust away from the edge of the cap, thereby uncovering the darker surface round the margin of the ice-cap. The spiral structure inside the cap is probably caused by a combination of wind erosion and the surface relief.

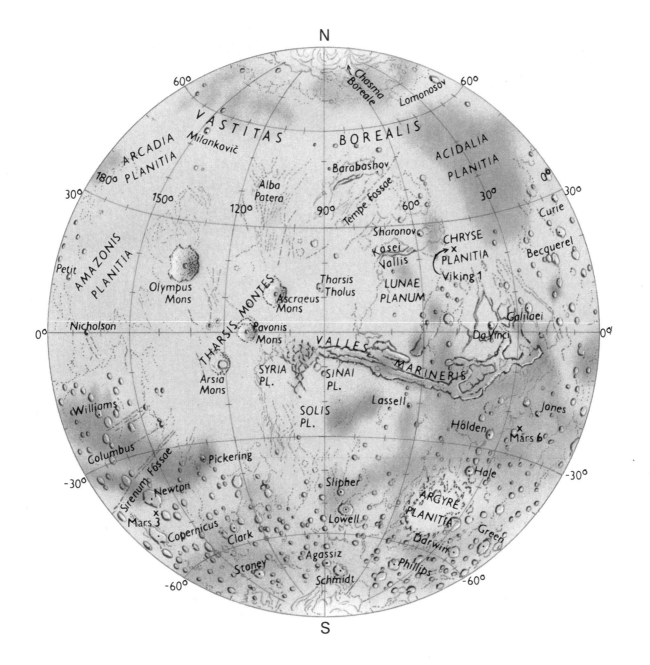

Bottom:
How the shrinking of the polar cap in the northern Martian hemisphere appears to a terrestrial observer in mid-spring (left), late spring (centre), and early summer (right). The part of the cap that evaporates chiefly consists of carbon dioxide, CO_2, but the part that remains throughout the summer consists of a thick layer of frozen water. The temperature of the surface of this ice is $-73°$ C.

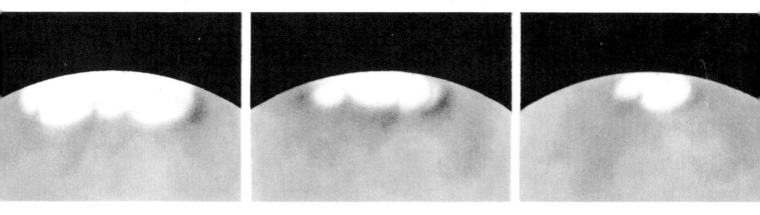

Mars

Canals and river beds

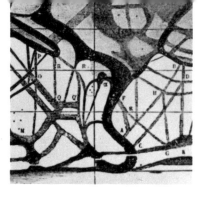

The mysterious 'canals' on Mars have exercised the human imagination since 1877, when they were depicted by the Italian astronomer Schiaparelli. The narow, dark lines visible on the planet's disc were even thought to be artificial canals, the work of Martians. Later observers, however, discovered that most of the 'canals' consist of rows of irregular spots, so they are not continuous lines, but optical illusions.

Close-up views of the Martian landscape as seen by the cameras of space probes show no signs of the classic 'canals'. In many places, however, they discovered entirely different canals — formations of natural origin resembling large, dry river beds hundreds of kilometres long. This is surprising, for under existing conditions water can only be present on the surface in the form of ice or water vapour. It seems, however, that there is a large amount of frozen water below the surface in the form of permafrost (like the frozen subsoil found in polar regions on Earth) and at greater depths there may even be liquid water. In the remote geological past, for instance in the period of intense volcanic activity, the temperature and atmospheric density on Mars may have been higher.

At that time, flowing water, released from the subsurface, may have slowly (in the form of a river), or rapidly (in the form of a catastrophic flood) shaped the landscape of the planet. Of course it is also possible that some of the 'dry river beds' were formed by flowing lava.

An entirely different type of 'canals' are the formations of tectonic origin, fissures, rilles, canyons, and the like. The best known of these is the huge Valles Marineris complex of canyons, measuring 150 to 700 km in width and having a length of 4,500 km, extending over more than a quarter of the planet's circumference (see map on p. 45). On the walls and floors of the canyons numerous traces of large landslides and continuing tectonic activity can be observed. The loose material is then further shifted and shaped by the wind.

In the case of such a large formation as Valles Marineris it should be possible to see it when observing Mars from the Earth. As a matter of fact, a classic albedo formation — the Coprates canal — follows the path of Valles Marineris precisely. This is one of the rare exceptions where an albedo feature has a true counterpart in a surface formation.

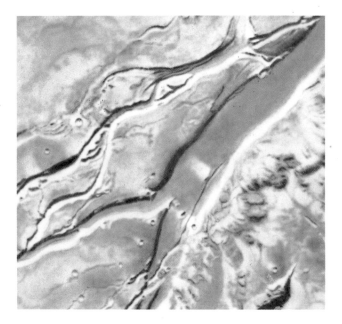

Left:
An approximately 60-km-long section of a complex of channels extending a distance of several hundred kilometres from the large volcano Elysium Mons. It is possible that these channels were formed by water released by the melting of permafrost ice during volcanic activity. However, they may also be lava channels.

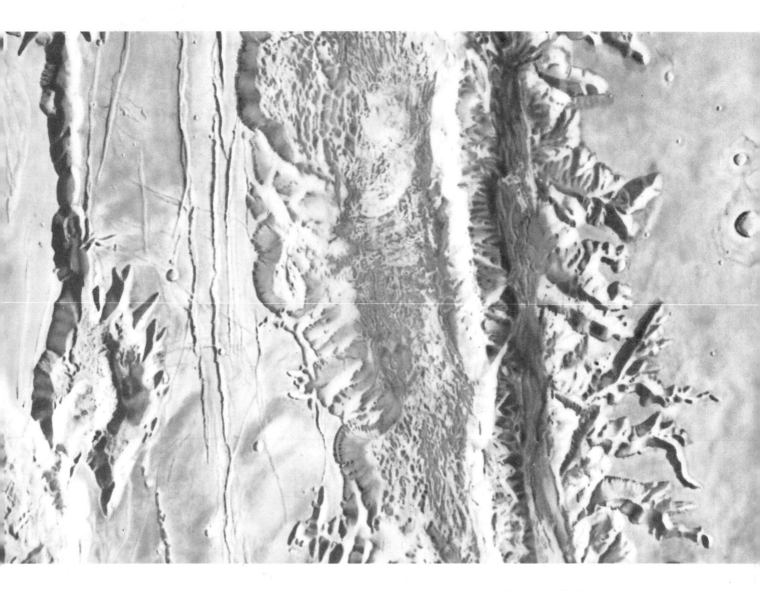

Above: A section of the huge Valles Marineris complex of canyons, approximately 110 km long. The lateral canals (at right) are up to 30 km long. The main canyon is 2 to 7 km deep.

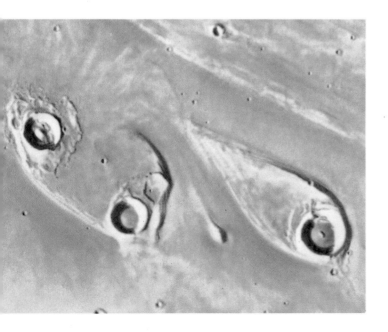

The teardrop-shaped 'islands' in the wide river bed in the Chryse region are most probably the result of erosion by water during an ancient catastrophic flood. The firm walls of the impact craters withstood the force of the water.

Mars

Craters and volcanoes

Volcanic activity of unprecedented proportions played an important role in shaping the Martian landscape. The main volcanic region is the Tharsis range in the western hemisphere (see map on p. 45) From the huge 'bulge' of solidified lava covering an area more than 2,000 km in diameter, with a height of 10 km, jut four large, and several smaller, volcanoes. The large volcanoes on Mars greatly resemble the shield volcanoes on Hawaii, which are similarly of considerable size; their bases on the ocean floor measure up to 120 km in diameter.

The volcanoes in the Tharsis region are of record dimensions. Heading the list is the volcano Olympus Mons (pictured at right) with a complex caldera that measures 80 km across and rises 25 km above the foot of the mountain. The diameter of the mountain's roughly circular base is approximately 500 km, and the remnants of old lava flows may be traced hundreds of kilometres farther away from the foot the mountain. These titanic dimensions indicate that the volcano must have been active for a very long time, perhaps thousands of millions of years, and it is possible that it may still become active occasionally to the present day.

Bright white clouds of ice crystals form above the mountain, particularly in spring; this cloud cap may be observed from Earth as the white patch Nix Olympica (see albedo map on p. 40).

Besides volcanic formations the surface of Mars is pockmarked with a great number of varied impact craters, which resemble the ones on other objects in the Solar System. In addition, however, there are a great many craters of a type that are sometimes called 'splash' craters (bottom right). The area round such a crater gives the impression that following the impact, the ejected material flowed like fluid mud in all directions. Presumably the cause of this phenomenon is the quantity of permafrost ice held in the subsurface layer. Impacts of large meteoritic bodies were accompanied by a marked rise in temperature at the site of impact. This melted the ice beneath the surface, creating a mixture of liquid solid ejecta and atmospheric gases; this then spread out round the crater and created the formations we observe now.

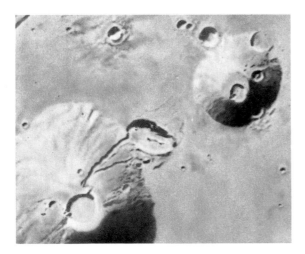

Left:
A pair of volcanic domes, similar to shield volcanoes. The larger of the two, Ceraunius Tholus (*tholus* is the Latin word for dome or mound), measures 150 km in diameter at the base. A 2-km-wide channel extends from the crater (caldera) at the top. The smaller dome, called Uranius Tholus, measures 70 km in diameter.

Right:
The perimeter of the volcano Olympus Mons, measuring 500 km in diameter, is rimmed by a steep scarp that varies in height and is as much as 6 km high in places (detail below).

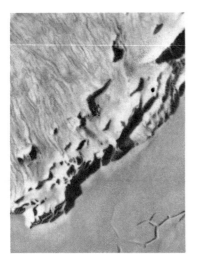

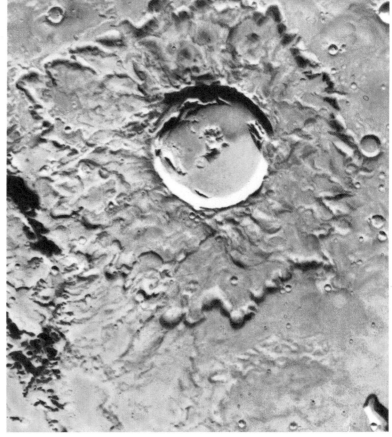

Right:
A typical impact crater 20 km in diameter. The ejected material was apparently liquid and formed several layers round the crater rimmed with raised edges (rims). Such 'splash' craters are only found on Mars.

Phobos

The Martian moons in close-up

The refractor of the Washington Observatory with which the satellites of Mars were discovered in 1877. Flammarion, *Astronomie populaire*, 1890.

In 1877, A. Hall, using a new refractor with 65 cm objective at the Washington Observatory, discovered two small Martian moons. They were named Phobos (Fear) and Deimos (Terror) after the mythological companions of the god of war. For almost 100 years they were known only as small, faint points of light, and nothing definite was known about them. There even existed fantastic ideas that both moons were hollow and were artificial. It was not until 1971, when Mariner 9 made its voyage, and the years 1976—1977, when Viking 1 and 2 journeyed into space, that the matter was cleared up.

Both moons are of a very irregular shape, which might be approximately likened to an ellipsoid with three unequal axes. They revolve round Mars in such a manner that their longest axes continually point towards the planet. Their surface is completely covered with craters and is blanketed by a layer of regolith tens to hundreds of metres thick. (Regolith is loose unconsolidated rubble of fragmented rocks and dust,

the product of countless impacts by meteoritic bodies in the distant past.)

Phobos measures 28 × 22 × 18 km and its volume is slightly more than 5,000 km³. It revolves round Mars at a distance of 9,400 km, once in 7 hours 39 minutes. The orbital period of Phobos is slowly becoming shorter, the satellite is descending towards the surface of Mars by about 9 m per century so that it should fall on the planet's surface in about 40 million years.

The most striking formations on Phobos are its largest crater, named Stickney (Angeline Stickney was the maiden name of A. Hall's wife), and the system of rilles fanning out from the crater. The density of Phobos is a mere 1.95 g.cm^{-3} (determined with the aid of the space probe Phobos 2 in 1989) so that the satellite may be compared to a porous mound of rock, rubble and ice. The surface of Phobos is very dark, reflecting only 7 per cent of sunlight. In respect of these features Phobos resembles certain types of minor planets, or cometary nuclei.

A schematic map of the surface of Phobos. The rilles and grooves are coloured red.

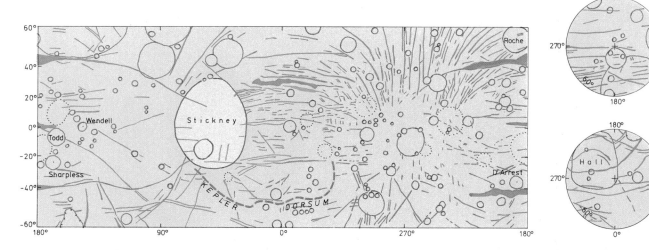

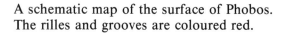

50

Left:
The most striking feature on Phobos is the crater Stickney, measuring 10 km in diameter. The surface of Phobos is furrowed with countless shallow grooves (below). The grooves are generally 100—200 m wide and 20—30 m deep. The parallel rows of small pits with raised edges might be places where gases escaped from subsurface ices along fissures. Phobos may have then manifested itself as a comet.

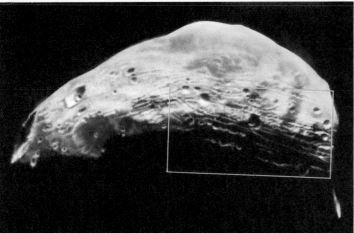

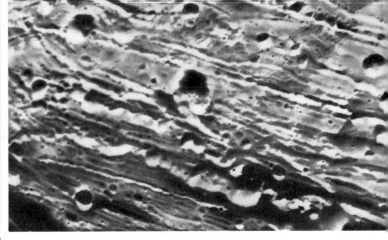

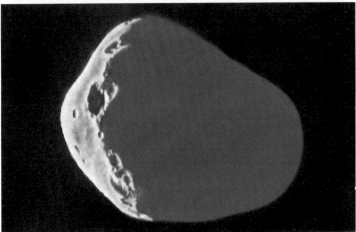

Left:
The night side of Phobos is slightly illuminated by the Sun's rays reflected from Mars, so that the whole outline of this irregular moon stands out.

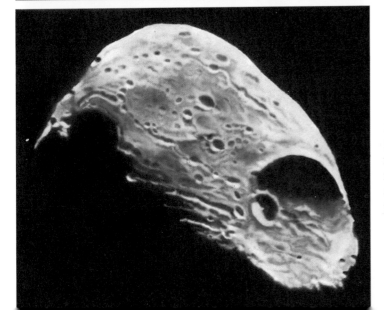

Left:
Stickney, the largest crater on Phobos, is on the right-hand margin of the picture. Oblique illumination gives this irregularly shaped moon a fantastic appearance. All pictures are based on photographs made by Viking 1 and 2.

Deimos

The Martian moons and asteroids

Mars according to
G. D. Cassini's observations,
2nd half of 17th century.

The smaller of the Martian moons measures 16 × 12 × 10 km, and revolves round the planet at a distance of 23,500 km in 30 hours 18 minutes.

When the general appearance of Phobos and Deimos is compared, the surface of Deimos seems to be smoother, and not as thickly pockmarked with craters as Phobos. Why? The answer was supplied by Viking 2, which was guided to a mere 28 km from Deimos, and which made photographs attaining a resolution of 2—3 metres (top right). These revealed that the surface of Deimos is also blanketed by craters but that they are obscured from view by layers of fine matter. The peculiar light-coloured spots visible on Deimos are also layers of fine matter, perhaps ejected during impacts. Grooves and rilles like those on the larger moon are not found on Deimos.

The question of the origin of the Martian moons is a matter of debate. From the known dimensions and mass, it is estimated that the density of the moons is approximately 2 g/cm³, which, among Solar System bodies, corresponds to a type of meteorites known as carbonaceous chondrites. Some types of asteroids that were formed in the outer half of the asteroid belt between the orbits of Mars and Jupiter (see p. 92) are presumed to be of the same composition. It is therefore a possibility that Phobos and Deimos are former asteroids that came within the gravitational field of Mars and were captured to become satellites of that planet.

Be that as it may, Phobos and Deimos — the smallest celestial bodies to be explored in great detail to date — serve as examples of the probable appearance and properties of asteroids. Future exploration of these bodies may yield important information about the origin of the Solar System.

A small schematic map of the surface of Deimos.

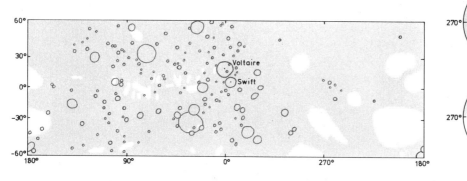

Although, from a distance, Deimos seems to be relatively smooth (right and bottom right), in actual fact it is pockmarked with small craters filled with fine matter (below). One side of the detailed picture actually measures approximately 0.5 km.

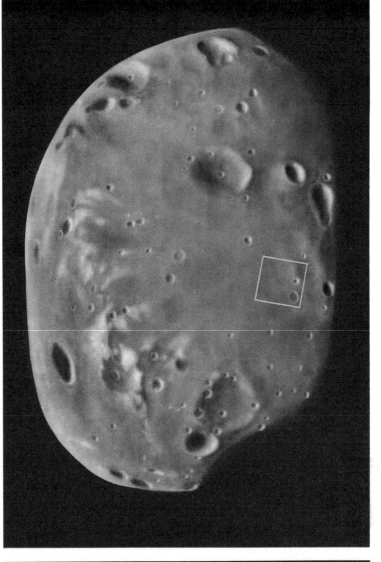

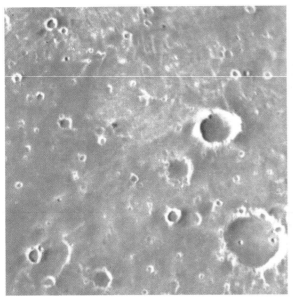

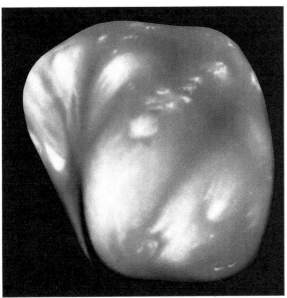

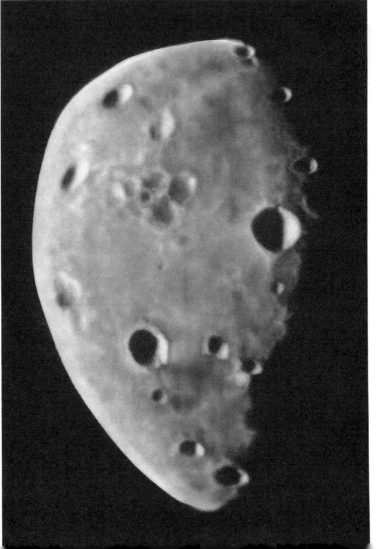

Above:
Deimos at 'full moon'. The irregular shape is clearly evident under this illumination where the observer is seeing the satellite as if the Sun were behind his back.

Jupiter

The appearance of the planet

Jupiter according to
Grimaldi's and Riccioli's
observations, mid-17th century.

Jupiter is the largest of all the planets, with a volume more than a thousand times that of the Earth, and a mass greater than that of all the other planets combined. It differs profoundly from the terrestrial planets. A substantial part of the planet consists of an atmosphere composed primarily of hydrogen and helium with traces of methane, ammonia and other compounds. The temperature and pressure increase markedly towards the centre of the planet, whilst the atmosphere becomes denser and its properties change. At a depth of approximately 50,000 km, the pressure is so great that hydrogen solidifies into a substance that behaves like metal.

Looking at Jupiter through a telescope, we see only cloud formations, which have the form of dark and light belts parallel to the planet's equator. By following the details in these belts we can observe the rapid rotation of the planet, which rotates round its axis once in a mere 10 hours. On account of this relatively rapid axial rotation, Jupiter is considerably flattened at the poles.

The appearance of the planet changes rapidly not only on account of its rotation, but also because of meteorological processes and the effects of the chemical properties of the atmosphere. The overall distribution of the belts and their distances from the equator, however, remain fairly constant. The cloud formations on Jupiter are of much longer duration than those on Earth. A unique feature is the so-called Great Red Spot, a reddish oval with a diameter bigger than that of the Earth, which has been observed by astronomers for more than a hundred years, and perhaps from as early as 1664.

The belts are produced by the atmospheric circulation. The light zones consist of cooler clouds at a great height. The dusky belts are relatively more transparent and it is possible to see to greater depths in these regions with thinner and lower-lying clouds. The coloration of the belts and their details show up well in photographs made at close range by spaceprobes. The colours are caused by various compounds that form at specific temperatures, and thus at certain heights in Jupiter's atmosphere. The temperature at the top of the uppermost cloud layer is −140°C, but in lower cloud layers it rises to 0°C.

Below:
The appearance of Jupiter in July 1973 (left) and October 1974 (right). The drawings show details visible from the Earth with a telescope.

Opposite:
The appearance of Jupiter based on photographs made by Voyager 1 in early March 1979.

Jupiter

Meteorological phenomena

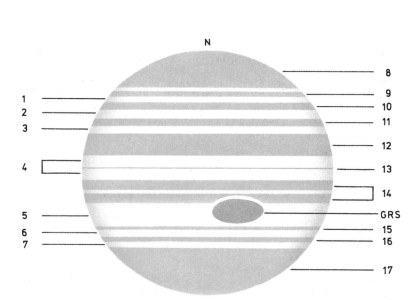

Changes in Jupiter's appearance — observations made in 1881—85.

Still pictures can only hint at the immense phenomena in Jupiter's turbulent atmosphere, where atmospheric velocities are much greater than those found in even the largest hurricanes on Earth. On Jupiter, of course, conditions affecting the circulation of the atmosphere are considerably different from those on Earth.

The main difference when compared with the Earth is that the source of thermal energy causing atmospheric mixing does not come primarily from the Sun but from the interior of the planet. Jupiter has not yet had time to cool down from when it was created; its interior is extremely hot and this provides the thermal energy, which heats the atmosphere from below. Masses of heated gas rise upward, carrying with them chemical compounds, which condense in the higher, cool layers, and form high clouds in the bright zones. Cooled gases then descend elsewhere, carrying cloud particles with them to lower, warmer levels, where the clouds evaporate and vanish. That is why descending currents are relatively cloudless and appear as dusky belts. The planet's rapid rotation produces strong currents parallel to the equator which cause the arrangement of the clouds in belts and zones.

The Great Red Spot (GRS) is the highest and coldest cloud formation on Jupiter. Masses of clouds rotate counterclockwise round the perimeter of GRS, as in anticyclones on the Earth; it is an atmospheric eddy. The GRS may thus be likened to an unprecedented storm — a hurricane with winds moving at a speed of more than 500 km/h. The white ovals, some of which have been in existence for more than 50 years, are also similar in character. The differences in coloration are probably due to the depths to which these eddies extend. The strong currents mix the atmosphere vertically, affecting the chemical composition of the clouds at various levels, and the formation of chemical compounds that colour the cloud formations.

The designation of the dark belts and light zones on Jupiter.

1 — North North Temperate Zone
2 — North Temperate Zone
3 — North Tropical Zone
4 — Equatorial Zone
5 — South Tropical Zone
6 — South Temperate Zone
7 — South South Temperate Zone
8 — North Polar Region
9 — North North North Temperate Belt
10 — North North Temperate Belt
11 — North Temperate Belt
12 — North Equatorial Belt
13 — Equatorial Band
14 — South Equatorial Belt
15 — South Temperate Belt
16 — South South Temperate Belt
17 — South Polar Region
GRS — Great Red Spot

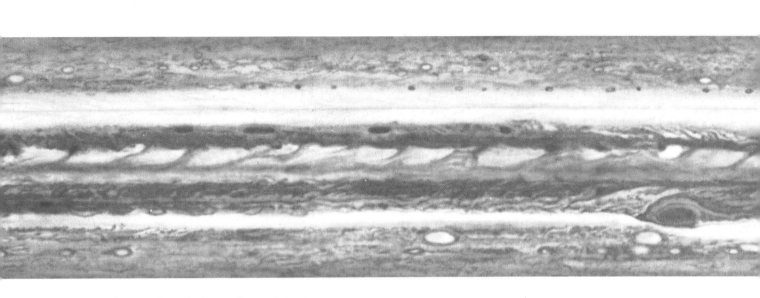

In the above picture the whole surface of Jupiter is spread out like a map, showing the appearance of Jupiter in early March 1979.

Below:
The Great Red Spot, a stable cloud formation with a diameter greater than twice that of the Earth. It is a huge anticyclone, as is the white oval at bottom right.
Both pictures are based on photographs made by Voyager 1.

Jupiter's satellite system

The Galilean satellites and the ring

Galileo's records
of the first observations
of Jupiter's satellites,
February 1610.

Jupiter is a veritable giant amongst the planets and its influence extends far out into the Solar System. First and foremost, Jupiter has powerful gravitational and magnetic fields; the planet's magnetosphere may even extend as far as the orbit of Saturn.

Its gravitational power is so great that Jupiter is capable of changing the orbits of comets and asteroids moving round the Sun, and has permanently captured so many moons and moonlets that its system resembles a small solar system. Up to 1990, 16 satellites had been discovered at first by observations from the Earth and later by spaceprobes. A list of these satellites is given on p. 222. Twelve of them are irregularly shaped, asteroid-like bodies several tens of kilometres in size.

In 1610, Galileo Galilei was the first to realize that the four small 'stars' passing alternately from one side of the planet to the other and back were satellites of Jupiter. They are called Galilean moons and, in the order of their distance from the planet, are named Io, Europa, Ganymede and Callisto. They can be seen readily even with a relatively small telescope or binoculars, and their movements can be observed from day to day — just as Galileo did.

Next to the picture of Jupiter and its moons on the opposite page is a diagram showing the positions of the moons at 6-hour intervals for ten consecutive days. It is possible to observe a number of interesting phenomena at the same time, such as the apparent close approach (conjunction) of two satellites, the transit of a satellite across the disc of Jupiter, the eclipse of a satellite, etc. Information about these phenomena is given in astronomical yearbooks.

Since 1979, when Voyager 1 first showed us close-up pictures of the Galilean satellites, they represent four completely new worlds.

Voyagers 1 and 2 also discovered another feature of Jupiter's system, invisible from Earth, in the form of a very narrow dust ring. The flat, thin ring extends from the upper layers of the atmosphere out to a distance of 53,000 km above the planet's clouds. The inner part of the ring is extremely thin and is, in all probability, composed of dust particles slowly falling in towards Jupiter. The ring is apparently continuously renewed from some source, perhaps from one of the inner satellites.

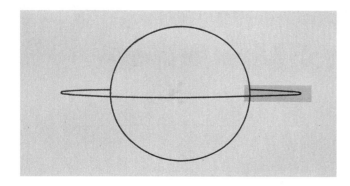

The dust particles forming the thin Jupiter's ring revolve round the planet between 47,000 and 53,000 km above the tops of the clouds. In the detail at right it is possible to distinguish the inner part of the ring, 5,000 km wide, and the outer, brighter part, 800 km wide.

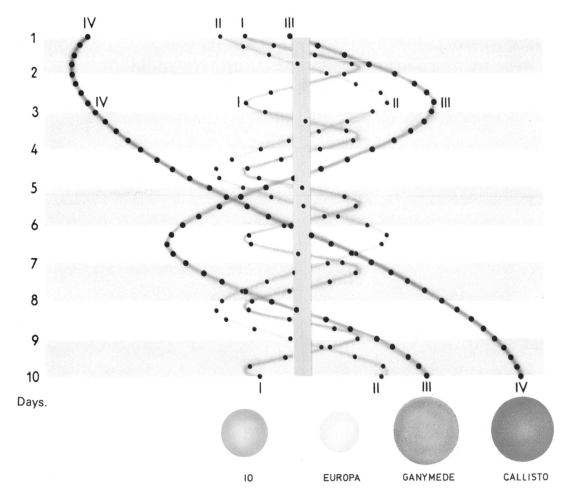

IV   II I III

1
2
3   IV
4
5
6
7
8
9
10

Days.

III

I II

I   II   III   IV

IO   EUROPA   GANYMEDE   CALLISTO

Comparison of the size of the Galilean satellites.

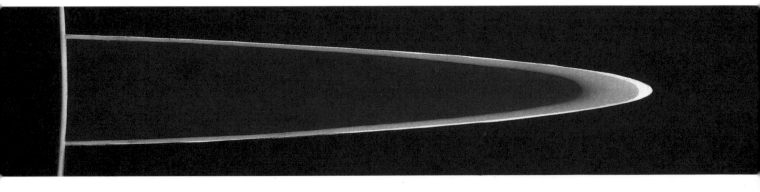

Io, Amalthea

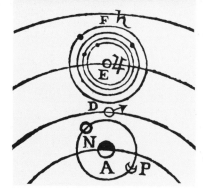

Earth, Mars, and Jupiter
and its satellites. G. Galilei, *Dialogus
de systemate mudni*, 1635.

Glowing with bright colours in the black void of space is an utterly incredible object produced by natural forces — Jupiter's satellite Io. Who would expect such a small body to be the scene of turbulent volcanic activity, the likes of which are unknown elsewhere? The surface of Io looks like a giant pizza, patterned with brown, orange, reddish, yellow, and white hues produced by sulphuric compounds, and with the black gaping throats of calderas and the black surface of lava lakes. There are no impact craters here, however, which means that the surface of Io is very young.

Io has a diameter of 3,630 km and a mean density of 3.6 g/cm³ — practically the same as the diameter and density of our Moon. If Io were to revolve round the Earth in place of the Moon it would probably be a similar dead body. Io, however, orbits relatively very close — at a distance of just 400,000 km — to gigantic Jupiter,

in the planet's extremely strong gravitational field. Here, great tidal forces are exerted that stretch the otherwise spherical moon in the direction of Jupiter. If Io revolved around the planet in a precisely circular orbit, it would always present the same side to Jupiter and the tidal bulge would always be at the same point. However, due to the gravitational perturbation of the moons Europa and Ganymede, Io's orbit is eccentric. This causes oscillation of the satellite in relation to Jupiter, which produces changes in the height of the tidal bulge at various points on the surface, as well as the movement of material in the satellite's interior. This 'kneading' and stretching heats Io to such a degree that the greater part of its interior is molten liquid. The 'fire' beneath the kettle in this infernal kitchen is stoked primarily by Jupiter.

(continued on p. 62)

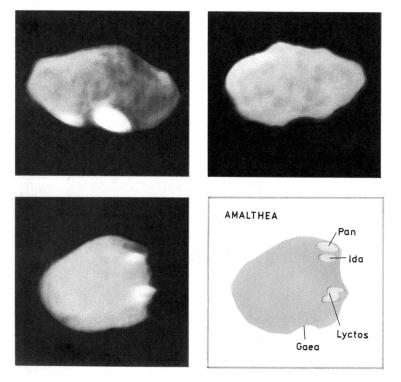

AMALTHEA. Three views (from Voyager) of the largest of the small Jupiter's moons. It is an irregularly shaped body measuring 270 × 170 × 150 km. There are craters on the surface, three of which have been named. Amalthea's red coloration is probably caused by particles of sulphuric compounds ejected during volcanic eruptions on Io.

Io

World of volcanoes

Jupiter with four satellites.
Details from the atlas
Harmonia macrocosmica,
Cellarius, 1763.

(continued from p. 60)

The entire surface of Io is one huge volcanic region, covered with sulphuric compounds of widely varying composition and form. The temperature at the surface is generally between −150°C and −200°C, but inside the matter ejected by the volcanoes the temperature is approximately 100°C and on the surface of the black sulphur 'lava' lakes as high as 380°C.

During explosive, long-lasting eruptions, the volcanoes on Io eject gases and fine particles of sulphur and sulphuric oxide to heights of 100—300 km, at a velocity of more than 3,000 km per hour. The particles fall back to the surface where they form a layer whose thickness increases by 1 cm in 3,000 years. Huge streams of lava flow from some of the volcanoes forming vast spreading layers. All this rapidly changes Io's surface. It can be assumed that in the 4.6 thousand million years of the Solar System's existence all of Io's material has gradually passed through the volcanic vents, remaining solid for a period and changing the surrealistic landscape of the satellite before returning into the molten interior once again.

The volcanoes on Io are named after mythological gods of fire. The most striking is the volcano *Pele*, the god of fire of Hawaiian mythology. *Prometheus* was a Greek deity, a Titan, who stole fire from the lightnings of Zeus for the benefit of Mankind. The volcano *Loki* is named after the Scandinavian god of guile and duplicity, who in many ways resembles Prometheus. Some volcanoes are irregular depressions, which are known as paterae.

Below: The volcano Ra Patera. Like bright orange threads, lava flows of sulphur compounds extend more than 200 km from the black vent of the caldera, which is 40 km in diameter.

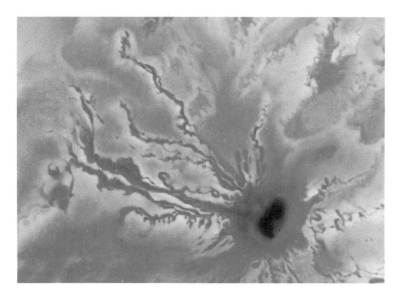

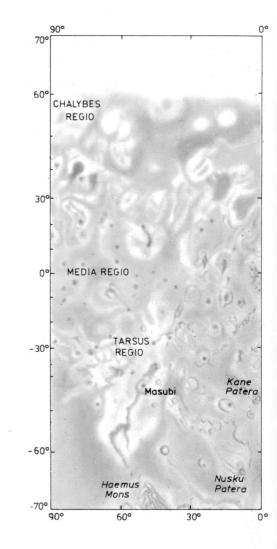

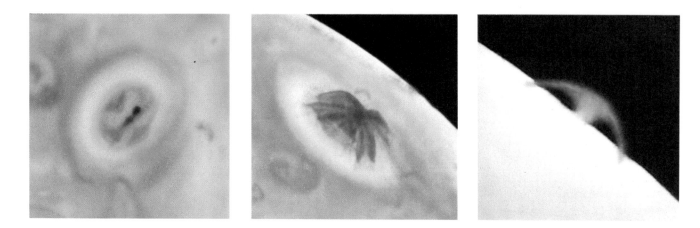

Left: The light ring marks the boundary of the area where ejected matter falls into the surface of Io.

Centre: Grey is used to emphasize the fountain of ejected matter.

Right: Above the limb of Io, gas and particles of sulphuric compounds spout to a height of 100 km where they form a giant 'umbrella' beneath which the matter again piles up on the surface. The particles are ejected at a velocity of more than 3,000 km per hour.

Three views of the active volcano Prometheus.

A general map of Io. Mercator projection, scale: 1:50,000,000. 1 cm at the equator is equivalent to 500 km.

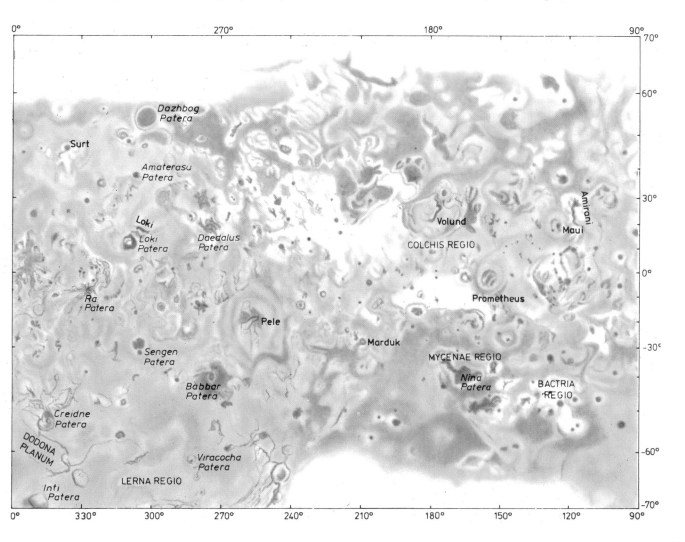

Europa

Jupiter with two satellites.
J. Hevelius, mid-17th century.

Imagine a smooth billiard ball about as big as our Moon. If the surface of the ball is covered with a layer of ice we will have a relatively good model for the Jupiter's satellite Europa.

With a diameter of 3,138 km and a mean density of 3.04 g/cm³, Europa is not much different from our Moon. If, however, it occupied the same place as our Moon it would appear about ten times brighter to a terrestrial observer. The surface of Europa is covered with a layer of ice, probably 75—100 km thick. The ice crystals reflect most of the Sun's light and this is the reason Europa is so bright.

Beneath the ice is a solid, rocky surface, which apparently shows through the relatively thin layer of ice in places appearing as dark spots. The possibility of liquid water between the solid surface and the ice cover cannot be ruled out.

The dark lines criss-crossing the surface are probably fissures in the layer of ice. The fissures are filled to the level of the surrounding surface, in all probability by water that penetrated to the surface and then froze. What caused these fissures is unclear. They range from several kilometres to tens of kilometres in width, and from several hundred to several thousand kilometres in length.

The dark lines on the map of Europa are called *lineae*. Their names are taken from the Greek myths about Europa; among them those of her father Agenor, her brother Cadmus, and her sons Minos and Sarpedon. *Macula* is the designation for a dark spot.

A general map of Europa. Mercator projection, scale: 1:43,000,000. 1 cm at the equator is equivalent to 430 km.

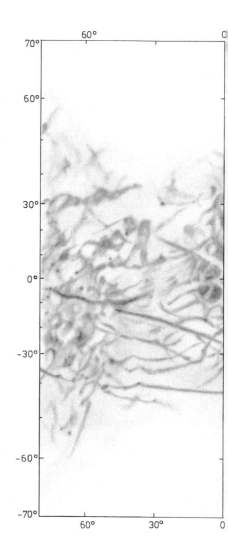

Visible on the smooth face of Europa are irregular dark spots and numerous narrow and long lines resembling fissures.

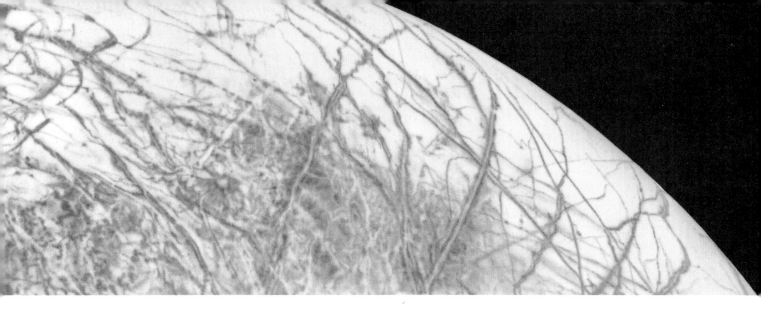

There are no surface irregularities of any consequence on even the most detailed photographs made by Voyager 2, which attained a resolution of 5 km. Only three impact craters were discovered on the entire surface of this satellite, each about 20 km in diameter. Europa appears to be the smoothest object in the Solar System.

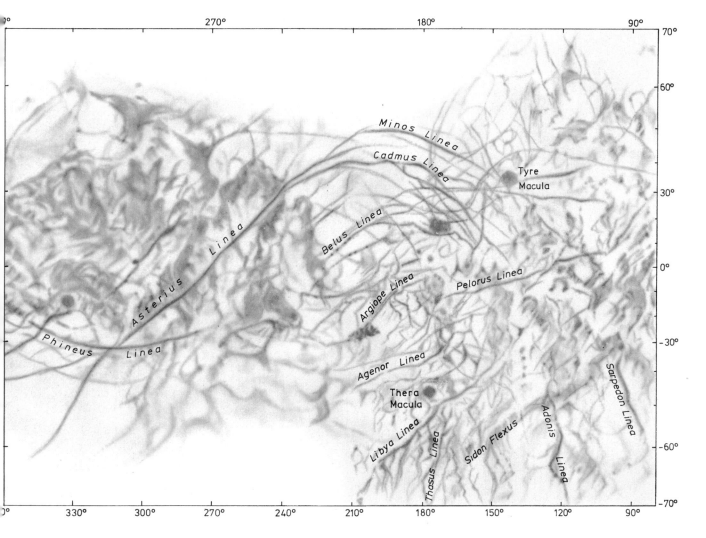

Ganymede

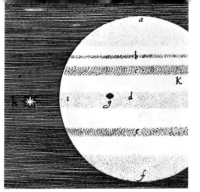

Jupiter according to
R. Hooke's observations,
2nd half of 17th century.

Viewed from a distance, Ganymede resembles our Moon — a disc with large dark- and light-coloured spots. When viewed from nearby, however, Ganymede's surface is quite different. This is not surprising, because the mean density of Ganymede is a mere 1.9 g/cm³ and a large part of its volume is apparently made up of ice. Ganymede's neighbour, the roughly equal-sized satellite Callisto, has a similar composition, but even these two related bodies do not have the same evolutionary history or surface appearance. We do not know why this is so.

Ganymede is the largest satellite in the Solar System; it measures 5,262 km in diameter, about 100 km more than Saturn's satellite Titan.

The dark regions on Ganymede are probably the oldest in terms of evolution. In the largest such region, Regio Galileo, the remnants of a former basin, similar to the formation Valhalla on Callisto, are preserved — a system of concentric, crooked ridges about 10 km wide and 100 m high, spaced 50 km apart. The centre of this basin was obliterated by later mountain-building movements.

A type of surface unique in the Solar System, but found in abundance on Ganymede, is that of the sharply defined, light-coloured stripes, hundreds of kilometres long, that criss-cross the surface of the satellite (picture opposite right). A closer view reveals that these stripes are a fur-

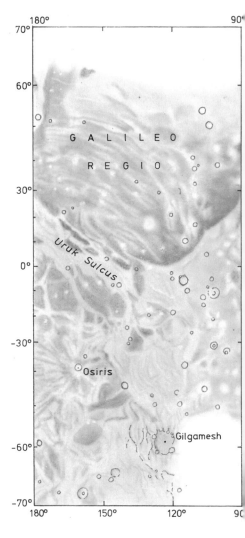

rowed surface resembling a ploughed field (picture at right). The apparently fairly shallow furrows are in fact ditches, walls, and long ridges approximately 1,000 metres high and spaced 10—15 km apart. The system of ridges intersect one another and one can observe faults, both with down-faulting and horizontal movements of parts of the crust along the faults, a phenomenon otherwise known only on Earth.

Ganymede is pockmarked with numerous impact craters with haloes of bright rays, evidently formed by ice thrown out by the impact.

The dark regions (*regio*) are named after the discoverers of Jupiter's satellites: Galileo, Marius, Nicholson, etc. The craters bear names linked with ancient civilizations (Babylon, Egypt, Sumer). *Sulcus* is a region of parallel furrows.

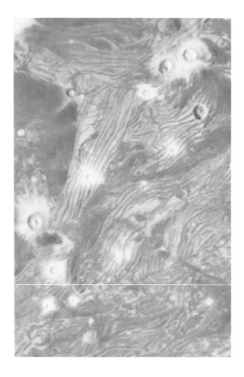

A general map of Ganymede. Mercator projection, scale 1:72,000,000. 1 cm at the equator is equivalent to 720 km.

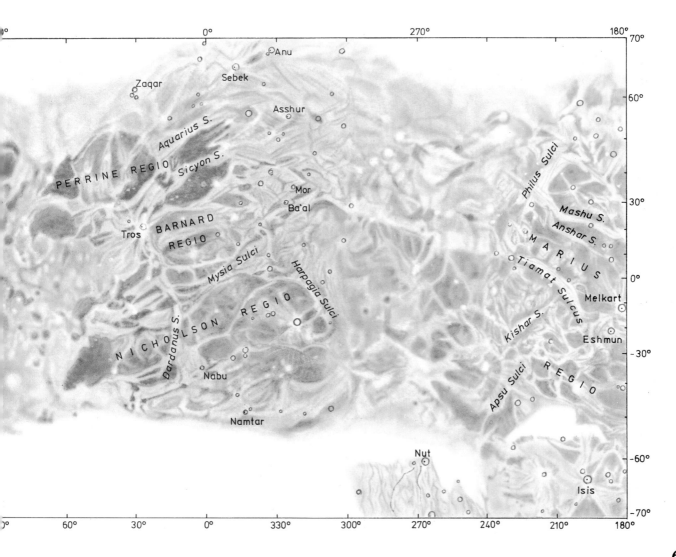

Callisto

Jupiter with its satellites
and their shadows. Flammarion's observations
of 25 March 1874.

On three of the Galilean moons there is plentiful evidence of the effects of internal forces that formed—and in the case of Io are still actively forming—their surfaces. The fourth moon, Callisto, is an exception. It is a dead icy world, scarred by traces of numerous impacts by meteoric bodies with impact craters covering the satelite's entire surface, almost without a break.

Unlike the Moon or Mercury, there are no craters on Callisto larger than about 150 km in diameter, and the preserved large craters are very shallow. Nor are there any high mountain ranges here. The surface of Callisto consists of ice with a certain proportion of rocky material. During the period of intense bombardment it apparently behaved like a slow-flowing ice sheet on which any high, or large-scale structures gradually sank down level with the surrounding landscape. Not only is the surface ice, but so is a large part of Callisto's interior; this is thought to be the case because this body, with a diameter of 4,800 km, has a mean density of 1.8 g/cm³, i.e. less than twice the density of water. There might even be liquid water beneath the surface. On the surface, however, the temperature is far below freezing: −120° C during the day and −190° C at night.

Two large, prominent impact formations, Valhalla and Asgard, are surrounded by large systems of bright features resembling the ripples that spread out from the spot where a stone has been dropped into water. They are probably a counterpart of the large basins on the Moon and Mercury, but different in character, typical of any icy body.

More than 80 craters on Callisto have been named, generally after figures from Scandinavian mythology. Valhalla was the great hall where Odin received and feasted dead heroes, fallen in battle, and Asgard was the heavenly residence of the Scandinavian gods, whence they ruled over mortals.

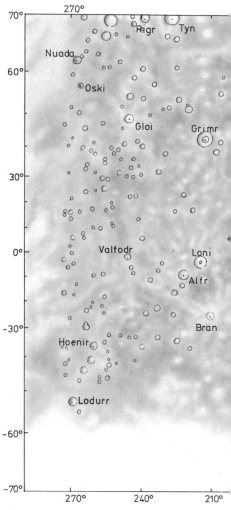

Left:
On the relatively dark surface of Callisto there are a number of bright spots — large craters more than 100 km in diameter. The striking brightness of the craters indicates the presence of ice in the moon's crust.

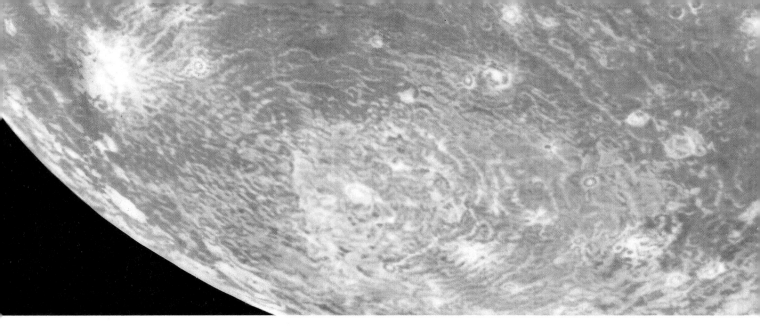

Top: The most striking formation on Callisto is the system of bright concentric rings that surround a lighter central region. This formation, Valhalla, is some 2,600 km in diameter and probably represents the result of an impact by a body the size of an asteroid. There is no central crater here, nor high ring mountains, as in the case of corresponding formations on our Moon (Mare Orientale), or on Mercury (Caloris Planitia).

A general map of Callisto. Mercator projection, scale 1:66,000,000. 1 cm at the equator is equivalent to 660 km.

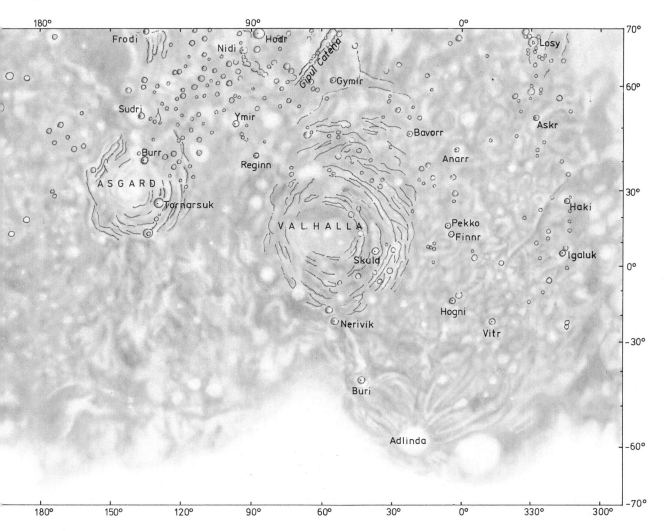

Saturn

Until the second half of the 1970s Saturn with its rings was considered to be a unique object — the only one of its kind. But 1977 marked the discovery of Uranus' system of rings, and two years later, Jupiter's ring was photographed for the first time by Voyager 1. Nevertheless, Saturn remains one of the most beautiful and most admired celestial objects.

Saturn is a major planet, very much like Jupiter. The body of the planet predominantly consists of hydrogen, and its mean density is correspondingly 0.69 g/cm³, the lowest of all the planets. Saturn's atmosphere likewise consists mainly of hydrogen, but the proportions of other gases differ from those in Jupiter's atmosphere. The flattening of the planet at the poles is very striking. This is caused by its rapid rotational speed (1 rotation in 10 hrs 40 min.); the planet's equatorial diameter is 120,660 km; the diameter at the poles is 98,000 km.

The pattern of belts on Saturn is much less distinct than on Jupiter and it is only after special processing of photographs of the planet that detailed cloud formations, in the form of variously coloured ovals, brown and red spots, and the like, show up clearly. The differences between the planets may be caused by different thermal processes affecting the circulation of the atmosphere, meteorological and chemical processes. It is colder on Saturn — at the top of the cloud layer the temperature is approximately −130°C — but the ratio between the thermal energy radiated from the interior of the planet and that received from the Sun is 2:1 (in the case of Jupiter it is 1:1). The greater proportion of internal energy may cause strong ascending currents and efficient mixing of the atmosphere. It may also be responsible for the extreme velocity of the currents, up to 1,800 km/h, that are observed in Saturn's equatorial belt.

The opposite page shows a picture of Saturn and its rings based on photographs made by Voyager 2. At the outer edge of the system of rings is the narrow F ring. Next in order is the bright A ring, divided close to the outer edge by the narrow Encke division. The widest and brightest of all is ring B, separated from ring A by the transparent Cassini division, which is about 5,000 km wide. Inside ring B is the very faint, so-called Crèpe ring, C. The thickness of the rings is no more than a few hundred metres. To the left of the planetary disc are the moonlets Tethys (top) and Dione, and visible as a black spot in Saturn's southern hemisphere is the shadow cast by Tethys. The rings also cast distinct shadows on the planet and, conversely, a piece of the rings disappears in the shadow cast by Saturn.

The appearance of Saturn's rings depends on the planet's position in its orbit around the Sun. Because the plane of the rings is inclined to the plane of Saturn's orbit, an observer on Earth alternately views their northern and southern sides. The period from the apparent 'edge-on' position (and disappearance) of the rings to the utmost opening of the rings (bottom) is always approximately 7.5 years.

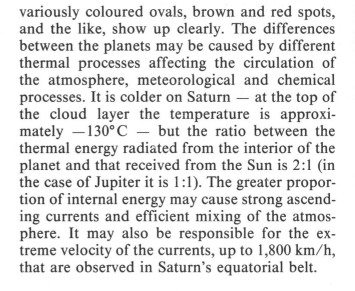

Saturn's rings

Observations of Saturn,
early 17th century.

Since the middle of the 17th century when they were discovered, the rings around Saturn were one of the greatest mysteries of the Solar System. In 1980 and 1981 the rings were photographed in unexpected detail by Voyagers 1 and 2 but this merely added to the number of questions. Ever since the late 19th century it has been known that the rings consist of numerous small particles, which range from grains of dust to boulders a few tens of metres across. The exact composition of this matter is not known, but we do know that there is an abundance of ice. What remains a puzzle, however, is the origin of the rings. They may have originated in their present form but they may also have come into being as the result of the disintegration of a former satellite.

Normally the two brightest rings A and B are visible from the Earth, separated by a seemingly empty space — the Cassini division. The faint, seemingly transparent C ring, also called the Crêpe ring, can only be observed with larger telescopes. Ring D extends all the way to the planet, but is extremely thin and transparent. Only from a spaceprobe is it possible to observe ring F, which is about 150 km wide. It is kept this width by two small moonlets, one circling the inside margin and the other the outside margin of the ring, and their gravitational effects shepherd any particles that might have a tendency to leave ring F back into the ring. Saturn's system also includes the extremely tenuous ring G, located about 30,000 km farther out than ring F, and, finally, ring E, which forms wide but tenuous cloud around the orbits of the moons Enceladus and Tethys.

Among the most interesting discoveries made by the Voyager spaceprobes was the fact that the main rings A, B, and C, are composed of an immense number — perhaps hundreds of thousands — of narrow concentric ringlets, which makes the rings resemble the surface of a gramophone record. Deriving a theoretical basis for the origin of such fine, complex structure will be very difficult.

Spaceprobes also made possible entirely new views of the unilluminated side of the rings. The darkest appears to be ring B, which is the thickest and least transparent to sunlight. The brightest are the Cassini division and ring C, where there are evidently fewer particles; what there are, however, scatter light strongly, as expected for ice particles.

Each of the main rings consists of a large number of narrow ringlets. Different colours are used for rings A, B and C.

The designation of Saturn's main rings. Compare with the pictures at top and bottom.

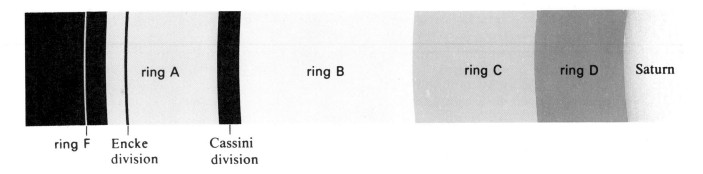

ring F | Encke division | ring A | Cassini division | ring B | ring C | ring D | Saturn

The appearance of Saturn's rings changes considerably when the side illuminated by the Sun (bottom) and the side that is not illuminated by the Sun (top) are compared. The explanation is given in the text.

Mimas, Enceladus

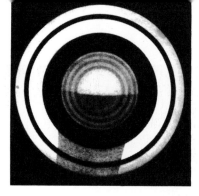

The true shape of
Saturn's rings. F. Arago,
Astronomie populaire, 1856.

Of all the planets Saturn not only has the richest system of rings but also of satellites. For a list of these see p. 222. Pictures, maps and characteristics of the nine largest satellites may be found on p. 74—81 in the order of their distance from Saturn.

Mimas is the smallest of the spherical satellites of Saturn. It measures 392 km in diameter and has a density of 1.4 g/cm³. Like the other larger satellites, Mimas is also a 'large dirty sphere of ice' pockmarked with impact craters. The most striking formation is the crater Herschel, which measures 130 km in diameter (one third of the diameter of Mimas!), is more than 10 km deep and has a wall rising 5 km above the surrounding landscape. The existence of such a large formation proves that, at the temperature of −200°C that exists here, ice attains the strength of rock.

Enceladus is the brightest moon, and gleams white from a distance. It measures 500 km in diameter and has a density of 1.2 g/cm³. Its surface is a great surprise — alongside the usual cratered areas there are regions with practically no craters at all, regions that are furrowed and undulating as if from local movements and thawing of an icy crust. These are obviously traces of the moon's relatively recent internal activity, caused, perhaps, by the tidal forces of neighbouring bodies (this mechanism functions on a larger scale in the case of the Jupiter's moon Io).

The names of the formations on Mimas are from the Legend of King Arthur and the Knights of the Round Table. An exception is the crater Herschel, named after the discoverer of the moons Mimas and Enceladus (in 1789). The names of the formations on Enceladus are from The Arabian Nights.

A general map of Mimas.
Lambert equal area projection, scale: 1:8,000,000

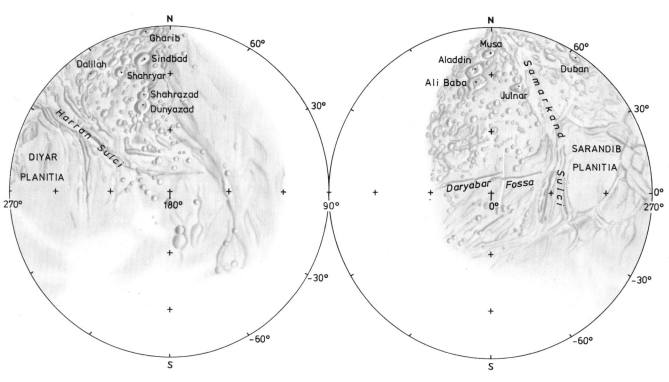

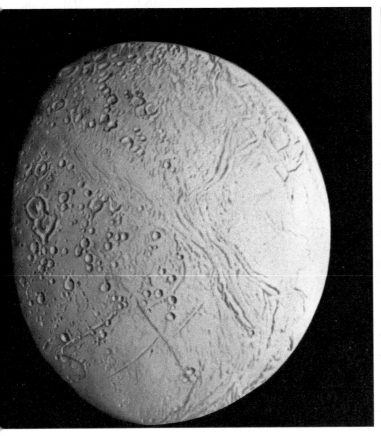

Top: Enceladus (left) and Mimas (right) depicted
to the same scale.

Right: Mimas with the crater
Herschel on the terminator.

A general map of Enceladus.
Lambert equal area projection, scale: 1:8,000,000

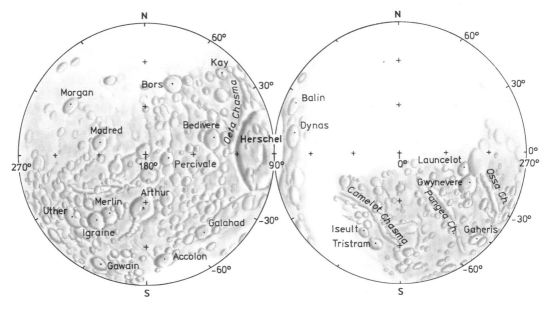

Tethys, Dione

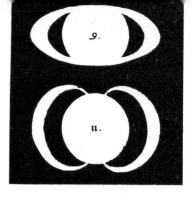

Tethys, with a mean density of 1.2 g/cm³, is a typical icy moon, a frozen 'drop' of water 1,060 km in diameter that is only slightly contaminated by rocky material. The most striking formation here is the huge valley, Ithaca Chasma, which is 50—100 km wide, 3—5 km deep, and so long that it covers practically two thirds of the satellite's circumference. At the northern end of the valley is the prominent crater Telemachos, which measures 100 km in diameter (opposite, top left). The valley probably originated as a fissure formed as the crust expanded when the interior of Tethys solidified (froze). Another noteworthy formation on Tethys is the giant crater Odysseus, measuring 450 km in diameter; it is the largest impact crater with a central mountain that has as yet been discovered in the Solar System.

Dione has the greatest density among all Saturn's icy satellites — 1.4 g/cm³. It has a greater concentration of rocky material in its core, which makes up about one third of the satellite's volume. The surface of Dione, pockmarked with craters, slightly resembles that of the planet Mercury. The largest crater (opposite, top right) is Aeneas, which has a diameter of 160 km; near the crater is a system of rilles. The hemisphere of Dione that permanently faces backward as the satellite orbits Saturn is darker, and covered with a large tuft of bright rays (opposite, bottom). This may be snow or hoarfrost formed following the escape of gases from the satellite's interior.

The names of the formations on Tethys, as every reader will recognize, are from Homer's Odyssey, and the names of the formations on Dione are from another great epic poem — Virgil's Aeneid.

A general map of Tethys. Lambert equal area projection, scale: 1:17,500,000.

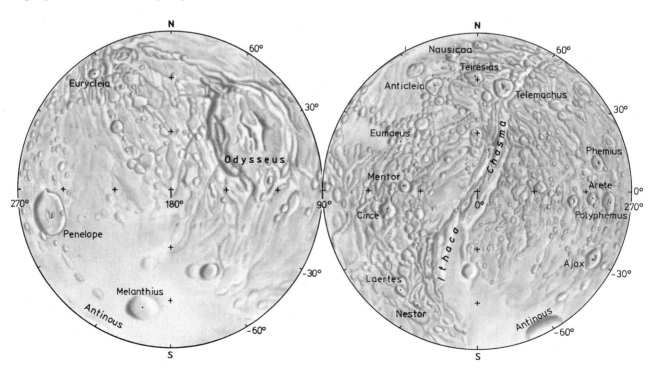

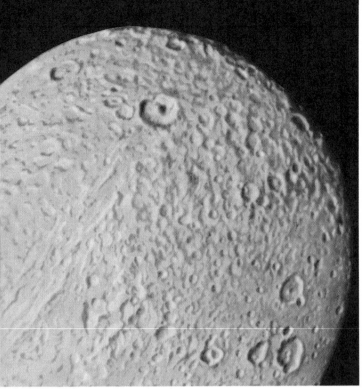

Above and left:
Tethys

Above and right:
Dione

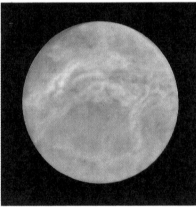

A general map of Dione. Lambert equal
area projection, scale: 1:17,500,000.

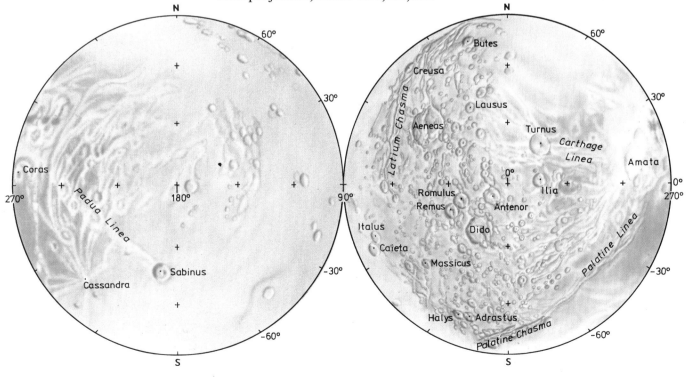

Rhea, Titan

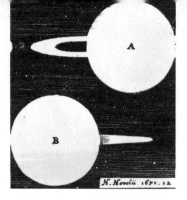

Drawings of Saturn
by J. Hevelius, 1671.

Rhea is the largest of Saturn's icy satellites: it measures 1,530 km in diameter and has a mean density of 1.3 g/cm³. The internal structure of this moon is very like that of the two preceding moons (Tethys and Dione) but its surface is the most densely pockmarked with impact craters; the largest of these, the crater Izanagi, measures 300 km in diameter. On the side of the moon that always faces away from Saturn there is a system of bright rays (opposite, top left). This may be hoarfrost formed from water vapour that escaped through fissures, as happened on Dione.

The nomenclature on the maps of this moon is taken from the legends of various cultures, related to the creation of the world.

Titan is the largest satellite of Saturn; its diameter is 5,150 km. This is the only satellite in the Solar System to have a dense atmosphere. The atmosphere, which is about 200 km thick, is filled with impenetrable clouds, making it impossible to see the surface. Titan is a completely cold body, and largely consists of water — ice; the mean density is a mere 1.9 g/cm³. The atmosphere consists predominantly of nitrogen and also contains about 1 per cent methane. The orange coloration of the clouds is apparently caused by complex hydrocarbons. The temperature at the surface of Titan is approximately —180°C, so methane may exist there in gaseous, liquid (as rain or lakes), as well as solid, states. The atmospheric pressure on the surface is 1.5 times as great as that on barth.

Bottom: A general map of Rhea. Lambert equal area projection, scale: 1:24,000,000.

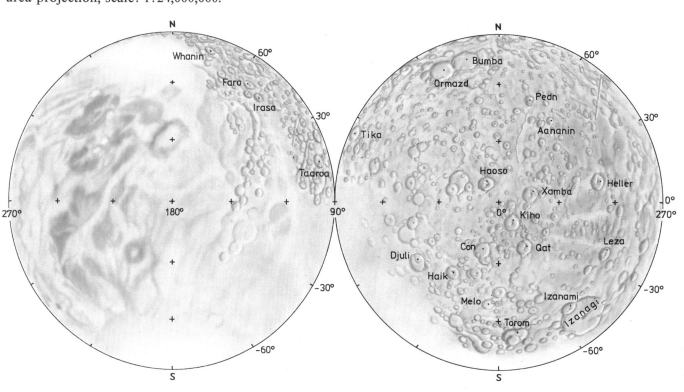

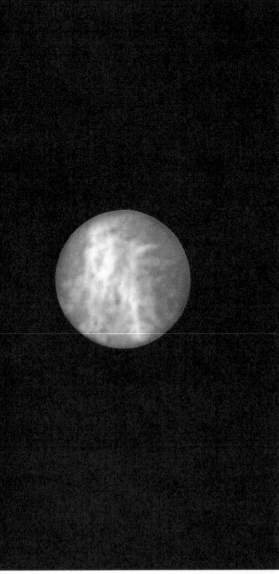

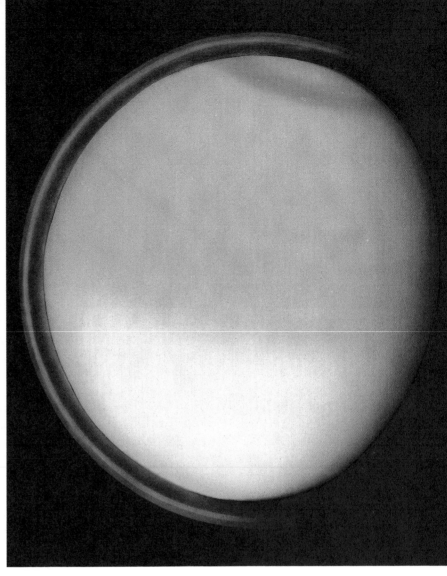

Above: Rhea (left) and Titan (right) depicted at the same scale. Only the surface of the clouds can be seen on Titan. The southern hemisphere is lighter in tint; in the northern hemisphere there is a dark band at the pole. The layers of bluish haze in the atmosphere are as much as 500 km above the surface of Titan.

Left: The surface of Rhea.

Hyperion, Iapetus, Phoebe

Drawings of Saturn
by J. Hevelius, 1655—56.

Hyperion is of an entirely irregular shape, resembling a hamburger that has not turned out right. Its approximate dimensions are $350 \times 234 \times 200$ km. On the surface there are numerous craters, surface irregularities and one prominent mountain ridge. Hyperion is probably a fragment of some larger body. Its rotation does not appear to be captured, unlike all the other satellites.

In Greek mythology Hyperion was the father of the sun god Helios. The craters on Hyperion are named after the gods of the Sun and Moon.

Iapetus is one of the greatest puzzles in Saturn's system. It was known from terrestrial observations that one of its hemispheres was extremely dark. Observations from the Voyager spaceprobes confirmed that almost all the leading hemisphere as the satellite orbits Saturn is almost coal-black; it reflects only 5 per cent of light. The opposite hemisphere, on the other hand, is bright — about as bright as dingy snow — and reflects 50 per cent of light. We do not know the composition of the dark material or its origin. It may be material 'captured' from outer space or material of internal origin. The mean density of 1.2 g/cm^3 indicates that Iapetus is also one of Saturn's icy moons. Its diameter is 1,460 km.

On the map of Iapetus there is a mysterious dark region named Cassini Regio after G. D. Cassini, who discovered this moon in 1671. Other names are from the Song of Roland. Roncevaux was the battle-field where Roland was slain.

A general map of Iapetus. Lambert equal area projection, scale: 1:24,000,000.

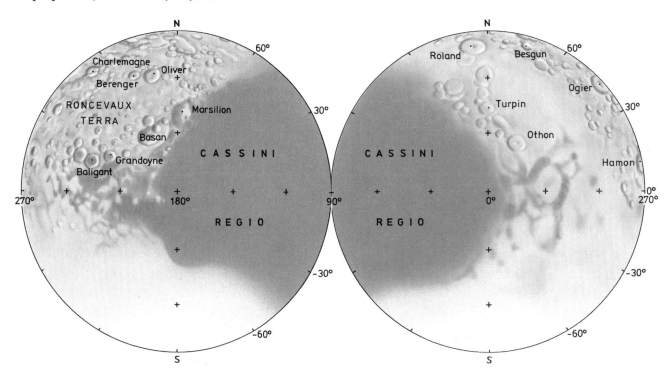

Above: Iapetus (left) and Hyperion (right depicted at the same scale. Visible on Iapetus is part of the dark region Cassini Regio.

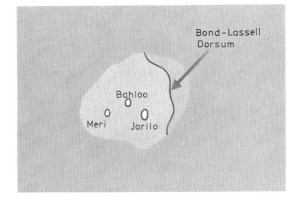

Above: The Bond-Lassell Ridge (Dorsum) is named after the discoverers of Hyperion (in 1848).

The most distant of Saturn's satellites, **Phoebe**, measures approximately 220 km in diameter. It was photographed by Voyager 2 from a great distance; the surface features could not be resolved. The satellite is almost as dark as the dark side of Iapetus.

81

Uranus, Neptune and Pluto

Le Verrier discovers
the eighth planet
by calculation. Flammarion.
Astronomie populaire, 1890.

Uranus was discovered in 1781 by W. Herschel. In 1986 the plant was explored for the first time at close quarters by Voyager 2. Uranus is a major planet and has a diameter four times that of the Earth. It has an extensive atmosphere about 11,000 km deep consisting of 88 per cent hydrogen and 12 per cent helium. The temperature at the top of the cloud layer is about —210° C.

The rotation of Uranus is quite extraordinary; its rotational axis is practically in the orbital plane. The period of rotation is approximately 17 hours. Even more extraordinary is the position of the planet's magnetic axis, which is inclined 58° to the rotational axis. Uranus has a strong magnetic field.

The English astronomer Adams and the French astronomer Le Verrier independently calculated the position of the eighth planet, which had indicated its existence by its gravitational effect on Uranus. Then on 23 September 1846 two Berlin astronomers Galle and D'Arrest found the planet **Neptune** less than one degree from the calculated position. In 1989 more detailed information about the planet was obtained by Voyager 2.

Neptune is very like Uranus in many respects: dimensions, greatly inclined magnetic field, composition of the atmosphere, period of rotation, and the like. Its density of 1,640 kg.m^{-3} makes Neptune the densest of the giant planets. Neptune has a substantial internal source of heat, for it radiates nearly three times more heat than it receives from the Sun. The temperature at the top of the cloud layer is approximately —214° C. The magnetic axis is inclined almost 47° to Neptune's rotational axis.

PLUTO

EARTH

CHARON

Pluto was discovered by the American astronomer C. Tombaugh on 21 January 1930. Pluto (diameter 2,280 km) forms a double planet with its satellite Charon (diameter 1,190 km). Pluto's surface is icy, its interior is composed of rock. Pluto has an extensive atmosphere composed primarily of methane and reaching more than 3,000 km above the planet's surface. Charon, the satellite, was discovered in 1978. It orbits Pluto once in 6,387 days. The double planet Pluto—Charon has not been explored by any probe as yet and there are no plans to launch such a probe in the near future. In terms of its size, mass and thin atmosphere Pluto is similar to Neptune's satellite Triton.

The planet Uranus (right) looks like a blue-green disc without conspicuous details—these are concealed by an impenetrable atmospheric haze (smog). Uranus's rings are dark an extremely narrow, ranging from hundreds of metres to several tens of kilometres in width. They are composed of fragments all larger than 1 m. There is only an insignificant amount of dust in the space between the rings.

The planet Neptune as observed by Voyager 2 in 1989. On the surface of the bluish cloud layer encircling the planet are dark bands, rapidly changing whitish clouds, and dark oval spots. The large grey spot, designated GDS (Great Dark Spot) in the centre of the planet's disc measures approximately 12,000×8,000 km and resembles the familiar Great Red Spot (GRS) on Jupiter. It is an atmospheric eddy rotating in counter-clockwise direction; the period of rotation is approximately sixteen days. The resulting hole in the blue methane cloud layer provides a glimpse of a deeper, darker cloud layer.

Neptune's two main rings are approximately 53,000 km and 63,000 km distant from the centre of the planet and only several tens of kilometres wide. Extending about halfway from the first to the second is a further faint ring. Closer to the planet is still another faint ring about 2,500 km wide. Neptune's rings are composed mainly of microscopic dust particles.

Miranda

Uranus with its satellites
(after G. Kuiper's photograph of 1948).
The largest terrestrial telescopes
show Miranda just like a small point
of light (see the arrow).

Until the fly-by by Voyager 2 in 1986 astronomers knew about the existence of only five of Uranus's satellites: Miranda, Ariel, Umbriel, Titania and Oberon. The probe's cameras revealed a further ten, all less than 100 km in diameter (see table on p. 222).

Miranda with a diameter of 562 km is the smallest of Uranus's five large satellites. Photographs made by Voyager 2, however, revealed one of the most bizarre bodies in the Solar System, with surprising signs of one-time geological activity.

Primarily these are two basically different types of surfaces: old, slightly undulating terrain pockmarked with craters, and young terrain with numerous faults, scarps, systems of low parallel ridges and furrows, dark and light bands, and the like. The three geologically young, ovoid or trapezoidal regions are marked as the 'corona' on the map of Miranda. In all probability they are the outcome of a process originating at the centre of the 'corona' and proceeding outward towards its edges. Remarkable, also, are the systems of tectonic faults resembling huge canyons or graben valleys 10—15 km deep and bordered by steep slopes up to 20 km wide. The largest of these commences at the illuminated scarps of Verona Rupes and continues along the edges of the Inverness Corona and Arden Corona regions to the edge of Miranda's disc.

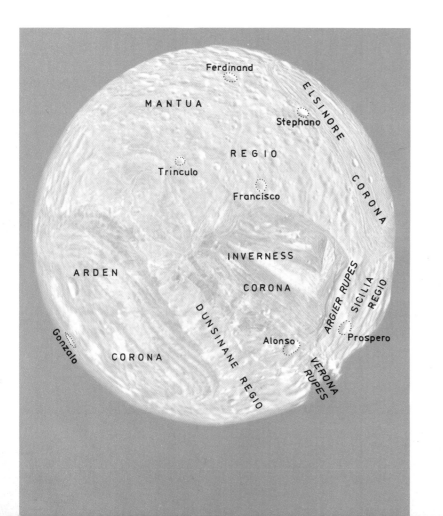

Names of formations on Miranda.
Miranda was discovered by G. Kuiper in 1948 who named it after the heroine of Shakespeare's comedy 'The Tempest'. The craters are likewise named after characters in the play. Other formations are named after important places in Shakespeare's plays.

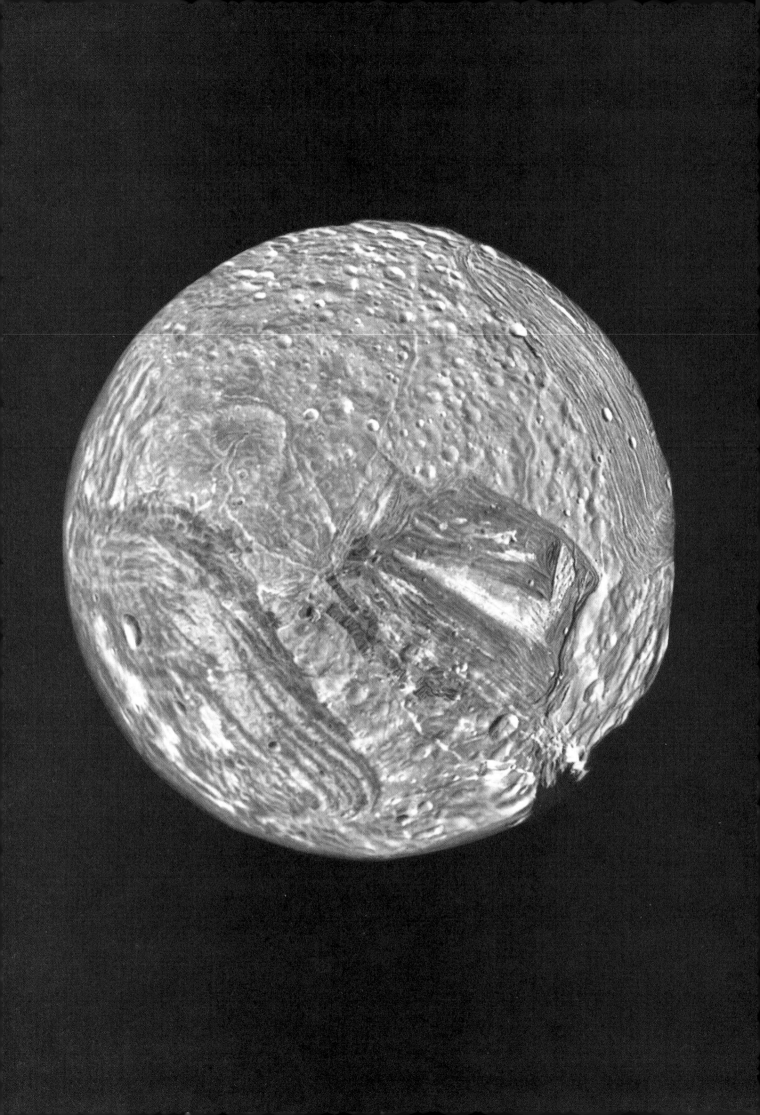

Ariel, Umbriel

122 cm reflector constructed in Malta in 1860 by W. Lassell, discoverer of Ariel, Umbriel and Triton.

During Voyager 2's flyby in 1986 only the southern hemispheres of Uranus's large satellites, permanently illuminated by the sun at the time, were explored. Examination revealed that all these satellites were geologically active in the past. The satellites are composed of about 50 per cent water ice and 50 per cent rock and the temperature at the surface is about −190° C.

Ariel (diameter 1,158 km) is the brightest of Uranus's satellites. Its surface is younger and more geologically diversified than that of the other satellites. The old surface, covered with impact craters, is greatly disrupted and dissected by a global system of faults and fissures forming long valleys and graben valleys. The origin of the faults is apparently connected with the expansion of Ariel's crust as the interior of the satellite froze. The broad floors of the valleys are filled with smooth material, that at one time flowed as streams of highly viscous ice. The youngest formations on Ariel are the impact craters with bright wall and surrounding haloes.

Ariel is a good spirit in Shakespeare's play 'The Tempest' and in Alexander Pope's satiric epic 'The Rape of the Lock'. The formations on Ariel are named after good spirits and spirits of light.

Umbriel (diameter 1,172 km) has dimensions and density similar to those of Ariel, but the surfaces and evolution of the two satellites are markedly different. Umbriel is the darkest of Uranus's large satellites, reflecting only 19 per cent of sunlight. Its surface may subsequently have been covered with dark dust and fragments from a dust cloud somewhere on Umbriel's orbit. The entire satellite is pockmarked with craters and there are also many large crater formations testifying to the fact that the surface is considerably old. There are no bright rays or haloes of bright material ejected from impact craters. Nor is there even any evidence of the action of internal forces. The brightest and at the same time most mysterious formation is the bright ring on the floor of the large crater Wunda at the edge of the satellite's disc.

In the said work by A. Pope Umbriel personifies dark and evil forces. The names selected for the formations on Umbriel are therefore those of spirits of evil and of the underworld.

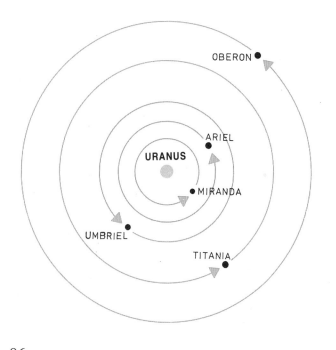

Of Uranus's fifteen satellites only the five largest can be observed from Earth, though they look merely like faint stars even through the largest telescopes. For a list of Uranus's satellites see p. 222. All the newly discovered satellites orbit Uranus closer than Miranda.

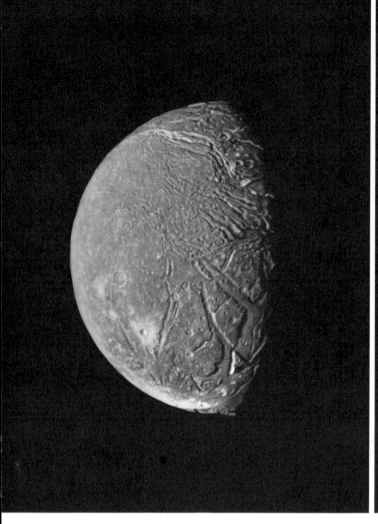

Above: Ariel
Below: names of formations on Ariel

Above: Umbriel
Below: names of formations on Umbriel

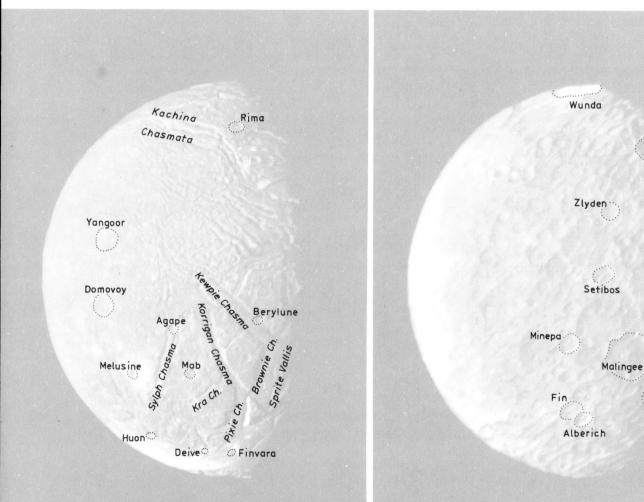

Titania, Oberon

Wiliam Herschel
discovers Uranus.
(Flammarion, *Astronomie
populaire*, 1890.

Titania (diameter 1,580 km) is the largest of Uranus's satellites. The entire surface is densely pockmarked with mostly small-sized craters from 10 to 50 km in diameter. On the part of the moon shown in the picture only 2—3 large impact craters 100—200 km in diameter are preserved. This testifies to a geologically relatively young surface. Striking is the extensive system of faults, some of them intersecting. Some slopes form graben valleys 20—50 km wide, 2—5 km deep, and up to 1,500 km long. In all probability the faults are the result of the expansion of Titania's crust in the final stages of the freezing of its interior. The youngest formations are the bright ray craters.

Titania is qeen of the fairies in Shakespeare's 'A Midsummer Night's Dream'. The craters were named after minor female characters and the other formations after certain places that figure in Shakespeare's plays.

Oberon (diameter 1,524 km) resembles Titania in size, density, colour and albedo, but the proportion of craters of different sizes differs markedly on the two satellites. Oberon has a greater percentage of large craters. The most prominent are two geologically young ray craters named Hamlet and Othello. The floors of both are covered with very dark material reflecting only 5—10 per cent of sunlight. Near the crater Macbeth there is a mountain approximately 20 km high on the edge of Oberon's disc. In all probability it is the central peak of a large impact structure several hundred kilometres in diameter. The great distance between Voyager 2 and Oberon made it impossible to obtain a more detailed picture of this satellite.

Oberon is king of the fairies in 'A Midsummer Night's Dream'. The craters on this satellite are named after tragic heroes in Shakespeare's plays.

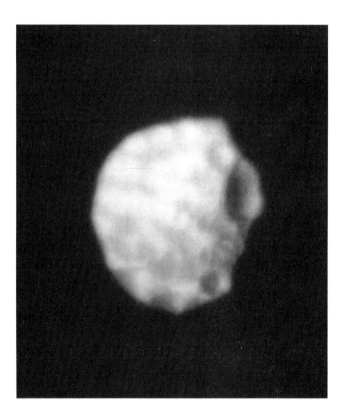

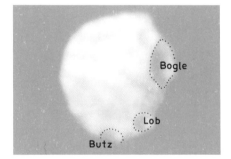

The moon named Puck is the largest of Uranus's ten satellites revealed by the photographs taken by Voyager 2. It is a celestial object of irregular shape measuring approximately 170 km at the longest. It is coal black and apparently pockmarked with numerous craters.

Puck is the name of a mischievous sprite in 'A Midsummer Night's Dream'. Three craters on this satellite are named after similar fairy-tale characters figuring in the mythology of various north European countries. The other nine satellites of Uranus are named after heroines in Shakespeare's plays.

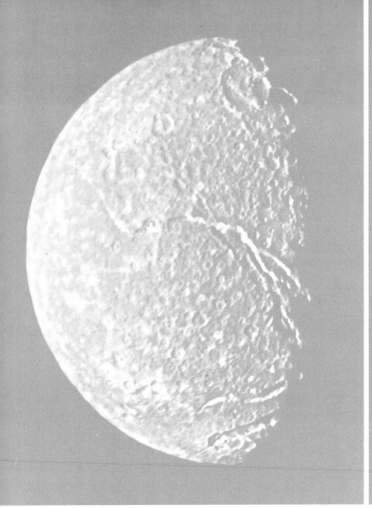

Above: Titania
Below: names of formations on Titania

Above: Oberon
Below: names of formations on Oberon

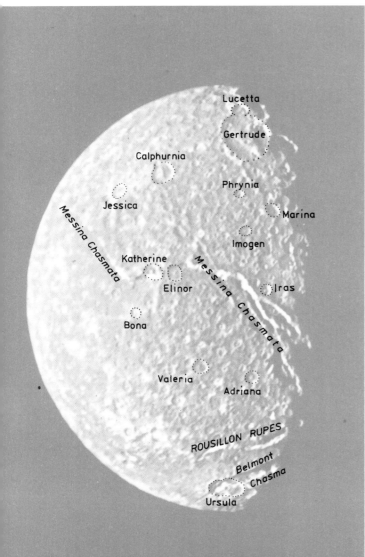

Lucetta
Gertrude
Calphurnia
Phrynia
Jessica
Marina
Messina Chasmata
Imogen
Katherine
Messina Chasmata
Elinor
Iras
Bona
Valeria
Adriana
ROUSILLON RUPES
Belmont
Chasma
Ursula

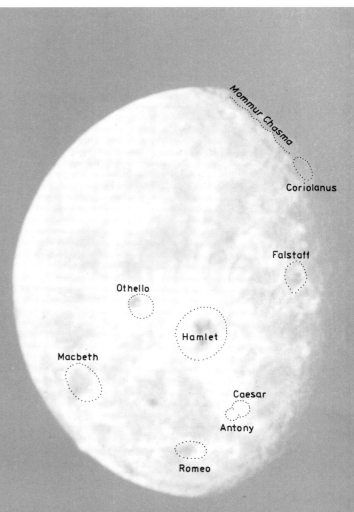

Mommur Chasma
Coriolanus
Falstaff
Othello
Hamlet
Macbeth
Caesar
Antony
Romeo

Triton

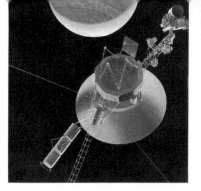

In August 1989 the American space probe Voyager 2 transmitted to Earth the first detailed photographs of Triton.

On its flight through Neptune's system Voyager 2 discovered six new satellites (see p. 222) and likewise transmitted to Earth detailed and surprising photographs of Neptune's largest satellite Triton, measuring 2,720 km in diameter.

Triton's crust, approximately 150—200 km thick, is composed mostly of water ice. Beneath this, in all probability, is an ocean of water, ammonia and methane. The core of rock and perhaps also metals represents about two thirds of Triton's mass. The temperature on the satellite's surface is —235° C. The surface is very bright, reflecting 70—90 per cent of sunlight. Brightest is the polar cap covered with ice and snow containing, in all probability, also nitrogen and methane. The most remarkable formations are the geysers of nitrogen rising vertically above the polar ice to a height of approximately 8 km, where the ejected material suddenly changes direction and extends parallel to the surface like a dark plume of smoke for a distance of more than 100 km. In several places on the polar cap there are dark elongated spots, apparently deposits of material from previous eruptions of nitrogen. Outside of and in line with the edge of the polar cap is a broad bluish band of frost. Frost volcanism also formed on Triton large calderas and extensive regions with ridged/warty surfaces called 'cantaloupe terrain'. This terrain is criss-crossed by a system of long furrows and low ridges. The small number of impact craters testifies to the fact that the surface of this satellite is relatively young. Triton has a very thin nitrogen atmosphere augmented from the geysers and also by the sublimation of nitrogen from the icy surface. Hazes were observed in the atmosphere and also small clouds at the terminator.

Names of water deities and spirits were chosen not only for Neptune, Triton and other satellites, but also for the formations on these bodies.

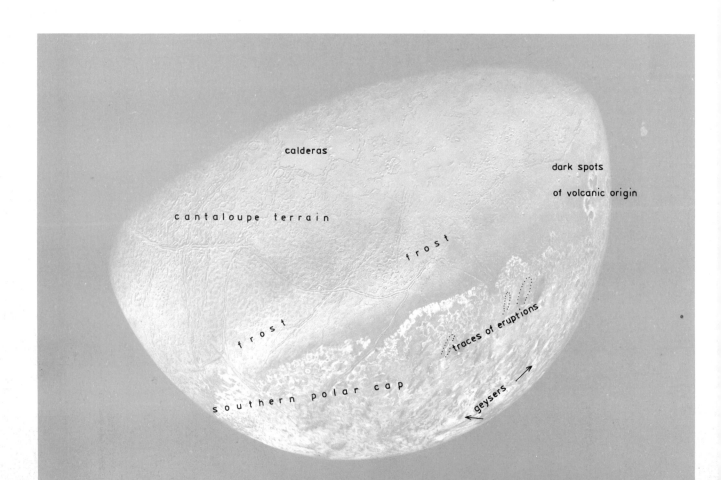

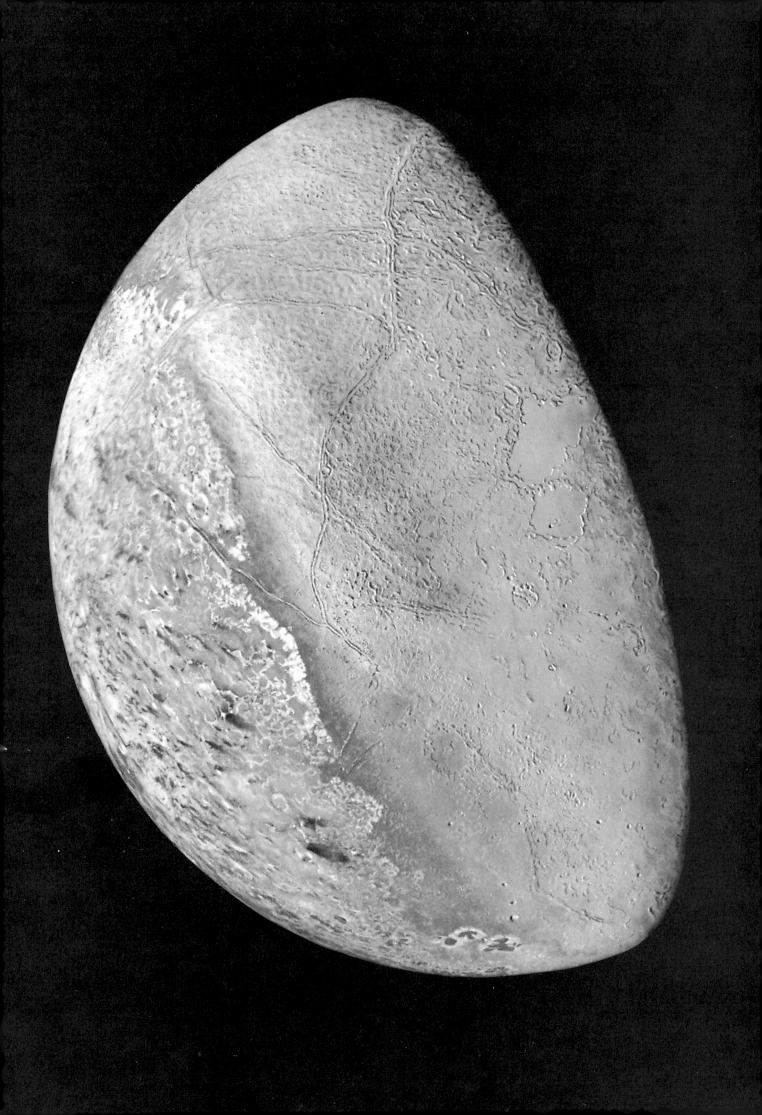

Between the planets

Asteroids, comets, meteors

The meteor shower
of 27 November 1872.
Flammarion, *Astronomie
populaire*, 1890.

Only rarely do the small and faint bodies of the Solar System attract our attention, but very occasionally they outshine — albeit only briefly — all the other objects in the heavens.

Least conspicuous are the minor planets, *planetoids*, or *asteroids,* that appear in the sky as faint stars visible only with a telescope. Thousands of these revolve around the Sun, mostly between the orbits of Mars and Jupiter (picture at bottom). A typical asteroid has a diameter of approximately 1 km and is irregular in shape.

Only about 110 asteroids have a diameter of more than 100 km. They are bodies of ice and rocks and may be similar in character to cometary nuclei. This is also borne out by the transformation of the asteroid Chiron into a comet as revealed in 1988.

The most striking of the small inhabitants of the solar system are the comets — or at least those that form long, bright tails when they are close to the Sun. However, most comets, of which there are perhaps thousands of millions, remain concealed at vast distances from the

Sun. More will be said about comets on pp. 94—97.

The smallest of the celestial bodies are the *meteoroids*. They are so tiny that they are not visible in outer space. If, however, a meteoroid enters the Earth's atmosphere (its velocity is 11—72 km/sec!) it heats up intensely, becomes molten, vaporizes, and flares up for a brief interval as a *meteor*. Meteors that are brighter than Venus are called *fireballs* or *bolides*; the light-path of fireballs may show sudden flares due to explosions; sometimes one may even produce sonic booms. The remnants of any such meteoroids that fall to Earth are called *meteorites*.

It is assumed that interplanetary material is a remnant from the period when the planets were formed, and that it consists of the original material, thus preserving information about the beginning of the Solar System. That is why these small celestial bodies are of such great interest to scientists.

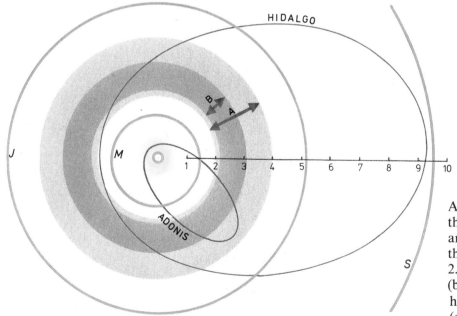

Asteroids revolve around the Sun primarily between 2 and 4 AU (belt A), with most of the orbits concentrated between 2.2 and 3.2 AU from the Sun (belt B). Some asteroids, however, have very eccentric orbits (e.g. Adonis and Hidalgo).

Below: Halley's comet as it looked after its passage round the Sun in 1986.

Above: In a photograph, an asteroid reveals its presence by its movement amongst the fixed stars.

Above: The trail of a bright meteor with three explosions.

Comets

The tail of a comet
points away from the Sun.
Gemma Frisius,
De astrolabo, 1583.

Of all celestial objects perhaps none have earned such a bad reputation in the past as comets, at one time believed to be omens of destruction. Nowadays we admire the beauty of this extraordinary natural phenomenon and regret that there are so few truly bright magnificent comets to be seen, less than a dozen each century. Every year, however, astronomers observe about ten faint comets visible only with a telescope. All-told some 700 comets have been observed to date and of this number only one-tenth have returned to the Sun two or more times.

What is a comet? First of all it consists of an irregularly shaped *nucleus* several kilometres in diameter, a large dirty snowball composed of water ice, various frozen gases, and silicaceous, carbonaceous and metallic dust particles. When a comet approaches the Sun its surface temperature rises and the ice begins to evaporate. The comet is beginning to waken. The gases liberated from the nucleus, together with the dust particles they carry, form a hazy cloud round the nucleus measuring several tens of thousands of kilometres in diameter; this is called the *coma*. A comet begins to be properly visible only when it is less than about 3 AU from the Sun. The coma and the nucleus together form the *head* of the comet, from which a *tail* of gas and dust particles usually begins to stream when the comet has approached the Sun to within a distance of about 1 AU. The tail is the comet's greatest ornament, and may extend for as much as several tens of millions of kilometres.

Near the Sun evaporation is extremely rapid; every second tons and even tens of tons of gas and dust escape from the nucleus in the form of streams spurting from the side of the nucleus facing the Sun. Solid particles are separated from the coma by solar-radiation pressure to form a *dust tail* that is usually curved, broad, and without internal structure. The gaseous molecules ionized by solar radiation form a *gas (ion) tail*, usually in the form of straight narrow rays directed away from the Sun. The tails of comets are extremely tenuous, as is shown by the stars that shine through the tail without any apparent diminution in brightness. Even more rarefied, and invisible to the eye, is the extensive *hydrogen corona* that may be even larger in size than the Sun.

Four examples of bright comets are illustrated on the opposite page: at top left is Comet West, observed in 1976, at top right Comet Mrkos, observed in 1957, at bottom left Comet Kohoutek, observed in 1973, and at bottom right Comet Humason, observed in 1962. The comets are named after their discoverers.

Parts of a comet: 1 — nucleus (a-a axis of rotation); 2 — jets of gas and dust; 3 — coma; 4 — cometary head; 5 — dust tail; 6 — gas (ion) tail; 7 — hydrogen corona. S indicates the direction to the Sun

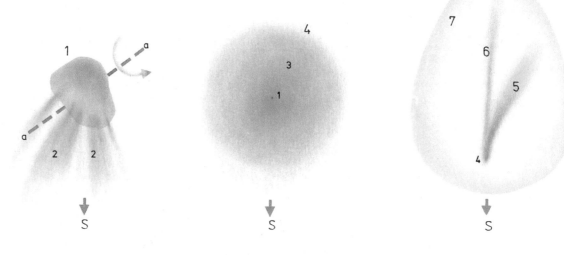

Halley's Comet

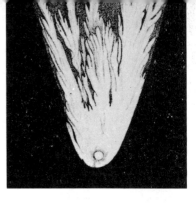

Drawing of a comet,
October 1811.

This comet bears the name of the prominent English astronomer Edmond Halley, who discerned that it is an object revolving round the Sun in an elongated elliptical orbit once every 76 years. He correctly predicted that the comet's next return would be in 1758. Later it was discovered that the first confirmed observation of Halley's Comet dates from the year 240 B.C.; since then the comet has returned to the Sun twenty-nine times. In 1910 it provided terrestrial observers with a grand spectacle but in 1986 conditions for the observation of the comet from Earth were extremely unfavourable.

This legendary comet is one of the brightest, most active and youngest of the comets and its orbit is precisely known. During its last return to the Sun it was the focus of attention of astronomers the world over and in March 1986 it was examined in detail by a whole swarm of spaceprobes. The Soviet probes Vega 1 and 2, and the West European probe Giotto were the first ever to observe the region of a comet's nucleus at close quarters.

The nucleus of Halley's Comet is a compact body of very irregular shape measuring about $16 \times 8 \times 8.5$ km. It resembles a potato in shape and its surface is blacker than coal. The nucleus revolves around its axis. The activity of the nucleus is remarkable: gaseous streams spurt from several places on the side illuminated by the Sun at a speed of several km/s, and carry with them particles of dust. The particles of cometary dust with masses greater than about 0.1 g fall back and form a very dark accumulated layer. Lighter, finer dust particles escape into the coma or into the tail. When it was near the Sun Halley's Comet lost more than 60 tons of water vapour, other gases and dust every second; i.e. more than 5 million tons of matter per day. The production of matter varies greatly, being related to the irregular shape of the nucleus and its rotation. At the time the spaceprobes made their fly-by the nucleus produced about 5 tons of material per second. The thick clouds of dust made photographing the nucleus extremely difficult. The total mass of the nucleus is about a billion (US:trillion = 10^{11}) tons and according to the observed mass-loss it may be presumed that the lifetime of Halley's Comet is about 1 000 orbits. During each orbit round the Sun the comet loses a surface layer about 1 m thick.

The orbit of Halley's Comet and its movement in the period 1910-1986.
The changes in speed in the comet's orbit are considerable: from 1.2 to 55 km/s. Marked in blue are the orbits of the planets Earth, Mars, Jupiter, Saturn, Uranus and Neptune. The planet will return to the Sun in the year 2061.

Top of p. 97: Head and part of the tail of Halley's Comet during its return in 1910. The direction of the Sun is towards the left.

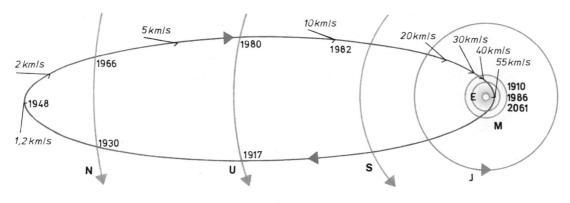

Below and right: Region of the nucleus of Halley's Comet according to observations made by the Giotto spaceprobe in March 1986. The dark outline of the nucleus (1) is visible against the faint background light scattered by dust. Visible on the outline of the nucleus (2) are surface irregularities several hundred metres high. Jets carrying fine dust particles (3) are spurting from the nucleus. The presumed outline of the part of the nucleus concealed by the jets is marked in light grey in the adjacent diagram (4). S indicates the direction of the Sun.

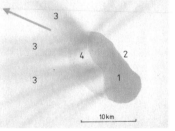

The Sun

The photosphere

A large sunspot.
Howlett, 16 October 1865.

The star called the Sun is not particularly outstanding amongst the thousands of millions of other stars that make up our Galaxy. For us inhabitants of the Earth, of course, the Sun is the most important star of all, the chief source of energy, light and heat, and source of life. It is also the only star that we can observe and explore from close at hand and in detail.

The blinding disc of the Sun is so bright that careless observers are in danger of having their eyes damaged or even of losing their eyesight. Only very exceptionally can we look at the Sun directly, when it is sufficiently dimmed by cloud, mist, atmospheric haze at the horizon, or the like. The Sun can be safely observed with a telescope by projection of the Sun's image through the eyepiece (see p. 219) or by the use of special reflecting filtres or other optical equipment.

What do we see on the Sun? When viewing it with the naked eye or with a telescope we see the lowest layer of the Sun's atmosphere — the *photosphere*, which is approximately 300 km thick and has a temperature of 6,000 K. Concealed from view beneath the photosphere is the Sun's interior. Rising from the interior to the surface are clouds of hot gases that produce a granular structure on the visible photosphere — *granulation* (bottom picture). It looks a little like boiling rice; the individual 'rice grains', however, measure 1,000 to 2,000 kilometres in diameter.

The so-called active regions in the Sun's atmosphere are areas where numerous changes take place, changes that as a whole are referred to as *solar activity*. The best-known result of this activity are *sunspots* that occur on the photosphere. These are areas with a lower temperature, approximately 1,500 K less than that of the surrounding photosphere. They generally occur in groups and their number fluctuates, reaching peak levels every eleven years or so; this is referred to as the eleven-year solar cycle. The picture on the opposite page shows how the Sun looks at a peak of solar activity. At the lowest level of activity, the Sun is 'clean', sometimes without any sunspots whatsoever.

On the photosphere, at the edge of the solar disc, we can see numerous bright patches called *faculae*. They often cover large areas, mainly in the vicinity of sunspots.

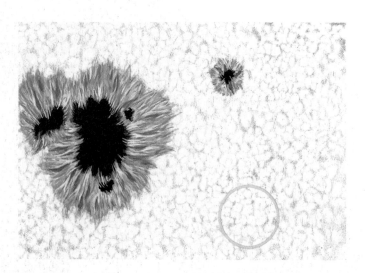

A fully developed sunspot consists of a dark *umbra* encircled by a lighter *penumbra*. The penumbra has a filamentary structure. Large sunspots may have a diameter greater than that of the Earth (blue ring).

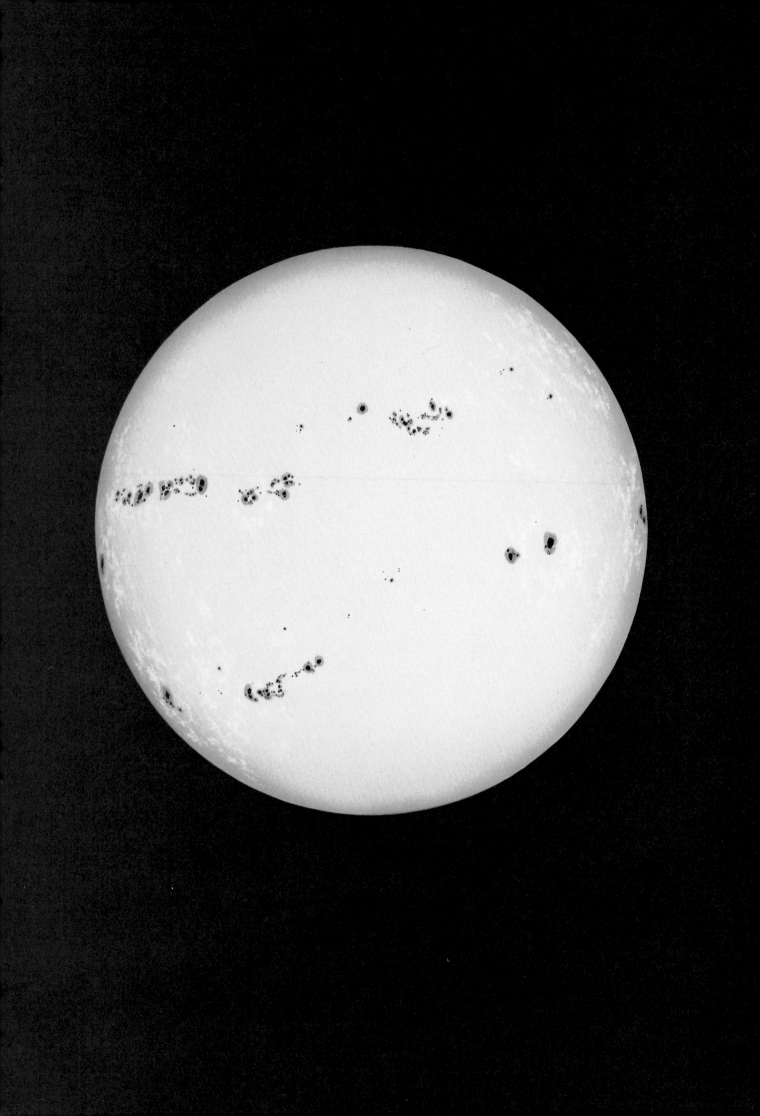

The Sun

The chromosphere and prominences

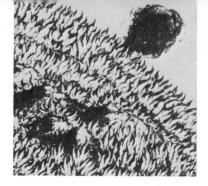

The Sun with sunspots
and prominences.
Kircher and Scheiner, 1635.

The Sun's atmosphere consists of three layers: the lowest is the *photosphere* ('luminous sphere'); above it, approximately 10,000 km thick, is the *chromosphere* ('coloured sphere'), and above that is the *corona*, extending far into interplanetary space.

The gases in the chromosphere are so rarefied that they are not detectable in visible light under normal observational conditions. They may be observed with the naked eye only for a very brief period during a total eclipse of the Sun, when the brilliant photosphere is completely obscured by the Moon; then we can see the chromosphere as a narrow pinkish border round the black lunar disc. The chromosphere radiates only in certain spectral lines (for an explanation of this term see p. 227), chiefly in the red light of hydrogen, in the Hα line. This can be used for observation of the chromosphere at times other than during a solar eclipse. With the aid of a special filter we can select the line Hα from the entire solar spectrum, thereby eliminating all interference from other light. We can then observe the chromosphere not only at the solar limb but also on the disc, as shown in the bottom picture.

Places where there is a strong and variable magnetic field frequently develop into active regions. Bright *flocculi* form in the chromosphere, particularly in the vicinity of sunspots. Occasionally an area of flocculi undergoes a sudden increase in brightness. This is a *chromospheric flare*, which is accompanied by the release of a vast amount of energy in many forms of radiation. This can have a pronounced effect also on various processes on the Earth. This is why the systematic observation of flares, and solar activity in general, is of great importance.

Extending upward from the chromosphere into the corona are luminous clouds and streams of plasma — the *prominences*, which are some of the most beautiful and most interesting phenomena in the Universe. The infinitely diverse forms and shapes, the stately and capricious movements, as well as the sheer scale of the phenomenon, which give a hint at the enormous energy hidden in the interior of the Sun, all combine to provide a grand spectacle.

A portion of the chromosphere as it appears above the obscured limb of the Sun's disc. The numerous columns of gas, spurting upward from the chromosphere, form sharp finger-like jets or spicules. The picture resembles a sea of fire above a blazing prairie. Solar prominences rise above the chromosphere.

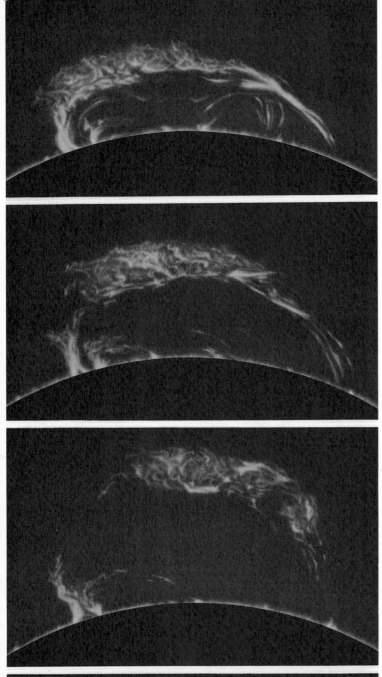

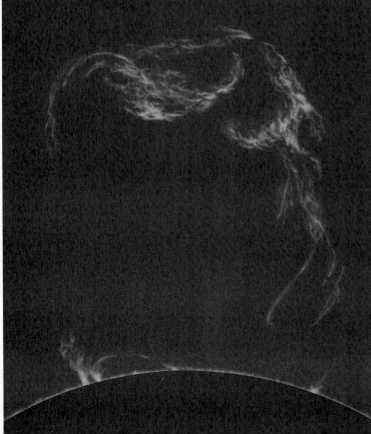

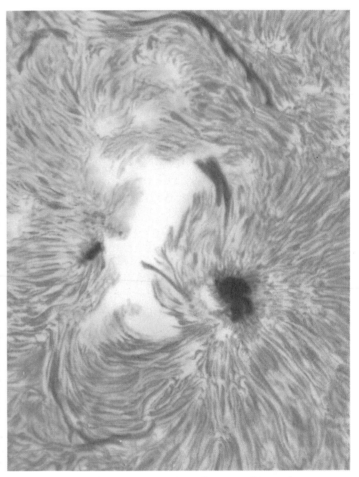

Above: The Sun's chromosphere in an active region around a group of spots, where there is a strong magnetic field. Threads of plasma—fibrils—form along the magnetic lines of force. The conspicuously dark, long threads are *filaments*—projections of a prominence onto the Sun's disc. The white spots are *flocculi*. The large white area in the centre is a *chromospheric flare*.

Left, from the top: The development of a huge prominence that in the space of six hours reached a height of 600,000 km.

101

The Sun

Corona

The corona during a total eclipse of the Sun, 1858.

Only few of us have the luck to see a total solar eclipse even once in our lifetime. For a few fleeting minutes and seconds we gaze in awe and wonder at this rare phenomenon, which has excited so many past generations of Earth's inhabitants. It is a lucky coincidence that the Moon is the size it is, and that the distance that separates it from the Earth is such that it appears to be about as big as the Sun in the sky. That is why, under certain circumstances, the Moon can briefly obscure the Sun, or rather its photosphere, so that a terrestrial observer can see the outermost layer of the solar atmosphere, known as *corona*, even with the naked eye. It is seen as a silvery glow whose brightness dims with increasing distance from the surface of the Sun. The brightness of the corona is a hundred thousand times fainter than the brightness of the photosphere. The gases in the corona are a million million times less dense than the air we breathe. The corona has a surprisingly high temperature: more than a million degrees.

The Sun's corona extends far into interplanetary space, way beyond the Earth's orbit. The Sun's general magnetic field shapes the corona and forms within it complex coronal rays and streamers along the magnetic lines of force (picture at right). Solar activity is closely linked to changes in the magnetic field (see pp. 98 and 100) and it influences the typical shape of the corona at the time of maximum and minimum solar activity.

With modern methods, it is possible to observe the corona at any time, not only during a total eclipse. Particularly effective is the exploration of the corona from outer space, where, among other things, observation of the Sun's X-ray radiation is not blocked by the Earth's atmosphere. This led to the discovery that there are relatively cooler, dark regions in the corona, the so-called coronal holes (picture at bottom), which are probably the source of streams of particles that penetrate far into space and also affect some processes on Earth.

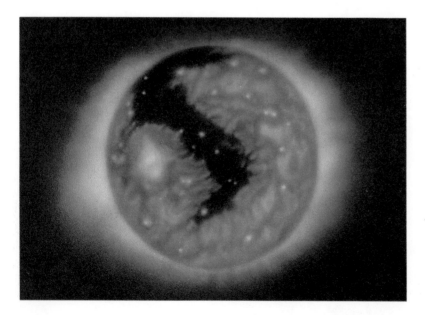

An X-ray picture of the Sun does not show the photosphere but only the hotter parts of the corona, which are projected onto the Sun's disc (the disc is much cooler and therefore dark). The large dark S-shaped spot is a coronal hole.

Typical shapes
of the corona at the time
of maximum (left)
and minimum (right)
solar activity.

Stars

The temperature-luminosity diagram

The scientist and the layman.
A medieval woodcarving.

The great diversity that exists among stars is graphically shown by the *temperature-luminosity* diagram, also known as the Hertzsprung-Russell diagram or HRD. A simplified version is shown on the opposite page. The stars are plotted in the diagram according to their temperature (or spectral class) and luminosity, L (or absolute stellar magnitude, M). The fraction $L:L_\odot$ is the ratio between the luminosity of the star and the luminosity of the Sun.

On p. 10 we have shown that the stars in the HRD cluster in certain groups and that they do not fill the whole of the diagram. The greatest number of stars, including the Sun ($\odot$) is located on the *main sequence* (line a). A large number of stars are found on the *giant* branch (g), fewer in the group of *supergiants* (c)—stars with an exceptionally great luminosity more than 10,000 times that of the Sun. Stars with the smallest luminosity are the *white dwarfs* (d), and the *red dwarfs* (b), which are ten thousand times fainter than the Sun and are thus difficult to observe, and even then only when relatively nearby.

These great differences in luminosity also go hand in hand with great differences in the size of stars. Shown in the top half of the picture on the opposite page are the dimensions of several stellar giants and supergiants, compared with the small dot representing the Sun, which here is shown with a diameter of only 1 millimetre. In the bottom half of the picture, on the other hand, the Sun appears huge when compared with the red and white dwarfs. Their small dimensions are emphasized by comparison with the Earth (brown circle).

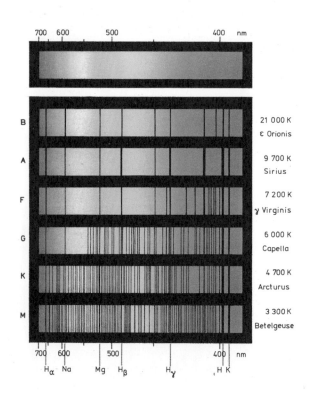

The picture at left shows examples of the spectra of certain bright stars and also gives their surface temperatures in kelvin (K). The wavelengths are in nanometres (nm). Shown at the top is a continuous spectrum. The stellar spectra contain numerous dark absorption lines — 'signatures' of the chemical elements present in the stars. The position of the lines of some elements is marked with symbols below. Stars are classified into spectral classes according to the presence and intensity of certain lines in their spectra. The *main spectral classes* are designated by the letters O, B, A, F, G, K, M. The differences between them are not due to differing chemical composition but mainly because of differences in the surface temperature of the stars.

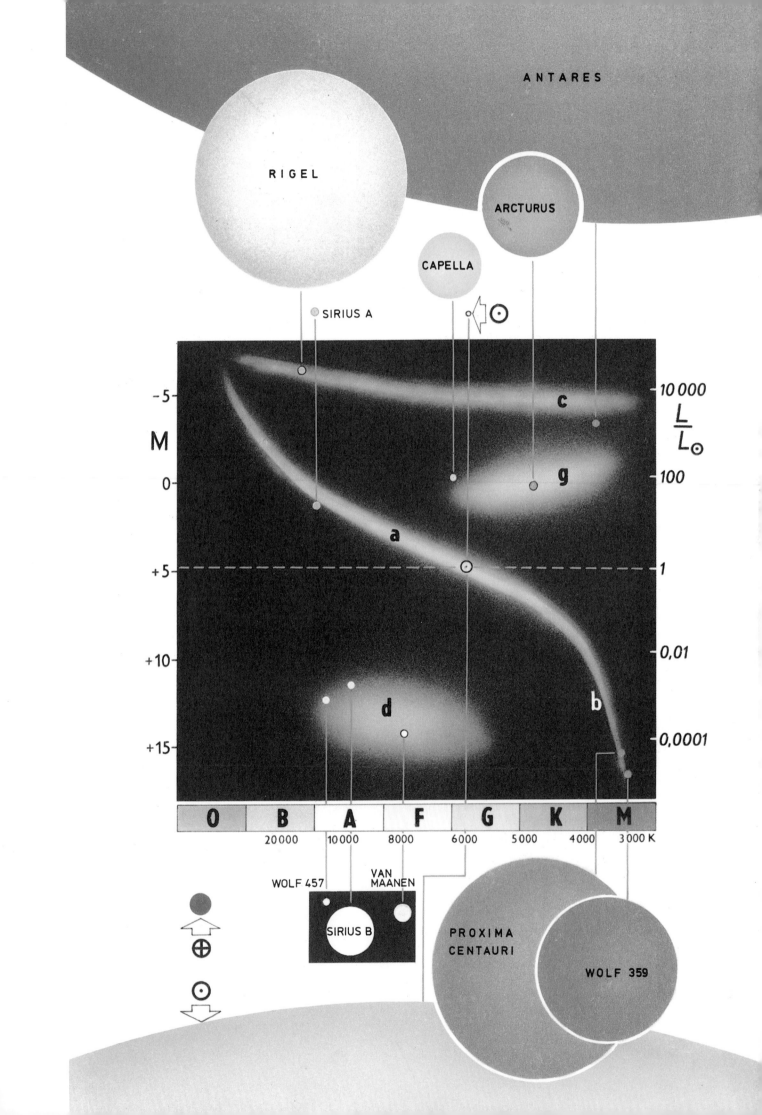

ANTARES

RIGEL

ARCTURUS

CAPELLA

SIRIUS A

M

−5

0

+5

+10

+15

O   B   A   F   G   K   M

20000   10000   8000   6000   5000   4000   3000 K

$\dfrac{L}{L_\odot}$

10 000

100

1

0,01

0,0001

a
b
c
d
g

WOLF 457

VAN
MAANEN

SIRIUS B

PROXIMA
CENTAURI

WOLF 359

Constellations in the region of the north celestial pole

Cepheus (detail). 14th century astronomical codex.

On the opposite page is the first of six charts, marked A-F, depicting the entire celestial sphere with both northern and southern skies. Together with the general chart on p. 214, charts A-F show the positions and boundaries of all 88 constellations. Thicker lines mark the boundaries of those constellations and groups of constellations that are shown in greater detail on the following pages, and accompanied by pictures of selected celestial objects. The *celestial coordinates* (right ascension and declination) on all star charts in this atlas are valid for epoch 2 000.0.

The most prominent constellation in the region of the north pole is *Ursa Major* (the Great Bear), part of which is the figure outlined by seven bright stars, and known as the Plough or Big Dipper. It is a constellation that is familiar to all observers in the northern hemisphere and is the best starting point for the novice. The line connecting the stars Dubhe and Merak points to the Pole Star (Polaris) in *Ursa Minor* (the Little Bear), also known as the Little Dipper. The Pole Star lies less than 1 degree from the north celestial pole (at the centre of the chart). Stretching between the two Bears is the constellation *Draco* (the Dragon) with a quadrilateral 'head'.

If we extend a line from the centre of the Plough to the Pole Star the same distance beyond the pole, we encounter five bright stars in the Milky Way marking the M- or W-shaped figure of the constellation of *Cassiopeia*. This is another of the familiar constellations in the northern sky. Near it lies the Double Cluster χ, h, in Perseus, visible to the naked eye as a small hazy cloud. Between Cassiopeia and Draco lies the faint constellation of *Cepheus. Camelopardalis* (the Giraffe) and *Lynx* (the Lynx) are referred to by amateur astronomers as 'invisible' constellations because they contain only very faint stars, and can be seen only under ideal conditions.

Key to symbols used in the constellation charts.

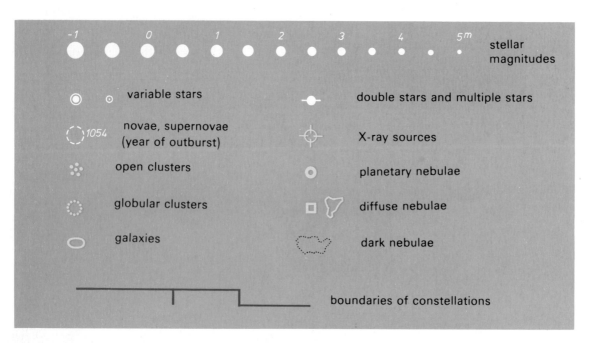

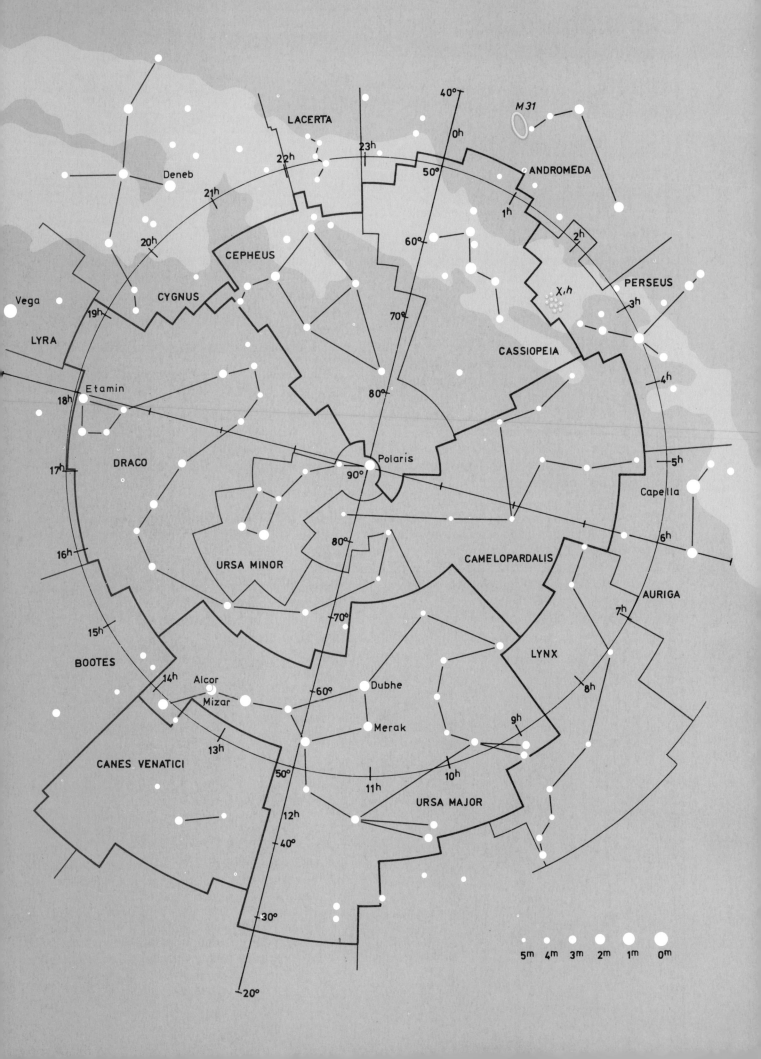

Camelopardalis

Camelopardalis—Cam—The Giraffe

Draco

Draconis—Dra—The Dragon

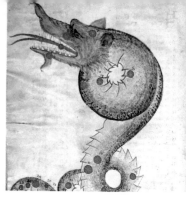

Draco (the Dragon) (detail).
14th century
astronomical codex.

Ursa Minor

Ursae Minoris—UMi—the Little Bear
(Little Dipper)

α Draconis—Thuban: mag. 3.6, spectral class A0, distance 215 light years. The Pole Star of the ancient Egyptians; in 2830 B. C. it was only 10' from the celestial pole.

α Ursae Minoris—Polaris—the Pole Star: mag. 2.0, spectrum F8, distance more than 300 light years; a supergiant 1600 times brighter than the Sun. A cepheid varying by mag. 0.1 with a period of 3.9696 days. Polaris is a close double, and the invisible companion revolves around it with a period of 30.5 years. It is less than 1° from the celestial pole and an important aid for orientation and navigation.

ν Draconis: double star visible with a small telescope. Mag. 4.95 and 4.98; separation between the two components 62"; both spectra A5, luminosity 11 times that of the Sun. The distance of the double star is 120 light-years.

NGC 6543 (top right): one of the brightest planetary nebulae, but with small angular di-

mensions (22" × 16"). The spiral structure is visible in photographs. The nebula's true diameter is nearly one third of a light-year, and its distance about 3200 light-years. The central star is very hot, mag. 9.5, temperature 35,000 K and with a luminosity nearly 100 times that of the Sun.

NGC 2403 (bottom right): a galaxy lying just outside the Local Group of galaxies. Visible even with binoculars as a large hazy patch. Mag. 8.8; angular dimensions 10' × 16'. Distance 8 million light-years. True diameter 37,000 light-years.

NGC 2523 (third picture from top): an unusual barred spiral galaxy. Mag. 12.7; angular dimensions 1.8' × 1.4'.

NGC 5866 (second picture from top): a galaxy observed edgewise showing a narrow, dark band along the equator. Mag. 11.1; angular dimensions 2.9' × 1.0'.

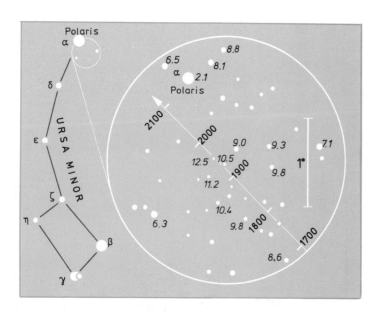

The position of the north celestial pole amongst the stars varies as a result of the Earth's precession. Polaris will be closest to the pole (27'31") in the year 2102. Faint stars with known magnitudes in the region of the pole (the North Polar Sequence) can be used to determine the faintest stellar magnitude visible with any given telescope.

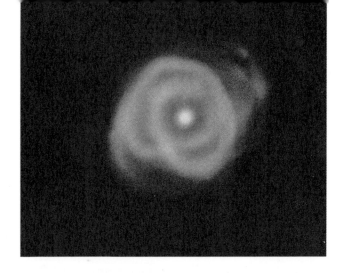

The planetary nebula NGC 6543 looks like a hazy
star when viewed through a telescope with a low
magnification. With greater magnification it looks
like a hazy disc, somewhat like the blurred picture
of a star, coloured blue-green. It is difficult to resolve the central star (mag. 9.5) against the bright
background of the nebula.

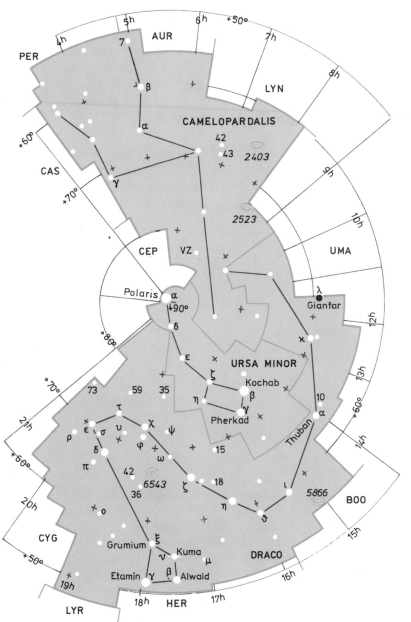

Cassiopeia

Cassiopeiae—Cas—Cassiopeia

Cepheus

Cephei—Cep—Cepheus

Cassiopeia (detail).
14th century
astronomical codex.

γ Cassiopeiae—Cih: an irregular variable star; a subgiant with B0 spectrum. In 1937 it reached maximum (mag. 1.6) when a gaseous envelope was ejected from the star. It then declined to below mag. 3.0 in 1940, afterwards rising to mag. 2.2. Distance about 100 light-years.

ρ Cassiopeiae: an irregular variable star, maximum 4.4, minimum 5.1 to 6.0 mag. The spectrum changes from F8 to M5. Distance about 200 light-years.

μ Cephei—Garnet Star: a bright reddish-orange colour. An irregular variable with magnitude range of 3.7 to 5.0. Estimated distance 800 to 1200 light-years. A red supergiant, several hundred times the Sun's diameter.

VV Cephei: an eclipsing binary, with mag. ranging from 6.7 to 7.4. Spectra M2 (red supergiant) and B9. The red supergiant was previously considered to be the largest known star (1600 times the size of the Sun); more recent measurements give a much smaller diameter (about 400 times that of the Sun).

SN 1572—Tycho's Star: at maximum it was bright as Venus (300 million times the Sun's luminosity), visible with the naked eye for 16 months. Distance more than 10,000 light-years. Remnants: radio radiation; an inconspicuous expanding nebula; no star that could be the remnant of the supernova has been identified.

M 52—NGC 7654: open cluster, studded with stars—about 200 stars within an area 12′ across. The calculated density in the centre of the cluster is more than 50 stars per cubic parsec. Estimated distance 3,000 to 5,400 light-years. True diameter 10—15 light-years.

NGC 7635—Bubble Nebula (opposite, bottom left): named after the unusual gaseous arc which resembles a large bubble. It may be an atypical planetary nebula or the remnant of a former nova.

NGC 147 and NGC 185: elliptical galaxies, companions of M31 (see p. 122).

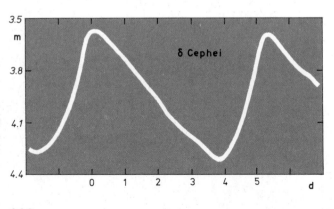

The light-curve of the pulsating variable δ Cephei. A typical example of the short-period variables, known as cepheids. δ Cephei is a supergiant about 30 times the solar diameter; at maximum its luminosity is 3,300 times that of the Sun; the distance of the star is slightly more than 1,000 light-years. The magnitude ranges from 3.6 to 4.3 with a period of $5^d8^h48^m$. For the importance of cepheids see pp. 11, 206 and 223.

Galaxy NGC 6946 (right). Visually this is a very faint object of about 11th magnitude. Angular dimensions 9.0′ × 7.5′; estimated distance between 10 and 20 million light-years. One of the closest galaxies outside the Local Group of galaxies.

The open cluster M52.

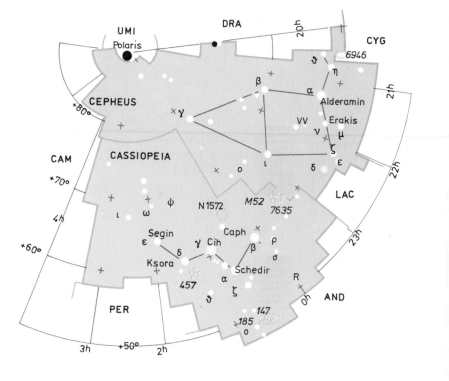

Cassiopeia A (below). The remnant of a supernova that probably erupted around 1680; a very intense source of radio emission; angular diameter about 4′; distance about 11,000 light-years. The faint nebular filaments are marked in red; invisible features emitting strong radio waves are marked in green.

NGC 7653

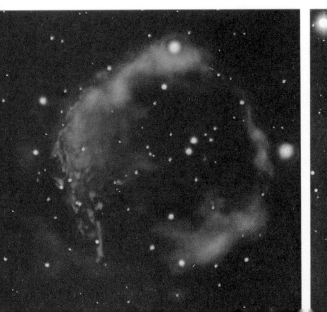

Ursa Major

Ursae Majoris—UMa—The Great Bear
(The Plough or Big Dipper)

Ursa Major
(the Great Bear)
according to P. Apianus,
Quadrans, 1532.

There is no doubt that of all the constellations, the most popular is the Great Bear, whose stars are a reliable aid in locating Polaris and the direction of the north celestial pole. This well-known group of seven stars catches the eye. It is, however, only a part of the entire constellation of Ursa Major, whose outline, consisting of fainter stars, we can identify from the chart. Note the 'snout' (o UMa), the 'front paws' (the triangle formed by the stars ϑ, ι and κ), and the 'hind paws' (the triangle ψ—λ—μ).

The seven stars forming the Plough are a rare exception in not being a purely accidental grouping of stars. Apart from the stars Dubhe (α UMa) and Benetnash (η UMa) the other five bright stars are travelling together through space, and form — together with 12 other stars at various points in the sky — a moving star cluster that is the closest of all star clusters. The centre of the Ursa Major Cluster is about 75 light-years away, and the true diameter of the cluster is approximately 30 light-years. The cluster moves through space at a speed of about 14 km per second in the direction of Sagittarius. The physical connection of the stars in the cluster bears witness to their common origin. The Hyades cluster in Taurus (see p. 143) is a similar formation.

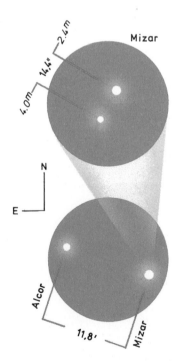

Mizar

2.4m
14.4"
4.0m

N
E

Alcor
11.8'
Mizar

Mizar and Alcor. The most familiar multiple star. Two stars are visible with the naked eye: bright Mizar (ζ UMa, mag. 2.4) and, 11.8′ farther east, fainter Alcor (80 UMa, mag. 4.0). Even with a small telescope it is possible to resolve Mizar into two components, mag. 2.4 and 4.0 with a separation of 14.4″. Mizar was the first double star to be discovered, (by Riccioli in 1650). Mizar's brighter component was also the first spectroscopic binary to be detected (Pickering, 1889). Mizar's fainter component has even been found to consist of three gravitationally bound stars. The distance of Mizar is 88 light-years.

Alcor is also a spectroscopic binary; it is a quarter of a light-year away from Mizar, and together with the latter participates in the movement of the other members of the Ursa Major cluster.

Galaxy M101—NGC 5457. One of the most beautiful examples of an Sc galaxy with pronounced spiral arms. Distance 15 million light-years; angular diameter 20′; true diameter about 90,000 light-years.

Below: **The Owl Nebula.** The planetary nebula M97—NGC 3587. Angular diameter 3′; low surface brightness. The distance is uncertain, but is estimated to be between 1600 and 10,000 light-years. The central star has a surface temperature of about 85,000 K.

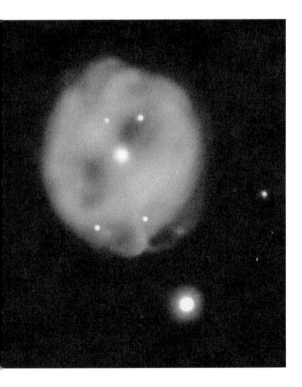

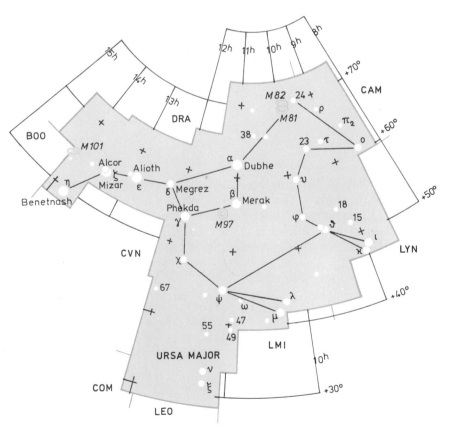

113

The group of galaxies in Ursa Major

Ursa Major
(the Great Bear).
Cellarius, *Harmonia macrocosmica*, 1763.

What is probably the closest group of galaxies outside the Local Group of galaxies is located inside the Great Bear. The centre of the group consists of a prominent pair of galaxies — M81 and M82 opposite left, with a separation of 38′, and easily visible even with a small telescope. The group has about twelve members and is approximately 9 million light-years distant.

M81 — NGC 3031 (opposite, bottom right) — when viewed through a small telescope the large nucleus of the galaxy looks like a small, oval, hazy cloud. Clearly visible in photographs are the extraordinarily symmetrical spiral arms, which prove to consist of clouds of stars. The lanes of dark interstellar matter emphasize the spiral structure inside the central part of the galaxy. The angular dimensions of M81 are 18′ × 10′; its true diameter is about 36,000 light-years. Its luminosity is equal to 20 thousand million Suns, and its total mass approximately is 250 thousand million solar masses.

M82 — NGC 3034 (opposite, top right)—a bright, irregular, spindle-shaped galaxy with an extremely unusual structure. It is divided by lanes of dark interstellar matter into numerous hazy patches. M82 is an intense source of radio emission, and has a strong magnetic field. Visible in photographs made with the largest telescopes is a system of filaments originating in the centre of the galaxy. The material in the filaments — with a volume of about 5 million solar masses — is expanding from the centre of M82 at a speed of almost 1,000 km/s! The angular dimensions of M82 are 7′ × 1.5′; its true diameter is about 16,000 light-years, and total mass 50 thousand million solar masses.

The distance between M81 and M82 is about 100,000 light-years. Radio observations reveal that the two galaxies are connected by a huge cloud of intergalactic gas. It may be that hundreds of millions of years ago M82 passed close to M81, which is much more massive, and that the gravitational effect of the latter could have caused the extraordinary phenomena now observed in M82.

A map of the central part of the M81 group, and two of the members of this group. The unusual elliptical galagy NGC 3077 (centre) is of 11th magnitude; has an angular diameter of 2.6′ and 'dwarf' dimensions: its diameter is a mere 6,000 light-years. The peculiar galaxy NGC 2976 (right), without distinct spiral structure, has similar dimensions.

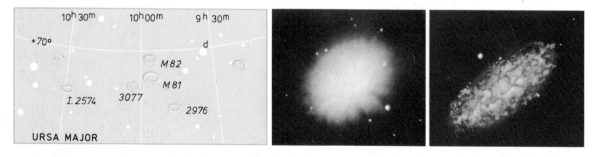

Canes Venatici

Canum Venaticorum—CVn—
The Hunting Dogs

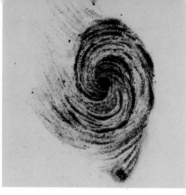

The galaxy M51
— Lord Rosse's observations.
Littrow, *Himmelsatlas*, 1854.

M3—NGC 5272 (opposite, centre). One of the richest and most beautiful globular clusters, visible even with binoculars. The angular diameter in a small telescope is 10′, in photographs up to 20′. The distance of M3 is between 35,000 and 40,000 light-years. Its diameter is about 220 light-years. The system contains at least half a million stars and it is estimated to be 10 thousand million years old.

M94—NGC 4736 (opposite, bottom). A bright, compact galaxy, which is practically circular in outline, visible even with a small telescope. The bright nucleus has an angular diameter of about 30″; the spiral structure is discernible over a diameter of more than 8′. M94 is about 20 million light-years away and has a true diameter of about 33,000 light-years.

M51—NGC 5194 (opposite, extreme right) — Whirlpool Galaxy. The first galaxy in which spiral structure was discovered (by Lord Rosse, 1845). It is one of the closest and brightest galaxies with a very pronounced spiral structure (type Sc according to Hubble's classification). Visual brightness 8^m; angular diameter 10′; true diameter more than 100,000 light-years; distance about 35 million light-years. Noteworthy, too, is the so-called satellite galaxy NGC 5195, apparently linked to the northern tip of one of the spiral arms of M51. In actual fact, however, the 'satellite' is in the background and is partly obscured by dark dust clouds in the arm of M51. The appearance that we see is the result of the mutual influence of two galaxies, NGC 5194 and NGC 5195, that came very close to one another several hundred million years ago, at which time the shape of M51 was changed and the ends of the spiral arms opened out. The smaller galaxy, NGC 5195, greatly deformed by the gravitational effect of NGC 5194, is now receding into the background, away from our Galaxy. Close encounters or collisions between galaxies, their course and consequences, can nowadays be modelled on suitable computers.

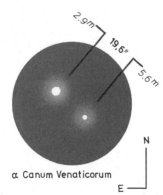

α Canum Venaticorum

α **CVn — Cor Caroli** (Charles' Heart) was named in honour of Charles II, King of Great Britain. A very popular double star for observation by the novice. Distance 120 to 135 light-years. The luminosities of the components are 80 and 7 times that of the Sun.

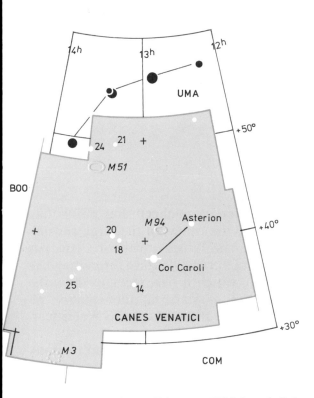

Right: The well-known Whirlpool Galaxy may be found about 3.5° southwest of the star η UMa. A small telescope will show a small hazy cloud with a bright centre.

M3—NGC 5272

M94—NGC 4736

Autumn constellations

Pisces (the Fishes)
(detail), 14th century
astronomical codex.

The division of the constellations into four groups according to the season of the year serves as a simple guide as to which stars are visible for the greater part of the night in the season concerned. This division into seasons applies to the northern hemisphere.

Dominating the autumn sky is the so-called *Square of Pegasus,* marked by the stars α, β, and γ Pegasi and the star Sirrah (α And) in the neighbouring constellation *Andromeda.* If we add to this 'square' the stars Mirach and Alamak in Andromeda and the star Algol in Perseus, the result is a figure resembling an enlarged version of the Plough (p. 106). This is the basic figure from which we proceed to find out way in the heavens. Above it is the prominent 'W' of *Cassiopeia,* south of Andromeda lie two small constellations: *Triangulum* (the Triangle) and *Aries* (the Ram).

The southeastern corner of the Square of Pegasus lies inside the broad 'V' of *Pisces* (the Fishes). The letter 'V' of the Fishes points like a large arrow to the centre of the large constellation of *Cetus* (the Whale). West of Cetus lies the inconspicuous constellation of *Aquarius* (the Water Carrier), which is best recognized by the triangular group of stars on the equator representing the 'jar' from which the Water Carrier is pouring water.

In the southern hemisphere we shall first try to locate the bright stars, Fomalhaut in the constellation of *Piscis Austrinus* (the Southern Fish) and Achernar in *Eridanus.* These two, together with Canopus in *Carina* (the Keel — see p. 202), form a conspicuous trio of stars lying approximately in a straight line, which will serve as a guide in finding one's way among the stars. South of Fomalhaut lies the pretty constellation of *Grus* (the Crane). The faint constellations of *Fornax* (the Furnace) and *Sculptor* (the Sculptor) can be located only under very good atmospheric conditions.

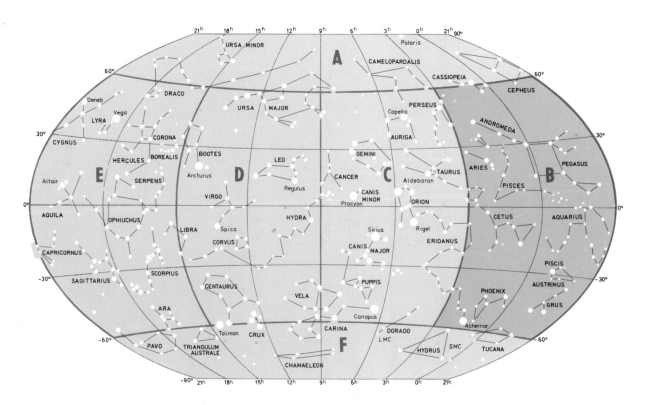

Andromeda
Andromedae—And—Andromeda

Triangulum
Trianguli—Tri—The Triangle

Andromeda
(detail). 14th century
astronomical codex.

In this region the most prominent objects are the two best-known galaxies in the Local Group of galaxies: M31 in Andromeda (see p. 122) and M33 in Triangulum.

M33—NGC 598 — Pinwheel Galaxy (top right). Type Sc. Visually it looks like a barely discernible hazy spot with an angular diameter equal to that of the Moon. It is difficult to observe because of its low overall brightness. In photographs, M33 has angular dimensions of up to 60′ × 35′. Extending from the small bright nucleus are two large main spiral arms and several auxiliary arms. In photographs made with larger telescopes, the arms are seen to consist of clouds of stars and it is possible to distinguish many types of objects such as we are familiar with in our Galaxy: variable stars, open and globular clusters, nebulae, etc. The distance of M33 is 2.4 million light-years; its diameter is about 60,000 light-years, and the total luminosity is equal to 3 thousand million Suns. The distance between M33 and M31 is about 570,000 light-years.

NGC 7662 (opposite, bottom left). A bright planetary nebula, which looks like a hazy star through small telescopes. With a larger instrument, one can see a faintly glowing ring and a central star. Angular dimensions 32″ × 28″; distance uncertain, estimated to be 1,800—5,600 light-years; the corresponding true diameter would be 20,000—50,000 AU.

NGC 891 (opposite, bottom right). An example of a spiral galaxy viewed edgewise, with a prominent band of dark interstellar matter along the main galactic plane. Angular dimensions 12′ × 1′; distance about 43 million light-years; true diameter more than 120,000 light-years.

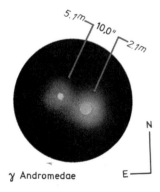
γ Andromedae

γ Andromedae—Alamak. One of the most beautiful, coloured double stars for observation with small telescopes. Distance about 260 light-years. In actual fact it is a group of four stars; two of the components are spectroscopic binaries.

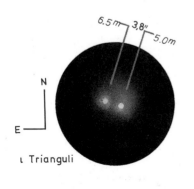
ι Trianguli

ι Trianguli. Distinct colour contrast. The distance of the double star is about 200 light-years. Both components are spectroscopic binaries.

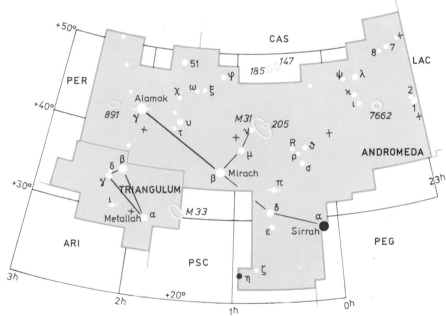

Above: The Galaxy M33 in Triangulum is located close to the line joining the stars α Tri and β And. Use a telescope with small magnification and a large field of view; conditions for observation must be very good with a dark sky.

NGC 7662

NGC 891

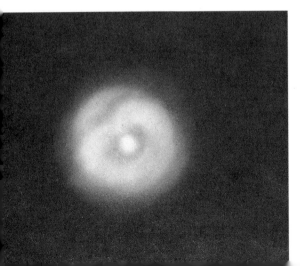

The Andromeda Galaxy

The galaxy M31
in Andromeda — W. Bond's
observations (ca. 1850).

M31—NGC 224 (large picture, right). Type Sb. Without doubt the most familiar galaxy, the only one of its kind in the northern sky visible without any trouble with the naked eye or binoculars. A telescope with a wide-angle eyepiece and low magnification is best for visual observation. In older literature, M31 is referred to as the Great Nebula in Andromeda, in recent literature it is usually called **the Andromeda Galaxy**. By determining the distance of M31 in 1923 (with the aid of pulsating cepheids — see p. 223), Dr. E. Hubble revealed the true nature of so-called spiral nebulae. M31 is the closest spiral galaxy, the largest member of the Local Group of galaxies, and one of the largest of all known spiral galaxies. Distance 2.2 million light-years; angular diameter from photographs 160′ × 40′; true diameter 110,000 light-years. The outer, barely discernible regions extend to a diameter of 4.5°, which corresponds to a true diameter of 180,000 light-years. The bright central region of M31, resembling an elliptical galaxy, is 12,000 light-years in diameter; in the centre of this region is the dense nucleus which measures 50 light-years in diameter and contains more than 10 million stars. In photographs made with the largest telescopes it is possible to distinguish individual stars in M31 — although naturally only the most luminous stellar giants. At the distance of M31 a star like our Sun would have a magnitude of 29.1; to date we have no means of observing such faint objects.

Satellite galaxies. Gravitationally linked to M31 are four dwarf galaxies designated by the numbers 221, 205, 185, and 147 in the NGC catalogue.

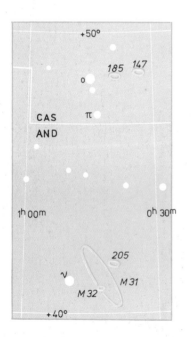

The positions of the four satellite galaxies of M31. 24′ south of the nucleus of M31 is galaxy M32—NGC 221, mag. 9.5, 3.6′ × 3.1′; diameter 2,400 light-years. 35′ northwest of the nucleus of M31 is the elliptical galaxy NGC 205; mag. 10.8, 8.0′ × 3.0′, diameter 5,400 light-years. About 7° to the north, in the constellation of Cassiopeia are galaxies NGC 185, mag. 11.8; 3.5′ × 2.8′; diameter 2,300 light-years (small picture, right) and NGC 147; mag. 12.1; 6.5′ × 3.8′; diameter 4,400 light-years (opposite page, inset).

Pegasus

Pegasi—Peg—Pegasus

Pegasus. 14th century
astronomical codex.

β Pegasi—Scheat. An irregular red giant, variable star. Magnitude variations from 2.1 to 3.0; distance 210 light-years; diameter up to 160 times the diameter of the Sun; surface temperature 3100 K; 5 solar masses.

M15—NGC 7078. A prominent bright globular star cluster; mag. 6.5; apparent diameter 12′. Distance 34,000 to 39,000 light-years; diameter about 130 light-years.

NGC 7479 (opposite, top left). A nice example of a barred spiral; a type SBb galaxy. A faint object, mag. 11.8; angular dimensions 3.2′ × 2.5′.

NGC 7814 (opposite, bottom right). Galaxy observed exactly edge-on with a prominent band of dark interstellar dust along the equatorial galactic plane. Type Sa/Sb; mag. 12.0; angular dimensions 1.0′ × 5.0′.

NGC 7331 (bottom). A spiral galaxy type Sb, dimensions and structure similar to those of our Galaxy. Angular dimensions about 10′ × 2.5′; mag. 10; distance about 50 million light-years; redshift 1050 km per second; total estimated mass 140 thousand million solar masses.

Stephan's Quintet (opposite, centre). A group of five galaxies, some of which are connected by 'bridges' of intergalactic matter. The marked differences in the redshifts of the individual members (as much as several hundred km/s) are surprising. It is probably an expanding or disintegrating group.

NGC 7331

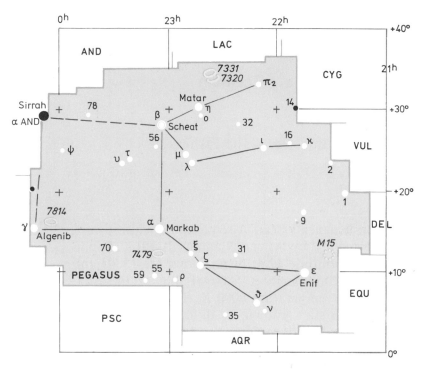

NGC 7479

Stephan's Quintet (right). A group of galaxies consisting of NGC 7320 (largest galaxy in the picture), and NGC 7317, 7318 A and B, and 7319. NGC 7320 has a red shift of 770 km/s; the other four members have red shifts of approximately 5800 km/s.

NGC 7814

Aries
Arietis—Ari—The Ram

Pisces
Piscium—Psc—The Fishes

Aries (the Ram)
(detail). 14th century
astronomical codex.

Van Maanen's Star. A remarkable white dwarf, discovered by A. van Maanen in 1917. Apparent magnitude 12.4; distance a mere 13.8 light-years. Luminosity 1/5800 of that of the Sun; surface temperature 6000 K. This is one of the smallest stars known, its diameter being calculated to be approximately 12,500 km, which is very close to the Earth's diameter. The mass of Van Maanen's star, however, is comparable with that of the Sun, so the density of the star is nearly a million times greater than the density of water, being about 1 ton per 1 cm³. The gravitational force on the surface of this star is 50,000 times greater than on the surface of the Earth.

γ Arietis—Mesarthim (below). One of the most familiar double stars, readily observed with a small telescope. Distance 160 light-years, total luminosity about 50 times that of the sun.

ζ Piscium (bottom). A nice double star for observation with a small telescope. Spectra A5 and F6; luminosity of the brighter component about 8—10 times that of the Sun. Distance 140 light-years.

The vernal equinox is not a celestial object, but nevertheless merits attention during examination of the constellation of Pisces. According to the accompanying chart we can estimate the position of this invisible, but very important point, where the celestial equator intersects the ecliptic. The vernal equinox has a similar function in the heavens as the Greenwich meridian has on Earth: it serves as the zero-point for the coordinate system that gives the precise position of objects on the celestial sphere (p. 223). The Sun is at the vernal equinox once a year, in spring, when day and night are of equal length. The vernal equinox slowly shifts along the ecliptic due to the Earth's precession; 2000 years ago it was located in the neighbouring constellation of Aries.

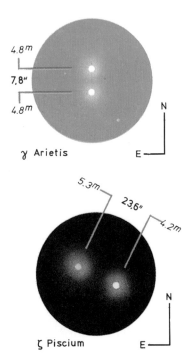

γ Arietis

ζ Piscium

α Piscium—Al Rischa (right). A double star that is continually becoming more difficult to observe due to the diminishing separation between the two components. Mag. 4.3 and 5.2; spectral types A2 and A3; period about 720 years. Periastron passage occurs in the year 2060. The distance of this double star is about 130 light-years.

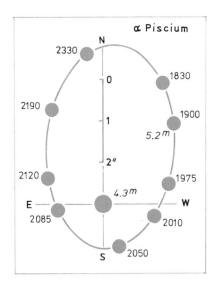

M74—NGC 628 (right). A large spiral galaxy, type Sc. Angular dimensions 10.6′×9.0′; mag. 11.0. The estimated distance, according to various authorities and methods, ranges between 25 and 42 million light-years.

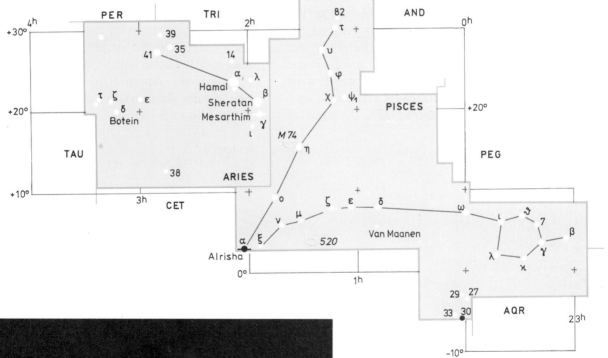

NGC 520 (left). A galaxy of unusual shape, which is probably ejecting matter. Mag. 12.4; angular dimensions 3.0′×0.7′.

127

Aquarius

Aquarii—Aqr—The Water Carrier

Capricornus

Capricorni—Cap—The Goat

Capricornus (the Goat),
P. Apianus, *Quandrans*, 1532.

NGC 7293—Helix Nebula. The largest and probably the closest planetary nebula. Angular dimensions $12' \times 16'$ (half the apparent diameter of the Moon!). The nebula is a spherical shell surrounding an extremely hot, 13^m central star, a dwarf with a temperature of more than 100,000 K. Recent data on the distance of the nebula range from 160 to 450 light-years. The true diameter of the Helix Nebula is about 1.75 light-years (at a distance of 450 light-years), the total mass of the nebula is 1/10 solar mass.

NGC 7009—Saturn Nebula (opposite, bottom left). A bright (8^m) planetary nebula, named by Lord Ross after the characteristic protrusions on either side of the bright disc. Angular dimensions $30'' \times 26''$; the bright condensations at the ends of the protrusions have a separation of $44''$. The central star is a blue dwarf with a surface temperature of 55,000 K. The distance of NGC 7009 is about 3,900 light-years; its true diameter 0.5 light-years.

R Aquarii (opposite, bottom right). An extraordinary variable star surrounded by a nebula. The star is a red giant with a diameter of 2—4 AU, showing irregular variations in brightness, ranging from 6^m to 11^m; average period 387 days. The temperature is 2,300 K at maximum. Distance 850 light-years. This is probably a close binary and the giant star is losing matter from the surface. It is enveloped by a cloud of gas and dust with an apparent diameter of $2'$. The nebula is changing and expanding.

M2—NGC 7089. A bright globular cluster; mag. 6.0; apparent diameter $11'$. Distance 50,000 light-years, true diameter about 160 light-years. It contains approximately 100,000 stars.

α Capricorni—Gredi (diagram beside the chart opposite). An optical double, readily resolved with the naked eye. The stars do not form a physical system. The brighter, α_2, is about 100 light-years distant; the fainter α_1 is about five times farther away.

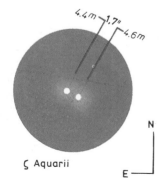

ζ Aquarii

ζ Aquarii (left). A pretty double star, which is a good test object for a small telescope. Distance 75 light-years. The true distance between the components is 100 AU.

The brightest parts of the Helix Nebula—NGC 7293 — look like two turns of a spiral (left and above). The object has a very low overall brightness and is best observed with a telescope with a wide-angle eyepiece and low magnification.

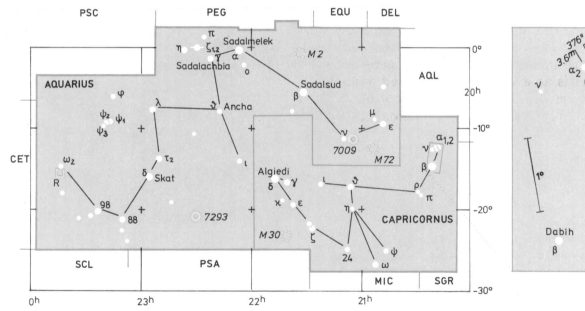

NGC 7009 — Saturn Nebula

R Aquarii

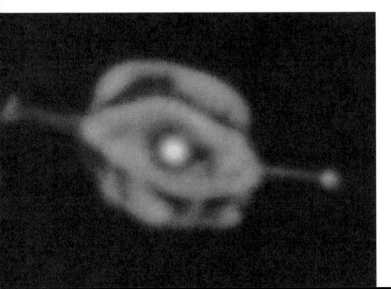

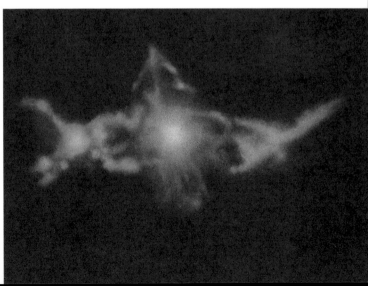

Cetus
Ceti—Cet—The Whale

Sculptor
Sculptoris—Scl—The Sculptor

Cetus (the Sea Monster)
(detail). 14th century
astronomical codex.

NGC 55 (top right). A flat, irregular galaxy of a type similar to the Large Magellanic Cloud. In photographs the spindle-shaped form has a length of 30′ to 50′; total mag. 7.8. This member of the Sculptor group of galaxies is one of the closest galaxies to the Local Group. The distance of NGC 55 is estimated to be between 7.5 and 9.8 million light-years according to various authorities. The true diameter is about 70,000 light-years, and its total mass 46 thousand million solar masses.

NGC 253 (right, second from top). A very bright, large galaxy; type Sc; apparent dimensions 22′ × 6′; total mag. 7.0. Next to galaxy M31 in Andromeda, NGC 253 is probably the most readily resolved spiral galaxy. It is the brightest member of the Sculptor group of galaxies. NGC 253 is an intense source of radio radiation. Its dimensions and distance are comparable to those of NGC 55.

Sculptor System (opposite, bottom right). An extreme example of a dwarf elliptical galaxy, reminiscent of a very sparse and indistinct globular cluster. Its apparent diameter is 75′ (!) but it cannot be resolved with small telescopes because the brightest stars are only magnitude 18. A member of the Local Group of galaxies. Distance 270,000 light-years; true diameter 5,500 light-years.

M77—NGC 1068 (opposite, bottom left). A spiral galaxy, type Sb; mag. 10.0; angular dimensions 2.5′ × 1.7′. Distance more than 60 million light-years, diameter about 40,000 light-years; total mass 100 thousand million solar masses. A strong source of radio radiation. M77 is one of the objects with active nuclei, known as Seyfert galaxies.

o **Ceti—Mira** ('The Wonderful')—the brightest and most familiar long-period variable star; the type star for its class, with a brightness that ranges approximately from mag. 2.1 to mag.10 with a period averaging 331 days. Mira's distance is 250 light-years; its true diameter 230 times that of the Sun. It is a red supergiant; at maximum it has a temperature of 2 500 K, at minimum 1 900 K. Mira is a double star; variations in the brightness of its companion range from 10^m to 12^m.

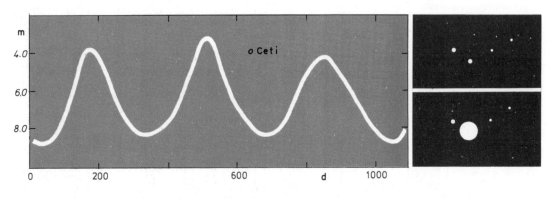

NGC 55

NGC 253

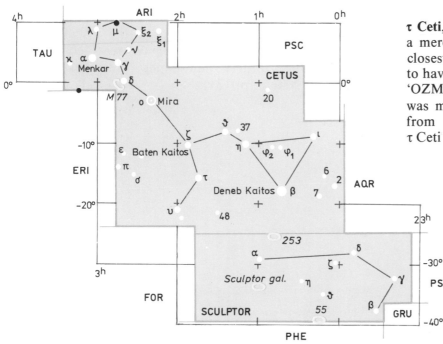

τ **Ceti**, mag. 3.50; spectrum G8; distance a mere 11.8 light-years. It is one of the closest solar-type stars, which is assumed to have a planetary system. As part of the 'OZMA' project starting in 1959, a search was made for signals of artificial origin from a hypothetical civilization in the τ Ceti system, but none were found.

M 77 — NGC 1068   Sculptor System

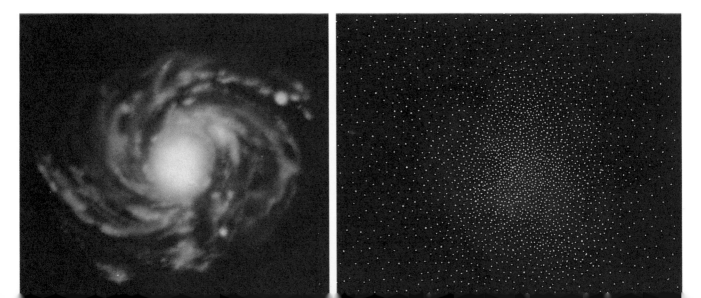

Fornax

Fornacis—For—The Furnace

Lord Rosse's large reflector, constructed in 1845. The diameter of the mirror was 180 cm.

Cluster of galaxies in Fornax. A compact system of galaxies on the boundary between Fornax and Eridanus. Apart from 18 bright galaxies there are several fainter objects in the cluster. This is one of the few regions in the sky where a group of galaxies can be observed visually in the field of view of a large telescope with a wide-angle eyepiece. Details, of course, show up only in photographs. Shown in the top picture is the barred spiral **NGC 1365**; its angular dimensions are $8.0' \times 3.5'$; the length of the 'bar' is 3′, which corresponds to an actual distance of about 45,000 light-years. The average distance of the cluster in Fornax is about 50 million light-years.

NGC 1398 (opposite, bottom left). Type SBb. Another example of a barred spiral with extremely narrow spiral arms. Mag. 10.7; angular dimensions $4.5' \times 3.8'$.

Fornax System (opposite, bottom right). A dwarf elliptical galaxy, a member of the Local Group of galaxies. Distance 630,000 light-years; angular diameter 6.5′; true diameter 15,000 light-years; total luminosity about 20 million times that of the Sun. The system resembles an extremely sparse globular cluster. It may only be observed with the largest telescopes; the brightest stars in the system have a magnitude of only 19^m. The two brightest objects in the picture are globular star clusters belonging to the system. Dwarf galaxies of this type are apparently quite common in the Universe, but they are so faint that outside the Local Group of galaxies they cannot be resolved even with the largest telescopes (see also Sculptor System, p. 131).

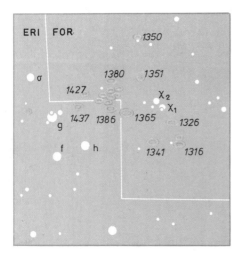

Cluster of galaxies in Fornax. The chart shows the positions of the brightest members of this group, which is on the boundary between Fornax and Eridanus.

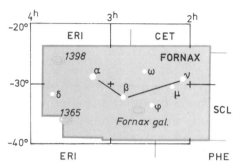

Galaxy NGC 1365 (left). Type SB; mag. 11.2. The third brightest member of the cluster of galaxies in Fornax. A very nice example of a barred spiral.

Fornax System

NGC 1398

Winter constellations

Lepus (the Hare).
14th century astronomical codex.

The winter sky is rich in bright stars, making it easy for beginners to find their way around.

The dominant constellation in the heavens is *Orion*, whose brightest stars form a distinctive quadrilateral with three regularly spaced stars in the centre. The whole group resembles a butterfly with outspread wings. According to the original notion of Orion as a hunter, this trio of stars is known as Orion's Belt. The northernmost star in the Belt lies close to the celestial equator. When extended northward, the Belt points toward the orange star Aldebaran in *Taurus* (the Bull). Further along this line lies the bright group known as the Pleiades. Between the Pleiades and Cassiopeia is a row of bright stars in *Perseus*. Highest in the group of winter constellations is *Auriga* (the Charioteer) with its bright star Capella, one of the brightest stars in the sky.

The line joining Rigel and Betelgeuse in Orion points to *Gemini* (the Twins), which is best located by the two stars Castor and Pollux.

According to mythology Orion the hunter was followed by his two dogs, a big one and a small one. The line joining the stars of the Belt points southeast to *Canis Major* (the Greater Dog) and the star Sirius, which is the brightest star in the whole sky. Between Sirius and Gemini lies *Canis Minor* (the Lesser Dog), with its bright star Procyon.

To help in locating objects in the sky beginners will find it best to become familiar with the polygon formed by the following bright stars: Capella, Aldebaran, Rigel, Sirius, Procyon, Pollux and Castor.

From Rigel in Orion we can follow the meanderings of the River Eridanus — i. e. the constellation *Eridanus* — all the way to the bright star Achernar. Following a line south from Sirius along the band of the Milky Way we come to *Vela* (the Sail) and *Carina* (the Keel). The star Canopus is the second brightest star in the night sky after Sirius and is often used as a navigation point in space flights.

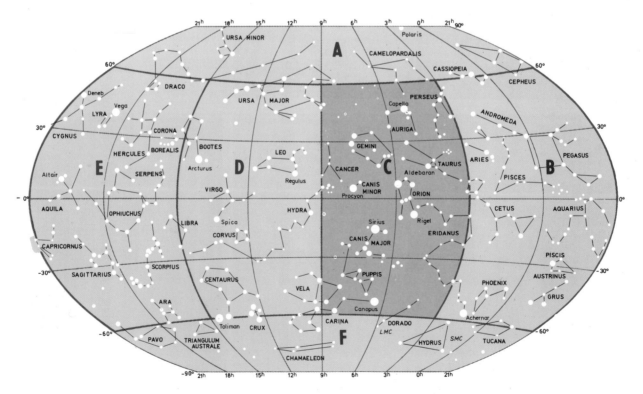

Perseus
Persei—Per—Perseus

Perseus
with the head of Medusa.
14th century astronomical codex.

β Persei—Algol (The Demon Star). The most familiar eclipsing binary. The fainter, cooler component, with diameter 3.8 times that of the Sun, regularly eclipses the brighter, hot component, which has a diameter 3.6 times that of the Sun. Algol's magnitude varies between 2.1 and 3.4 with a period of $2^d20^h48^m56^s$.

α Persei star cluster — a moving cluster comprising more than 100 stars round α Per. A beautiful object for observation with prismatic binoculars or a small telescope. Its distance is 570 light-years.

Illustrations on opposite page from top to bottom:

Double Cluster, χ, h Persei (NGC 884 and 869). A classic example of an open cluster, visible even with the naked eye as a small hazy cloud. A beautiful subject for observation with a telescope with a wide-angle eyepiece and low magnification. Each of the clusters has an apparent diameter of 30′ and a true diameter of about 70 light-years; both clusters are very young. NGC 884 is 8,150 light-years distant and is about 11.5 million years old; NGC 869 is 7,000 light-years distant and 6.4 million years old.

NGC 1275 (Perseus A). An unusual galaxy, which is an intense source of radio emission and X-ray radiation. Matter (the filaments seen in the picture) is being ejected from the galaxy at a speed of more than 2,400 km/s. The object's magnitude is 13.0, and its distance about 300 million light-years.

M34—NGC 1039. A bright open cluster; apparent diameter as much as 40′, containing approximately 80 stars. Distance 1,500 light-years, true diameter 17 light-years.

M76—NGC 650 (opposite, bottom right). A faint planetary nebula called the Little Dumbbell. Irregular in shape, 140″ × 70″; central star 16.5^m. Data as to distance are uncertain (ranging from 1,750 to 8,000 light-years).

NGC 1499 — California Nebula (opposite, bottom left). A diffuse nebula with angular dimensions of 145′ × 40′. It is difficult to observe visually.

Nova Persei 1901 (left). A drawing based on a 1949 photograph showing the expanding cloud of matter ejected into space by the nova explosion. On 23 February 1901 the nova attained the maximum magnitude of 0.2. Before the outburst it was a star of 13^m, at maximum it was 200,000 times greater than the Sun. It continues to vary in brightness between 11.0^m and 14.0^m.

Double Cluster, χ, h Persei

NGC 1275

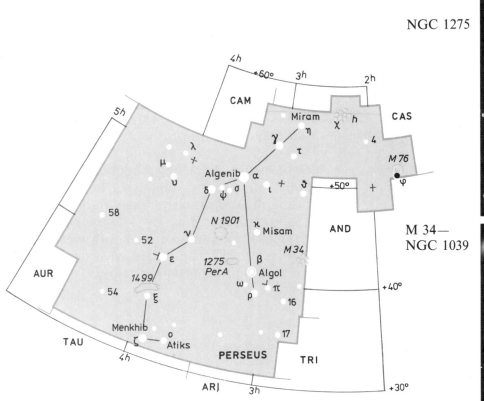

M 34—
NGC 1039

NGC 1499

M 76—NGC 650 ↘

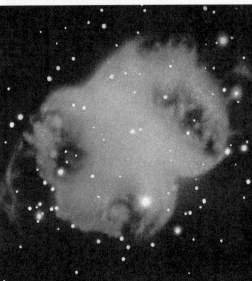

Auriga

Aurigae—Aur—The Charioteer

Gemini

Geminorum—Gem—The Twins

Gemini (the Twins).
Cellarius, *Harmonia macrocosmica*, 1763.

α Aurigae—Capella. The sixth brightest star in the sky, yellowish, mag. 0,06. Distance 45 light-years. A spectroscopic binary; component A has a diameter 13 times that of the Sun, and component B 7 times, the other two components are red dwarfs.

ε Aurigae. A very strange eclipsing binary, mag. 3.0 to 3.8. Distance 3,300 light-years. The bright component is a supergiant with a diameter 180 times that of the Sun. The character of the other, eclipsing component is not known with certainty.

There are three particularly bright open clusters in Auriga:

M36—NGC 1960. Contains approximately 60 stars of mag. 9 to 14, distance 1,400 light-years.

M37—NGC 2099 (opposite, top right). The richest cluster in Auriga, a beautiful object for observation even with a small telescope. Contains about 150 stars, mag. 9—12.5. Distance 4,600 light-years, diameter 25 light-years. It is more than 200 million years old.

M38—NGC 1912. An irregular, sparse group of about 100 stars. Distance 4,200 light-years, diameter about 25 light-years.

M35—NGC 2168. A bright, large star cluster (apparent diameter more than 0.5°), on the limit of visibility with the naked eye. Contains about 120 stars of magnitude 8, some bright stars form crooked rows. Distance 2,200 light-years, diameter 30 light-years, total luminosity 2,500 times that of the Sun.

NGC 2392 — A planetary nebula, called the Eskimo or Clown (opposite, bottom right). Around the central star of magnitude 10.0 there is a bright inner ring 19″ × 15″ separated by a dark gap from an outer ring with an apparent diameter of 40″. The estimated distance is between 1,400 and 3,600 light-years.

α Geminorum—Castor. A sextuple system: components A, B and C can be resolved with a telescope; each is a spectroscopic binary. A model of the system is shown below. The two C components are red dwarfs. The distance of Castor is 45 light-years.

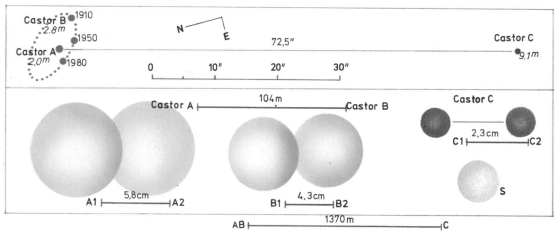

Above: The gas and dust nebula IC 405, illuminated by the star AE Aurigae. The distance is 1,600 light-years and the diameter is 9 light-years. This is an instance of a chance encounter between a rapidly moving star and a cloud of interstellar matter.

M37—NGC 2099

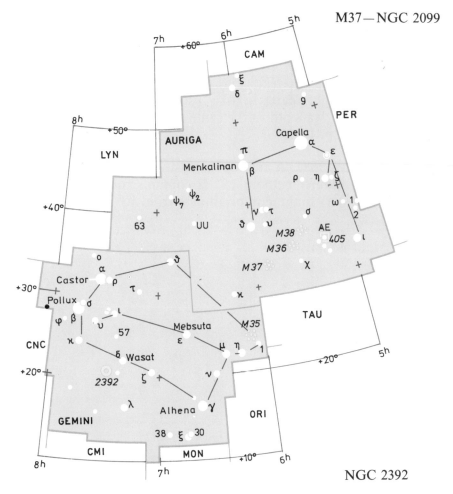

Below: Star clusters in Gemini. In the centre of the picture is the striking bright star cluster M35, in the upper left-hand corner is the rich, but very faint, open cluster NGC 2158.

NGC 2392

Cancer
Cancri—Cnc—The Crab

Lynx
Lyncis—Lyn—The Lynx

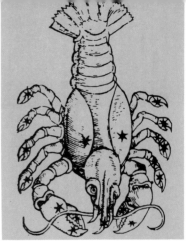

Cancer (the Crab).
P. Apianus, *Quadrans*, 1532.

M44—NGC 2632—Praesepe (The Beehive) — top right. A large, bright, open cluster visible even with the naked eye as a hazy patch. A very fine object for observation with binoculars or a small telescope. Its angular diameter is more than 1°. The cluster contains about 200 stars ranging in brightness from 6.3^m to 14^m, there are 80 stars brighter 10^m. The distance of the cluster is 525 light-years, and its true diameter is about 40 light-years. M44 is estimated to be 400 million years old — the same as the Hyades in Taurus (p. 142).

M67—NGC 2682. A rich open cluster, with an apparent diameter about 15′. It contains more than 500 stars ranging in brightness from 10^m to 16^m. The distance is 2,500 light-years. This is one of the oldest known open clusters, being about 100 thousand million years old.

NGC 2419 (opposite, bottom). Our own Galaxy's most distant globular cluster, sometimes called an 'intergalactic tramp'. The drawing shows the position of the object, 210,000 light-years distant from the centre of the Galaxy, and 182,000 light-years from the Sun. The true diameter of the cluster is 380 light-years and its luminosity is 175,000 times that of the Sun. Practically all the known globular clusters are located round the centre of the Galaxy inside a spherical cloud with a radius of 65,000 light-years (dots in the drawing).

ζ **Cancri.** A remarkable multiple star. Components A and B form a binary with a period of 59.6 years. Component C is evidently also a double star revolving round the AB pair with a period of 1,150 years. The distance of the system is 70 light-years.

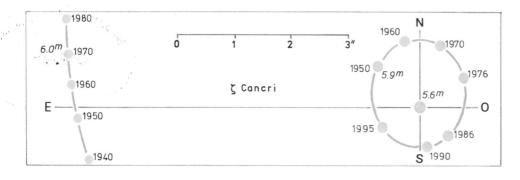

M44
—NGC 2632
—Praesepe

Right: **NGC 2623** in Cancer—an unusual galaxy with long filaments. It resembles the similar peculiar galaxy, NGC 4038 in Corvus (p. 168).

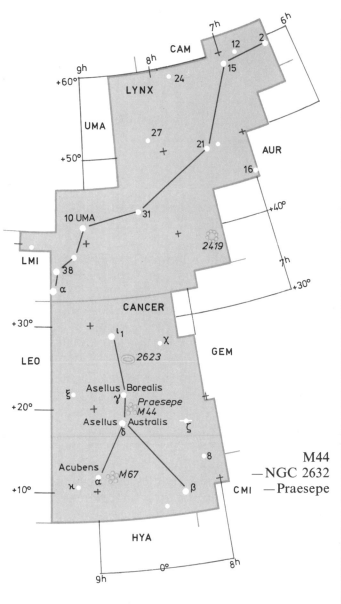

NGC 2419

141

Taurus
Tauri—Tau—The Bull

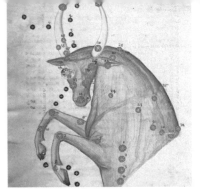

Taurus (the Bull) (detail).
14th century astronomical codex.

α Tauri—Aldebaran. The bright star in the 'eye of the Bull', a vivid orange colour (spectrum K5), mag. 0.86. This is an orange giant with a surface temperature of about 3,400 K and a diameter 40 times that of the Sun. Its distance is 68 light-years.

λ Tauri. A bright eclipsing binary, whose variations in brightness (from 3.3^m to 4.2^m with a period of 3.95 days) can be observed with the naked eye. The brighter component, of spectral class B, is partly eclipsed by the fainter companion of spectral class A. The distance between the two components is about 14 million km and the binary's distance from the Sun is 400 light-years.

The Hyades. A conspicuous open cluster with a triangular outline forming the 'head' of the Bull in pictorial representations of this constellation. Binoculars are the most suitable instrument for observation. The triangle formed by the Hyades has an apparent width of 3.5° and a true size of about 8 light-years. The average distance is 135 light-years, and the visible cluster forms the nucleus of a much larger cluster about 80 light-years in diameter, whose stars are spread out over an area with a radius of about 25°. All the stars in this cluster are moving together through space along parallel paths. This is why it is called the Taurus Moving Cluster. In 50 million years the cluster will be so far away that it will only be visible with a telescope and will then have an apparent diameter of 20'. From the observed spatial velocities of the stars of this group it is possible to derive the distance of the Hyades with reasonable accuracy and the relationship between the two factors may then be used to determine the distance of more distant groups of stars.

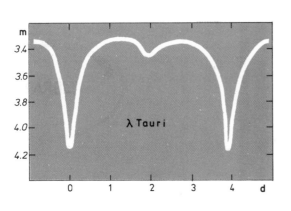

The light-curve of the eclipsing binary λ Tauri shows the continuous changes in brightness that are found in binaries of the β Lyrae type. The secondary minimum that occurs when the companion is partly eclipsed by the brighter component is easily discernible.

142

Orange Aldebaran adorns the Hyades like a bright gem (right), but is not a member of this cluster, because it lies about halfway between the centre of the Hyades and the Sun.

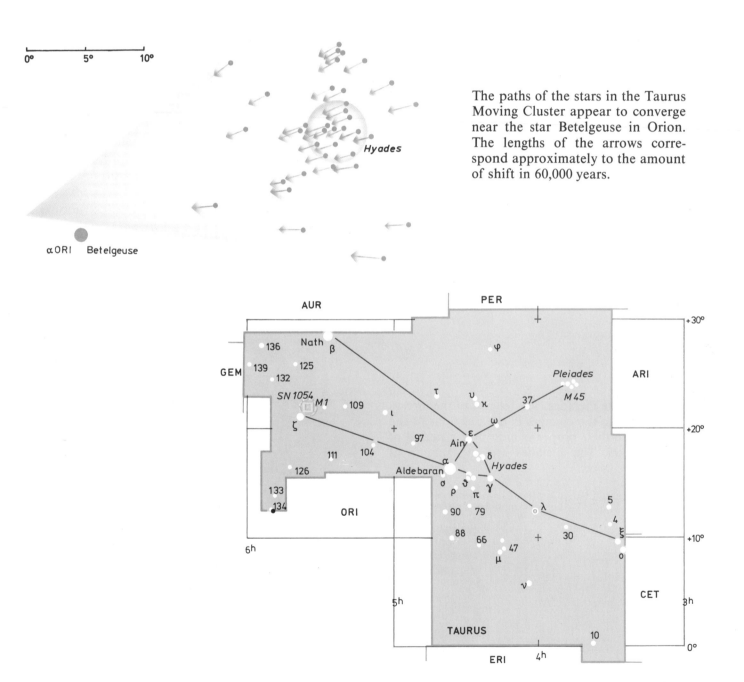

The paths of the stars in the Taurus Moving Cluster appear to converge near the star Betelgeuse in Orion. The lengths of the arrows correspond approximately to the amount of shift in 60,000 years.

Pleiades Star Cluster in Taurus

Taurus (the Bull) (detail). Cellarius, *Harmonia macrocosmica*, 1763.

M45—Pleiades. The most familiar open cluster and a favourite object for observation by amateurs. Six or seven stars may be readily seen with the naked eye, but under excellent observing conditions the experienced observer may see 9—11 stars, or even more. Good binoculars or a telescope with a large field of view show the Pleiades as a beautiful group containing many tens of stars and photographs reveal that their number runs into hundreds, although we know only about 250 actual members.

The nine brightest stars have specific names; they are spread out over a space about 7 light-years in diameter. The entire cluster, however, is much bigger, and some of its members are as much as 20 light-years from the centre. The distance of the Pleiades is 410 light-years, i. e. about three times the distance of the Hyades. Like the Hyades, the Pleiades is an example of a moving cluster. The stars in the Pleiades travel through space at a speed of 40 km/s, but it will take more than 30,000 years for the Pleiades to shift in the sky by the equivalent of the apparent diameter of the Moon.

The brightest of the stars in the Pleiades, Alcyone, is a giant of spectral class B, about 10 times the diameter of the Sun and 1,000 times more luminous than the Sun. The other bright stars in the Pleiades are also hot stars of spectral class B. All are rotating rapidly, particularly Pleione, which rotates round its axis 100 times faster than the Sun.

The beauty of the Pleiades is heightened by the silvery veil of diffuse nebulae which envelops the whole cluster and is illuminated by the brightest stars. The nebulae are made visible by light from the stars, which is scattered by dust particles (this is a typical example of a reflection nebula). Under ideal observing conditions the nebulae in the Pleiades may even be observed visually. Their filamentary structure is visible in photographs; the inset at right shows the nebula around the star Merope.

A chart of the Pleiades. The lengths of the arrows correspond to the changes in the positions of the stars due to their proper motion over a period of 20,000 years. The Pleiades are an example of a moving cluster.

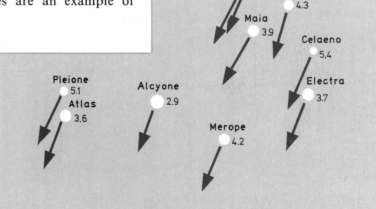

Crab Nebula in Taurus

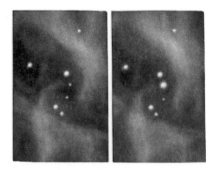

The Crab Nebula.
W. Herschel's observations.

M1—NGC 1952—Crab Nebula. The best-known supernova remnant and perhaps the most remarkable celestial object of all. The supernova outburst was recorded in Chinese chronicles. In July 1054, according to these records, a 'guest star' appeared in the heavens close to the star ζ Tauri. For several weeks it was visible even in daylight, like Venus, then it became fainter, and one and a half years later could no longer be seen. The distance of M1 (6,500 light-years) indicates that at maximum the luminosity of the supernova was 400 million times that of the Sun. The gigantic outburst scattered the greater part of the star in all directions, giving rise to a nebula that today has a diameter of almost 10 light-years, and is still expanding.

Even in small telescopes M1 may be observed as an elongated hazy cloud measuring 5′ × 3′. In 1844 Lord Rosse first observed the delicate filaments extending from the nebula like the legs of a crab — hence its name. Recent photographs clearly show the double structure of M1. The tangled filamentary structure shows up clearly in red light. The system of filaments lies within a more transparent, shapeless cloud, that shows up in blue light.

The Crab Nebula is an intense source of radio and X-ray emission. The most interesting remnant of this former celestial firework, however, is the collapsed remnant of the original star, a neutron star approximately ten kilometres in diameter, with the incredible density of about 1 million tons per 1 cm³, a very high temperature and strong magnetic field. The neutron star rotates at a rate of 30 revolutions per second and gives rise to a *pulsar*, radiating energy in pulses spaced precisely 0.03309 seconds apart. At the same time the pulsar emits 100 times more radiation in X-rays than it does in visible light, and 10,000 times more than at radio frequencies.

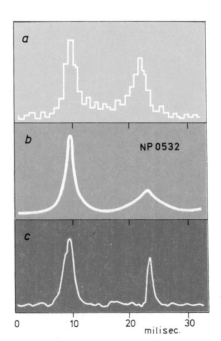

The pulsar in the Crab Nebula has the same period in the X-ray region (a), in visible light (b) and at radio frequencies (c). However, the shapes of the pulses differ.

Visual changes in a pulsar. At left the pulsar is at minimum, at right it is at its brightest.

The Crab Nebula has a very complex filamentary structure. The interior of the nebula is expanding at a speed of about 700 km/s, while part of the external filamentary envelope is receding from the centre at a speed of 1,800 km/s. The arrows in the bottom picture show the presumed expansion of the nebula during the next 250 years.

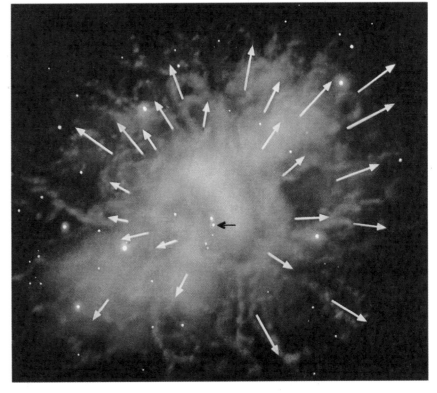

147

Orion
Orionis—Ori—Orion

Orion (detail).
14th century astronomical codex.

α Orionis—Betelgeuse. An irregularly pulsating red supergiant, spectral class M, varying in magnitude from 0.2 at maximum to below 1.2 at minimum. Surface temperature 3 100 K; luminosity about 14,000 times that of the Sun (at maximum). Typical orange coloration, visible with the naked eye. Distance 520 light-years. This is one of the largest stars known, ranging in diameter between 550 and 920 times that of the Sun. With a mass of about 20 solar masses the density of Betelgeuse is less than one ten-thousandth the density of air.

β Orionis—Rigel. A white supergiant with a diameter 50 times that of the Sun; the seventh brightest star in the sky; magnitude 0.14. Estimated distance between 540 and 900 light-years. Its luminosity is 57,000 times that of the Sun, making it one of the most luminous stars known (absolute magnitude —7.1). A 6.7^m companion is 9″ distant at position angle 202°.

ζ Orionis—Alnitak. A triple star with two close components (1.9^m and 5.5^m) having a separation of 2.6″. The third component (10^m) is 57.6″ away from component A at position angle 10°. The distance of the triple star is about 1,600 light-years.

Group of nebulae near the star ζ Orionis (opposite, right).
NGC 2024 — A bright, complex diffuse nebula divided from north to south by a dark band.
IC 434 — A large, faint nebula, with a sharp boundary along the eastern edge and becoming increasingly less distinct in a westward direction until it fades into nothingness. Standing out distinctly against the background of this nebula is the dark nebula B33.

B33—Horsehead Nebula. The most familiar dark nebula (bottom right). It is probably part of a larger cloud of dark interstellar matter marking the eastern edge of the bright nebula IC 434, and absorbing light from more distant stars (this is the cause of the marked difference in the number of stars on either side of the edge of IC 434). The estimated distance of the Horsehead Nebula is 1,200 to 1,600 light-years.

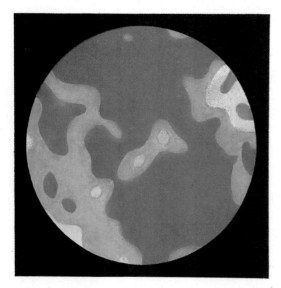

It is impossible to see any star as a disc, even with the largest telescopes. In 1975 Betelgeuse was the first star for which modern image-processing methods were able to construct an image of the disc, showing regions of different brightness (i. e. cooler and warmer).

Group of nebulae
near the star
ζ Orionis.

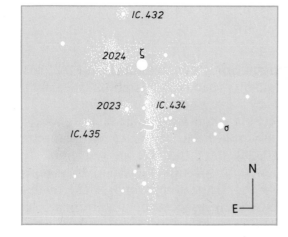

IC. 432

2024   ζ

2023   IC. 434

IC. 435   σ

N

E

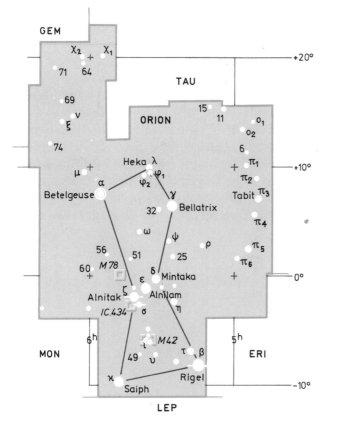

GEM

χ₂   +   χ₁

71   64

69

ν

ξ

74

TAU

15

11   o₁

o₂

ORION

6

μ   +   π₁   +10°

Heka λ   φ₁   π₂

α   φ₂   Tabit π₃

Betelgeuse   γ

32   Bellatrix   π₄

ω   ψ

56   51   25   ρ   π₅

60 M78   π₆

+   δ   +
ε   Mintaka   0°

Alnitak ζ   Alnilam

IC.434 σ   η

6ʰ   M42   5ʰ

MON   49   ι   τ β   ERI

υ

χ   Rigel   -10°

Saiph

LEP

+20°

A cloud of dark interstellar matter, dust and gas,
shows up against a more distant bright nebula as
the silhouette of a horse's head one light-year in
height.

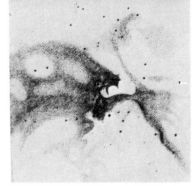

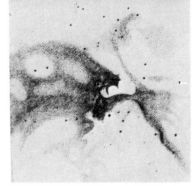

Great Nebula in Orion

ORI

The Great Nebula
in Orion. F. Arago,
Astronomie populaire, 1856.

M42—NGC 1976—The Great Nebula in Orion.
This is the most familiar diffuse nebula, and the one that is most popular with amateur astronomers and most often photographed. It can only be described in superlatives. It is easily visible with binoculars, and with a telescope it is a truly magnificent object, where it is possible to distinguish many details. In photographs, especially colour ones, it is beautiful beyond words. It was the first nebula to be photographed successfully (by Henry Draper in 1880).

The Great Nebula is a huge complex of interstellar gas, dust and molecules. Its distance is given as 1,300 to 1,900 light-years, and the diameter of M42 is about 30 light-years. The nebula's visible radiation is excited by the radiation of stars embedded in its interior, primarily the ultraviolet radiation from the very hot components of the multiple star ϑ Orionis (the Trapezium), and other hot stars. The gas in the nebula (chiefly hydrogen) is ionized by the stars' radiation, and recombination of the ionized atoms produces radiation in the region of visible light. Some of the light from M42, however, is also caused by the light of stars being scatterd by dust particles in the nebula. The Orion Nebula is aptly called a stellar cradle; its total mass would suffice for the formation of about 10,000 stars the size of our Sun. The 'older' generation of stars created in M42 is represented by the Trapezium, which is the nucleus of an expanding association of hot stars, less than 1 million years old. The younger generation comprises stars that are still enveloped by embryonic clouds of dust and gas, and are only detectable by their infrared radiation. They are less than 100,000 years old and form thc corc of the Orion Molecular Cloud immediately behind M42.

Shown at the top of the opposite page is the bluish nebula **NGC 1977**; in the centre is the small nebula **M43**, separated by a dark band from the brightest, central part of the great nebula M42. The bright star at the bottom of the picture is ι Orionis. The delicate shades of colour in the nebula cannot be perceived visually, they can only be recorded in photographs.

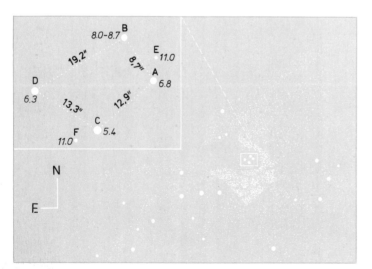

The multiple star **ϑ Orionis** is in the centre of the brightest part of M42. Marked on the chart at left are the magnitudes and angular separation between the components. The brightest components A, B, C and D form a quadrilateral called **the Trapezium**—a very popular object for observation by amateurs.

Canis Minor

Canis Minoris—CMi—The Lesser Dog

Monoceros

Monocerotis—Mon—The Unicorn

Canis Minor
(the Lesser Dog).
P. Apianus, *Quadrans*, 1532.

α Canis Minoris—Procyon. Magnitude 0.35 and the eighth brightest star in the heavens. One of the closest stars, distance 11.3 light-years. Spectrum F5; diameter 2.3 times that of the Sun; surface temperature 7,000 K; 6 times the solar luminosity. Its companion, called Procyon B, is a white dwarf, magnitude 10.8, whose diameter is only twice that of the Earth but whose mass is 65 per cent of the Sun, and whose density is 140 kg/cm³! Procyon B may only be resolved with a large telescope.

NGC 2237+2244. The Rosette Nebula (NGC 2237) is a diffuse nebula, surrounding the open cluster NGC 2244. The Rosette Nebula is very difficult to observe visually, but the central cluster can be resolved easily with binoculars. The cluster consists of hot stars of spectral class O and B, and is physically connected with the nebula; it is possible that the intense radiation of these young stars has 'swept' the nebula's central region clear of gas and was thus responsible for the present appearance of the Rosette Nebula. In photographs, the Rosette Nebula is one of the loveliest formations of its kind. Its irregular ring has an angular diameter of 80′ and a true diameter of about 55 light-years. The distance of the nebula is about 2,600 light-years and its mass is estimated to be 11,000 solar masses. Clouds of interstellar matter that absorb radiation show up as dark patches against the background of the glowing nebula. Most remarkable of these are the small spherical clouds, measuring only a few seconds of arc in diameter, and known as globules (detail top right). Their true diameters are estimated to be between 1,000 and 200,000 astronomical units and their mass between 0.1 and 70 times that of the Sun. It is believed that stars are born from collapsing globules.

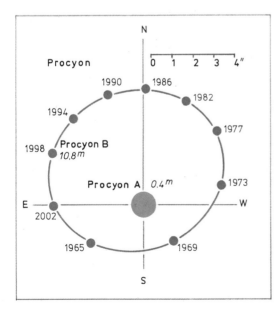

Left: The apparent orbit of the double star Procyon.

Right: The proper motion of Procyon over 1,000 years, compared with the apparent diameter of the Moon (0.5°). In 1 year Procyon shifts 1.25″.

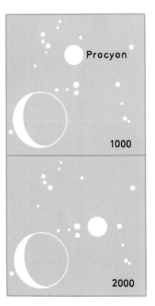

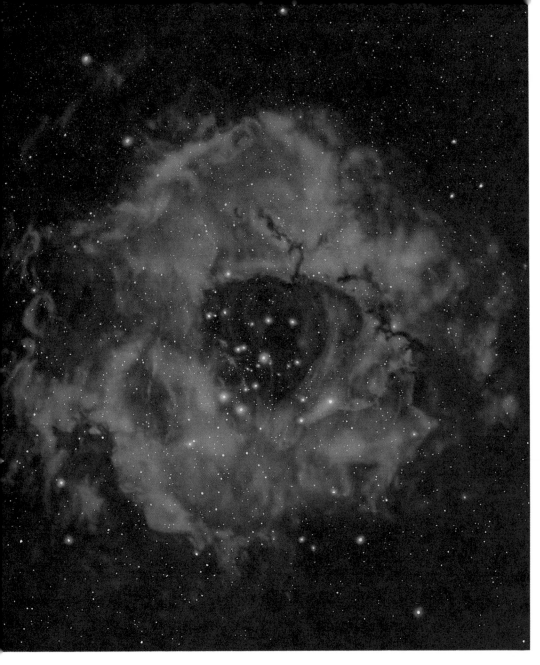

The inconspicuous constellation of Monoceros, overshadowed by its majestic neighbour Orion, contains some of the loveliest nebulae in the heavens: The Rosette Nebula (above) and the Cone Nebula (see p. 155).

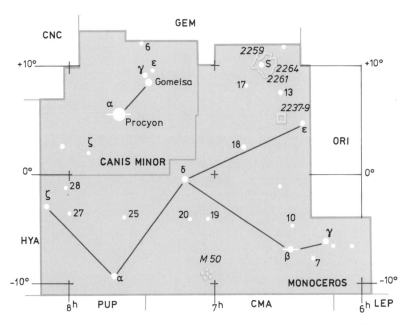

Star Clusters and Nebulae in Monoceros

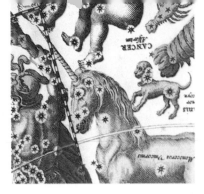

Monoceros (the Unicorn).
Cellarius, *Harmonia macrocosmica*, 1763.

NGC 2264. An open star cluster linked to a diffuse nebula. A vast cluster sometimes called the Christmas Tree because of the resemblance (opposite, top left). In the sky the 'tree' is 26′ high (nearly the apparent diameter of the Moon), in reality its height is 20 light-years. The cluster has about 150 members and is 2,600 light-years distant. The brightest member is the star S Monocerotis (opposite, top and centre left), a very hot white giant of spectral class O with a luminosity 8,500 times that of the Sun. Analysis of the physical characteristics of the stars in NGC 2264 shows the extremely low age of this group — most of its members are only 1—2 million years old.

The cradle of the Christmas-Tree stars is evidently the large nebula that surrounds the cluster. It is too faint for visual observation, but photographs reveal its immense size and numerous interesting details, the most remarkable of

which is the dark Cone Nebula. This stands out in sharp outline against the glowing nebula, as a dark cone 6 light-years high.

NGC 2261. Hubble's Variable Nebula. A very unusual gaseous nebula surrounds the even more unusual variable star R Monocerotis. The appearance of the nebula, which resembles the tail of a comet, changes in details very rapidly and irregularly, sometimes even from one day to the next. The star, or rather object, R Mon, is hidden in the southern tip of the nebula; its brightness varies irregularly between 10^m and 12^m approximately, and it is an intense source of infrared radiation. It is possible that we are observing the birth of a star here, one that is still surrounded by circumstellar dust which absorbs its radiation, becomes heated, and thereby becomes a source of infrared radiation.

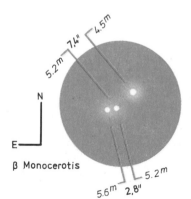

β Monocerotis

β Monocerotis. A very nice triple star for observation with a small telescope; all three components are roughly of equal brightness. The distance of the system is about 150 to 200 light-years.

Cluster NGC 2264 and its related nebulosity.   The dark Cone Nebula.

Below: The changes in the appearance of Hubble's Variable Nebula are not caused by motion of material in the nebula but by changes in illumination, i. e. by the movement of shadows cast by the dark matter surrounding the central star. The diameter of the nebula is about 1 light-year.

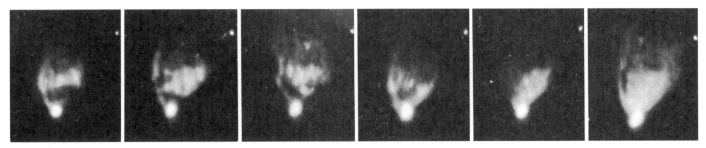

27 April 1919   19 December 1919   9 October 1920   29 December 1921   24 October 1922   26 October 1933

Eridanus

Eridani—Eri—The River Eridanus

Eridanus (the River Eridanus)
(detail). Cellarius, *Harmonia
macrocosmica*, 1763.

α Eridani—Archernar. The ninth brightest star in the sky, mag. 0.53. A very hot blue giant with a surface temperature of 14,000 K and luminosity 650 times that of the Sun. Distance 120 light-years.

ε Eridani. An inconspicuous 3.7^m star, one of the closest to our Sun—a mere 10.8 light-years distant. Its dimensions, mass, spectral class and luminosity are similar to those of the Sun and that is why in 1959 it became one of the subjects of Project 'OZMA'—the search for signals from possible alien civilizations. To date, all such experiments have produced negative results.

o₂ Eridani (40 Eridani). An exceptionally interesting triple star (bottom). Because of the system's proximity (16 light-years) it affords a rare chance to observe a white dwarf — component B — even with a small telescope. This was the first star of this kind to be recognized (in 1910).

The diameter of o Eridani B is slightly more than twice the diameter of the Earth, but its mass is equal to practically half the mass of the Sun, so its density is almost $100 \, kg/cm^3$. The force of gravity on the surface of this star is 37,000 times greater than on Earth. Also of interest is component C — a red dwarf of extremely low mass, a mere 0.2 of the Sun's mass, and a luminosity only 0.0008 times that of the Sun. The system has an extremely rapid proper motion, 4.08″ per year.

NGC 1300. One of the best examples of a barred spiral galaxy, type SBb. Apparent stellar magnitude 11.3; angular dimensions 6.0′ × 3.2′; very bright centre.

NGC 1232. A galaxy (type Sc) with numerous spiral arms; magnitude 10.7; angular dimensions 7.0′ × 6.0′.

The triple star o₂ Eridani. Relative magnitude of components A, B, C and the Sun (left). Apparent orbit of components B and C (centre). Appearance of the triple star viewed through a telescope (right).

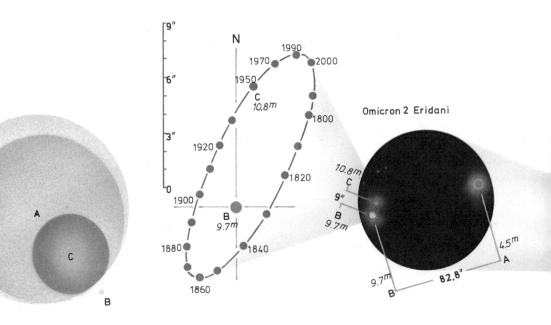

Galaxy NGC 1300.

Galaxy NGC 1232.

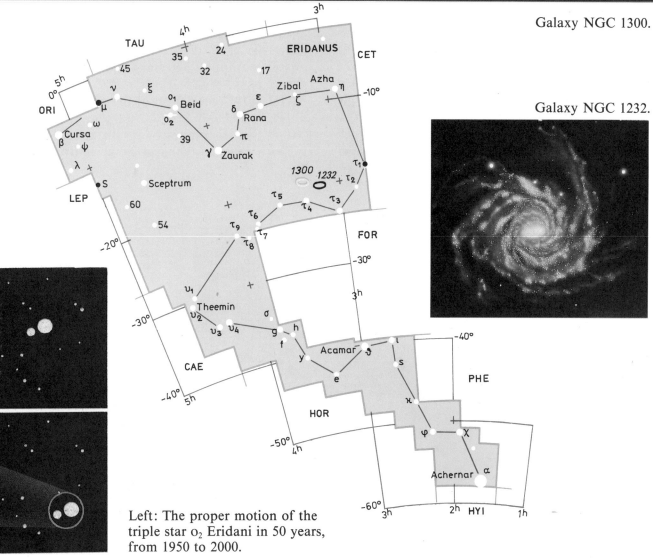

Left: The proper motion of the triple star o₂ Eridani in 50 years, from 1950 to 2000.

157

Canis Major

Canis Majoris—CMa—The Greater Dog

Puppis

Puppis—Pup—The Stern

Canis Major (the Big Dog)
(detail). 14th century
astronomical codex.

α Canis Majoris—Sirius. The brightest star in the sky, a true ornament of the winter nights. Magnitude −1.4, a brilliant white colour that sometimes, due to scintillation, appears to be all the colours of the rainbow. Its distance is 8.7 light-years — it is the fifth closest star. Spectral class A1, diameter 1.8 times that of the Sun; surface temperature 10,000 K, 23 times the solar luminosity.

Sirius' companion, Sirius B, is famous. It is the best-known white dwarf. Its existence was predicted by Bessel from observed variations in the proper motion of Sirius A in 1834—44. Sirius B was discovered by A. Clark in 1862, but not until 1915 did astronomers determine the character of this unusual star, whose mass is almost the same as the Sun's, but which has a diameter of only about 30,000 km and a density of about 130 kg/cm³. The magnitude of Sirius B is 8.65, but it is masked by the glare of Sirius A and a large telescope is necessary to see it.

L₂ Puppis. A semi-regular variable star, whose brightness ranges from 3^m to 6^m with an approxi-mate period of 141 days. A red giant of spectral class M5; distance about 200 light-years. Pulsation of the star is the reason for its variability.

NGC 2362. A very pretty group of about 50 stars of 7.5^m to 13^m, surrounding the star τ CMa (4^m) and lying within a circle of 6′ radius. Distance 4,600 light-years. One of the youngest star clusters known, about 1 million years old. The cluster mostly consists of giant, high-luminosity stars of class O and B.

M41—NGC 2287. A very bright cluster, visible with the naked eye and resolvable with a small telescope. It contains about 100 stars with magnitudes ranging from 7 to 13. Apparent diameter 30; true diameter about 20 light-years; distance about 2,350 light-years.

NGC 2477. The richest of the many star clusters in Puppis. There are 300 stars within a circle of 20′ radius. Estimates of its distance vary markedly (between 3,000 and 9,000 light-years).

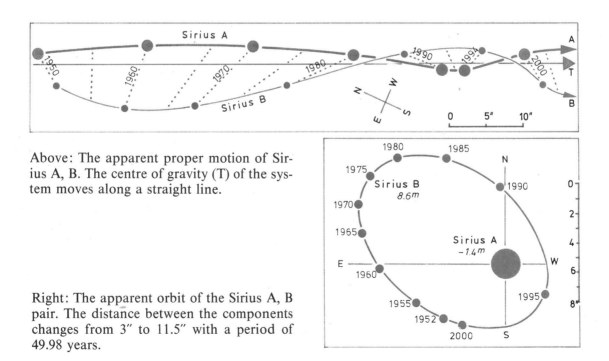

Above: The apparent proper motion of Sirius A, B. The centre of gravity (T) of the system moves along a straight line.

Right: The apparent orbit of the Sirius A, B pair. The distance between the components changes from 3″ to 11.5″ with a period of 49.98 years.

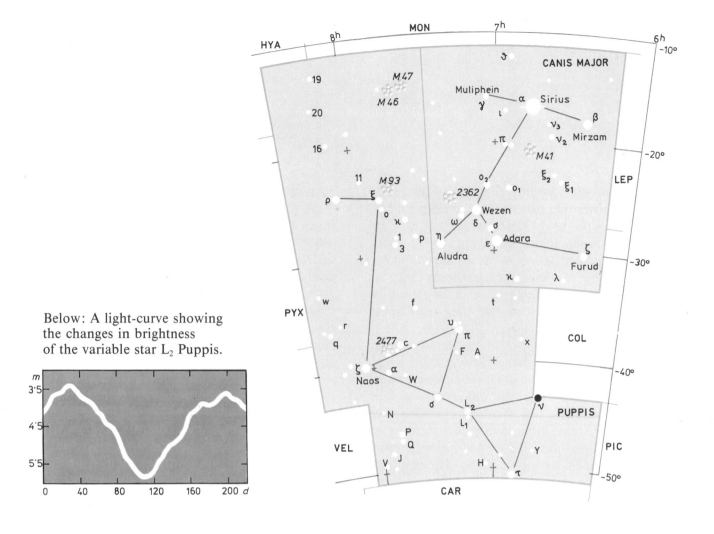

Below: A light-curve showing the changes in brightness of the variable star L₂ Puppis.

Below: The loveliest open clusters in the constellations of Canis Major and Puppis: left NGC 2362, centre M41, right NGC 2477.

Spring constellations

The celestial sphere
below the horizon.
P. Apianus, *Cosmographica*, 1535.

This part of the sky has relatively few bright stars, but is rich in galaxies and clusters of galaxies. Fig. 3 on page 12 shows that a line extending at right angles to the galactic plane points to the constellation of *Coma Berenices* (Berenice's Hair). This part of the sky, outside the Milky Way, contains a 'galactic window' that offers us a view of external regions of space.

In the northern sky we shall start with the familiar seven bright stars marking the Plough in *Ursa Major* (the Great Bear). The line joining stars Dubhe and Merak points southward to *Leo* (the Lion). Leo is easily recognized by the group of stars resembling a large crescent or reversed question mark; in pictorial representations this marks the lion's mane. The brightest star in Leo, Regulus, lies on the ecliptic. If we extend the arc of the handle of the Plough (the tail of Ursa Major) towards the equator, we encounter the orange star Arcturus in *Bootes* (the Herdsman). Farther along this arc, below the

equator, we come to the bright star Spica in *Virgo* (the Virgin). The three stars Regulus, Arcturus and Spica form the so-called 'Spring Triangle', which serves as a useful guide in finding our way about the sky. Stretching below this triangle is the long constellation of *Hydra* (the Water Snake), whose 'head' lies below Cancer (see map on p. 169). Between Hydra and Virgo lies the small but pretty constellation of *Corvus* (the Crow) and beside it the fainter *Crater* (the Cup).

South of Hydra lies a beautiful section of the Milky Way with the two most familiar constellations in the southern sky—*Crux* (the Southern Cross) and *Centaurus* (the Centaur). To see these constellations there is no need to journey all the way to the southern hemisphere. The Southern Cross is visible just above the horizon from the Tropic of Cancer (i.e. latitude +23.5° North). However, we can see the Southern Cross without any lengthy travel at all — in the artifical sky of the nearest planetarium.

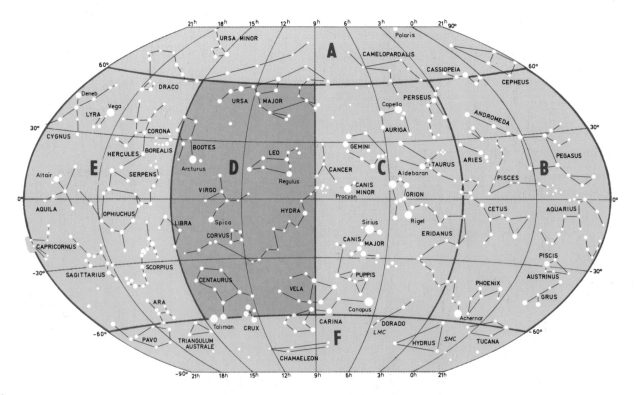

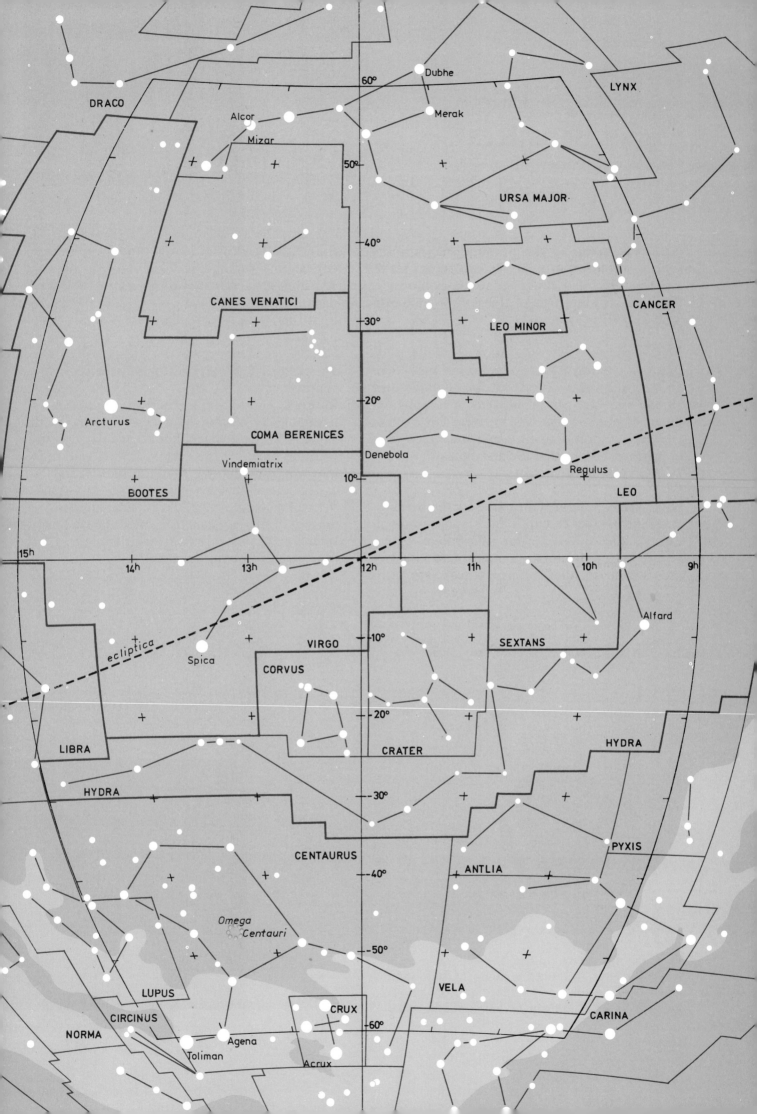

Boötes
Boötis—Boo—The Herdsman

Coma Berenices
Comae Berenices—Com—
Berenice's Hair

Boötes (the Herdsman).
14th century
astronomical codex.

α Boötis—Arcturus. Magnitude −0.06, and the fourth brightest star in the sky. An orange giant, spectrum K2; 115 times the Sun's luminosity; diameter 25 times that of the Sun; distance 37 light-years.

M64—NGC 4826 (opposite, top left). The Black-Eye Galaxy. A spiral galaxy of type Sa or Sb, with extraordinarily striking dark dust clouds near the central nucleus. The apparent dimensions are 7.5′ × 3.5′; viewed with a small telescope it looks like a hazy 8ᵐ star. According to various authorities the distance of M64 is 20 to 25 million light-years.

NGC 4565 (bottom right). One of the loveliest and most typical examples of a large spiral galaxy observed edge-on. Along the galactic equator are dark dust clouds that absorb the light of the clouds of stars, forming the spiral arms round the brightly glowing, broad, central condensation. The angular diameter of the object is 15′, and its apparent brightness is 10.5ᵐ. The distance of NGC 4565 is about 20 million light-years and its true diameter is about 90,000 light-years.

The cluster of galaxies in Coma Berenices, whose central part is shown in the picture opposite, top right, contains more than 1,000 galaxies and is about 400 million light-years distant. In the sky this colossal system has an angular diameter of more than 3°; the corresponding true diameter would be about 20 million light-years.

The giant elliptical galaxy NGC 4889 near the centre of the cluster is the brightest object, and yet it only appears like a star of 13th magnitude. The cluster is moving away from the Earth at a speed of about 6,800 km/s.

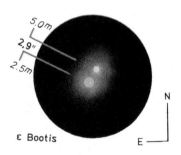

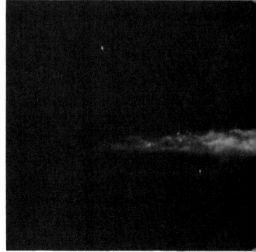

Below: Galaxy NGC 4565, which we observe edge-on. The dark clouds of interstellar dust and gas along the median galactic plane are very distinct.

Above: **ε Boötis—Izar.** One of the loveliest double stars with a marked colour contrast. The brighter component is yellow-orange, and its luminosity is about 500 Suns, the fainter component is bluish to greenish. The distance, according to various measurements, is between 200 and 300 light-years.

162

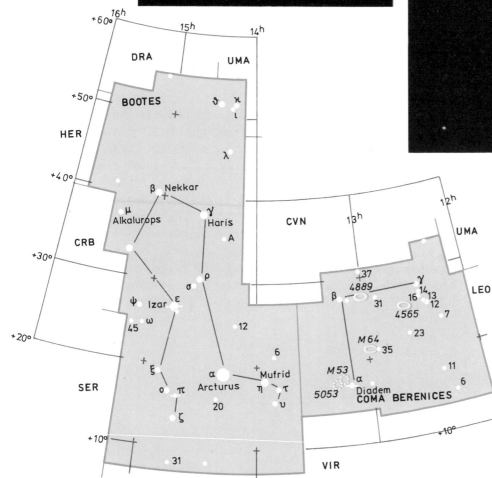

The Coma cluster of galaxies. The brightest galaxy is NGC 4889.

Leo
Leonis—Leo—The Lion

Sextans
Sextantis—Sex—The Sextant

Leo (the Lion) (detail).
14th century
astronomical codex.

α Leonis—Regulus. One of the brightest stars in the spring sky, magnitude 1.4. Distance 85 light-years. The star is five times as large and 160 times as bright as the Sun. The surface temperature is 13,000 K. Regulus is only 0.5° from the ecliptic, which is why the Moon and bright planets can occasionally be seen close to it.

M65 and M66 (NGC 3623 and NGC 3627). A pair of bright galaxies that can be seen together in the field of view of a telescope with low magnification. Both galaxies have a brightness of about 10^m and apparent diameters of about 8′; the distance between them is 21′. The distance of the pair is estimated to be about 29 million light-years, in which case the diameter of M65 would be 60,000 light-years and that of M66 would be 50,000 light-years. The true distance between the two galaxies is about 180,000 light-years.

M95 and M96 (NGC 3351 and NGC 3368). This pair of bright galaxies lies about 9° east of Regulus. The brighter of the two, M96, (type Sb and mag. 10.2), has an apparent size of 6.0′ × 4.0′. M95 is fainter; it is a type SBb galaxy, which makes it look like the Greek letter θ (theta); its apparent dimensions are 4.0′ × 3.0′. It seems that both galaxies are members of the same group as the nearby M65 and M66, and hence all are roughly the same distance from Earth — about 29 million light-years.

NGC 3115. A very bright galaxy of 10th magnitude, spindle-shaped, with apparent dimensions of 4.0′ × 1.0′. It is classified as a greatly flattened, elliptical, E7 galaxy, but it may also be a type SO galaxy observed edge-on. No dark dust band is discernible, however. The distance of NGC 3115 is estimated to be between 21 and 25 million light-years, and the true diameter of the galaxy at about 30,000 light-years or less.

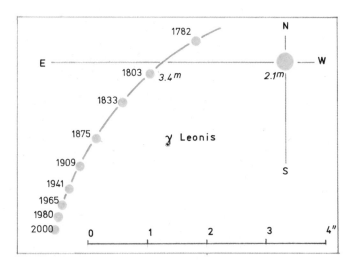

The apparent orbit of the double star **γ Leonis — Algieba**. The components are magnitudes 2.1 and 3.4, and are coloured orange; the period is not precisely known, it may be between 400 and 700 years. The distance is about 90 light-years. A very good object for observation with larger telescopes.

NGC 3115 — A bright, spindle-shaped galaxy in
the constellation of Sextans.

Bright spiral galaxies in Leo (right, from top to bottom):

M65—NGC 3623, type Sb galaxy with bright nucleus

M66—NGC 3627, type Sb galaxy with broad spiral arms

M95—NGC 3351, barred spiral galaxy

M96—NGC 3368, type Sa galaxy.

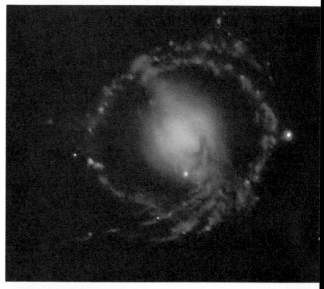

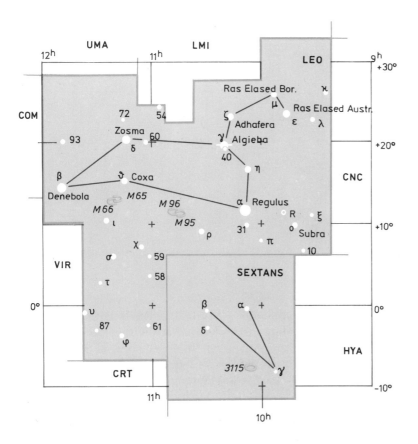

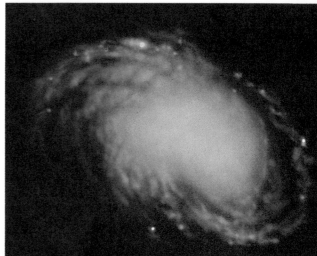

Virgo
Virginis—Vir—The Virgin

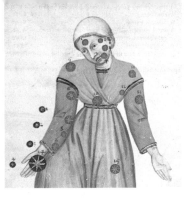

Virgo (the Virgin)
(detail). 14th century
astronomical codex.

α Virginis—Spica. A 1st magnitude star (its magnitude is precisely 1.00), with diameter 8 times that of the Sun. Luminosity 2300 times that of the Sun; spectrum B1; distance 275 light-years. The name Spica means 'ear of corn', which is held by the Virgin in her hand in pictorial representations of the constellation.

The Virgo Galaxy Cluster. At top left, opposite, is the central region of this large cluster, which numbers about 3,000 members. It is the closest of the large clusters of galaxies so that several tens of bright galaxies may be observed with amateur telescopes (for example, the elliptical galaxies M84 and M86, shown in the picture). The cluster is more than 40 million light-years distant.

M87—NGC 4486. One of the largest members of the Virgo Cluster. A bright elliptical, E1 galaxy, mag. 9.7, apparent diameter 3′. It is one of the most massive and most luminous galaxies known; its mass is about 800 thousand million solar masses. At the same time it is one of the strongest sources of radio radiation, designated 'Virgo A' or by the number 3C 274 (Third Cambridge Catalogue of Radio Sources). The powerful radio radiation and also very strong X-ray emission go hand in hand with a bright 'jet' extending more than 4,000 light-years from the nucleus of the galaxy. Streaming from the nucleus is a jet of electrons, accelerated by a strong magnetic field to immense speeds; this gives rise to high-energy synchrotron radiation. These processes might be caused, for example, by a supermassive black hole in the nucleus of the galaxy.

M104—NGC 4594. The well-known **Sombrero Galaxy**, one of the clearest examples of the presence of a band of dark interstellar matter in the equatorial galactic plane. M104 is a type Sa or Sb spiral galaxy that we observe practically edge-on. It is about 40 million light-years distant and its diameter is more than 100,00 light-years. The redshift in the spectrum of M104 corresponds to a recessional velocity of 1 100 km/s.

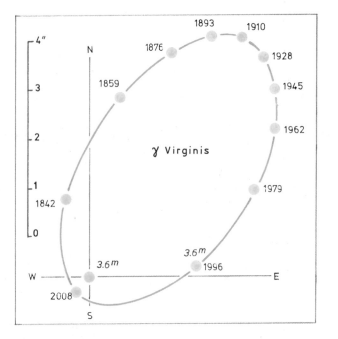

The double **star γ Virginis**, called **Porrima**. Both components of this very pretty visual double are of equal brightness: +3.65^m. The orbital period is 171 years; at periastron the separation of the components is 3 AU, their greatest separation is 70 AU. This double star is 32 light-years from the Earth.

The elliptical galaxy M87 with the jet of material from the nucleus. It is the Virgo A radio source.

The Virgo Galaxy Cluster.

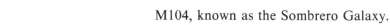

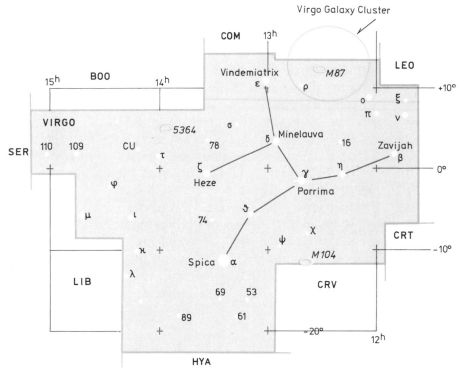

NGC 5364 in Virgo, a very nice example of a type Sb galaxy.

M104, known as the Sombrero Galaxy.

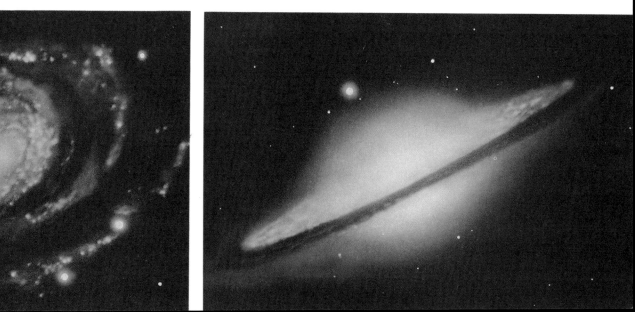

Corvus

Corvi—Crv—The Crow

Hydra

Hydrae—Hya—The Water Snake

Corvus (the Crow).
14th century astronomical codex.

Hydra is the longest constellation in the sky and is also the largest in terms of area. The head of this monster rises above the equator towards the constellation of *Cancer* (the Crab) and its snake-like body winds across the southern sky all the way to *Libra* (the Scales).

α Hydrae—Alphard is of 2nd magnitude and is the brightest star in Hydra. It is 95 light-years distant and its luminosity equals 110 times that of the Sun.

M48—NGC 2548. A fairly faint, but large, open cluster readily observed with binoculars. Its apparent diameter is about 42′ — in other words it is bigger than the disc of the Full Moon. The distance of M48 is about 1,700 light-years, and its true diameter is more than 20 light-years.

NGC 3242. A planetary nebula, whose inner elongated ring resembles an eye with apparent dimensions of 26″ × 16″. The outer and fainter envelope has a diameter of 40″. The central 11th magnitude star is very hot, with a surface temperature of about 60,000 K. As in the case of most planetary nebulae, authorities differ markedly in their estimates of its distance, ranging between 1,900 and 3,300 light-years. The true diameter of the nebula is probably more than 0.5 light-year.

NGC 4038/39—Ring-Tail Galaxy. A very peculiar pair of galaxies where the internaction of their gravitational fields has produced this strange formation (opposite, top right). We may speculate whether this is the result of the collision of two galaxies. It is obvious, however, that the two galaxies came so close to one another that a great many of their stars, and a large amount of interstellar material, were torn from their original orbits, and drawn out into intergalactic space. This may also account for the extraordinarily long, curved filaments extending north and south from the two galaxies. The distance of this celestial object is about 90 million light-years, and the true diameter of the pair is about 100,000 light-years. A similar formation is located in the constellation of Cancer (see p. 141).

The 'head' of Hydra is not a star cluster but a chance grouping of six stars, which are actually at greatly different distances, ranging from one hundred to four hundred light-years. The northernmost of the six, ε Hydrae, is a multiple system with five components — a quintuple star.

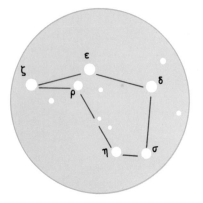

The bright planetary nebula NGC 3242.

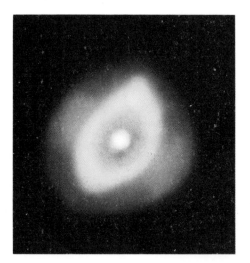

Right: An example of the interaction of two galaxies. In short-exposure photographs the two colliding galaxies NGC 4038/39 look like chains of hazy stars (detail). Longer exposures reveal fainter parts of the galaxies, particularly the long curved 'tails' extending far out into intergalactic space.

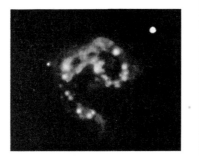

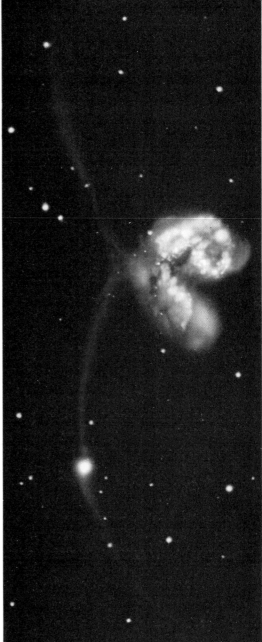

The open cluster M48—NGC 2548.

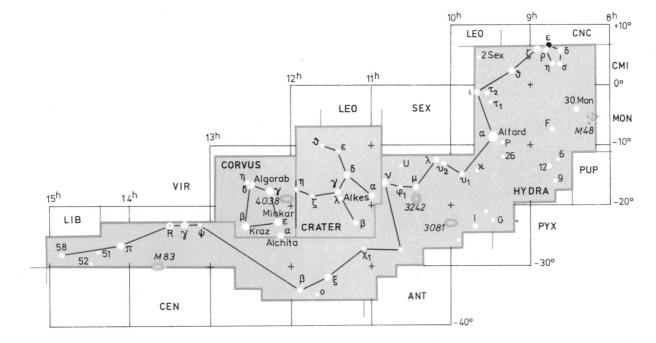

Galaxy M83 in Hydra

The head of Hydra
(the Water Snake).
14th century astronomical codex.

M83—NGC 5236. One of the brightest and most beautiful galaxies in the southern sky. Its elegantly curved spiral arms create the impression of dynamic, whirling movement by clouds of stars round the centre of this island universe.

In the sky M83 looks like a hazy object of 8th magnitude with angular dimensions of $10' \times 8'$. The true diameter of M83 is about 35,000 light-years, about one-third of the diameter of our own Galaxy. The distance of this object is about 12 million light-years.

M83 is a type SBa barred spiral galaxy. About one-third of all known spiral galaxies have a bar. This is a straight, usually spindle-shaped feature consisting of stars and interstellar matter, which extends from opposite sides of the galaxy's central condensation. Each end of the bar is then the point from which the main spiral arms spring. We do not know why many galaxies have bars.

The orange coloration of the bar and central region of M83 indicates the predominance of older, cooler, and hence 'redder' stars. In the galaxy's spiral arms, on the other hand, the pre-dominant colour is the blue of young, hot and very massive stars that were formed recently and are undergoing rapid evolution. Large clouds of ionized interstellar hydrogen glow red to pink. They are the cradles of new stars, which are born here in great numbers.

The spiral structure of M83 is made more conspicuous by the rich pattern of dark bands and clouds of interstellar dust and gas, which may be followed all the way into the bright nucleus of the galaxy. Despite appearances, these dark lanes are by no means empty — they contain an immense quantity of non-luminous interstellar matter which absorbs radiation from more distant stars and, in addition, numerous faint, dim stars.

Scattered thinly over the entire picture are stars of varying brightness that belong to our Galaxy. We look out through these into outer space as we try to understand the turbulent evolutionary processes, demonstrated on the scale of a whole galaxy, in this exquisite island the Universe.

The position and light-curve of the long-period pulsating variable **R Hydrae**. At maximum it sometimes attains magnitude 4.0 when it is easily visible with the naked eye; at minimum it is usually about 250 times fainter and may be seen only with a telescope. The period of R Hydrae is less than 400 days; its distance is about 325 light-years.

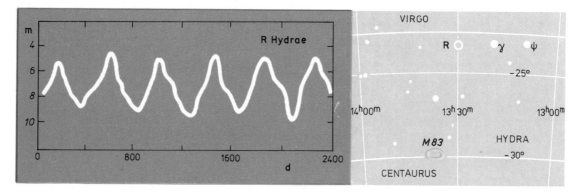

Summer constellations

Cygnus (the Swan).
P. Apianus, *Quadrans*, 1532.

The shimmering band of the Milky Way serves as an excellent guide for finding the constellations in this part of the sky. The Milky Way passes through the most important landmark, the so-called 'Summer Triangle', formed by the bright stars Vega, Deneb and Altair. Blue-white Vega in *Lyra* (the Lyre) is one of the brightest stars in the heavens. Deneb lies in the tail of *Cygnus* (the Swan), which flies with outspread wings along the Milky Way. Altair in *Aquila* (the Eagle) is accompanied on either side by fainter stars, so the three rather resemble Orion's Belt. North of Altair lie two of the smallest constellations — *Sagitta* (the Arrow) and *Delphinus* (the Dolphin).

West of Vega lies the large but inconspicuous constellation of *Hercules*, whose faint stars are arranged in a mirror-image of the letter K. Between Hercules and Boötes (see the spring constellations, p. 160) lies the beautiful constellation of *Corona Borealis* (the Northern Crown) with the bright star Gemma. Below Corona Borealis is *Serpens Caput* (Head of the Serpent). Serpens itself appears on both sides of *Ophiuchus* (the Serpent Bearer). The second part of the constellation, *Serpens Cauda* (Tail of the Serpent), stretches all the way to *Aquila* (the Eagle) and extends across the two branches of the Milky Way.

Of the zodiacal constellations along the ecliptic the most readily recognized is *Scorpius* (the Scorpion) with its red star Antares. West of Scorpius we find *Libra* (the Scales) and east of Scorpius, in the brightest parts of the Milky Way, lies *Sagittarius* (the Archer). West of the latter on the ecliptic is *Capricornus* (the Sea-goat). Located south of Sagittarius is a regular crescent of faint stars marking *Corona Australis* (the Southern Crown). South of Scorpius lies the clearly visible constellation of *Ara* (the Altar) which resembles a crude drawing of an armchair.

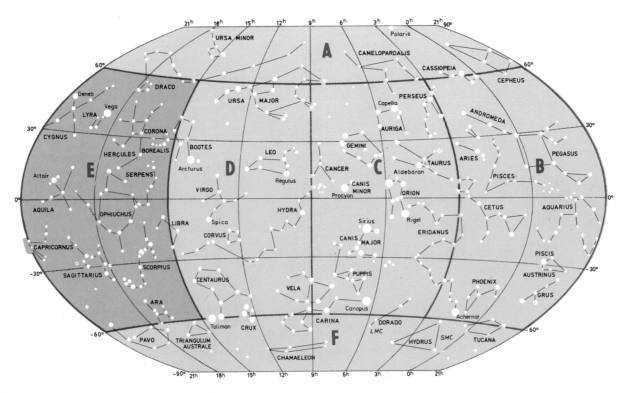

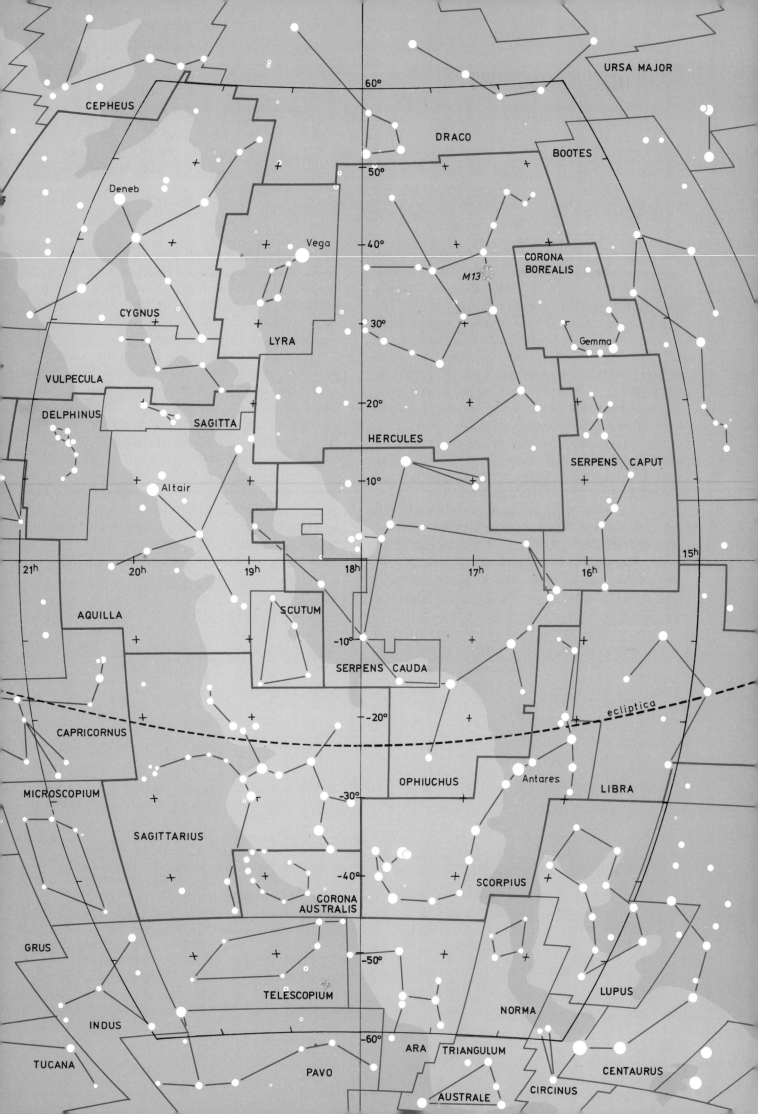

Corona Borealis

CRB

Coronae Borealis — CrB — Northern Crown

Corona Borealis
(the Northern Crown).
14th century astronomical codex.

The cluster of galaxies in Corona Borealis. Galaxies may be considered as the basic building blocks of the Universe. They are not isolated, independent of their surroundings, but occur in higher systems consisting of tens, hundreds or even thousands of members bound together by the force of gravity. Such systems are called clusters of galaxies. One example of a very remote and rich object of this kind is the cluster of galaxies in the very small, but conspicuous, constellation of Corona Borealis.

Within a small area equivalent to the disc of our Moon there are more than 400 galaxies. Part of this cluster is shown in the picture on the opposite page and it requires a good deal of imagination to grasp its true dimensions. The circular discs with nearly sharp outlines represent the stars of our Galaxy, between which we are gazing out into the vastness of outer space. The small hazy lenses and ellipses scattered over the picture are galaxies. Their light travels more than one thousand million years before it reaches the Earth. They are so remote and so faint that they can only be photographed with large telescopes; the brightest galaxy in this cluster has an apparent magnitude of about 16.5.

The individual galaxies in the cluster follow complex orbits. They can approach closely and affect one another by their force of gravity; galaxies may even collide, their structures may change, or there may be instances of 'cannibalism', when a more massive galaxy 'swallows' one that is less massive.

These galaxies lie at a distance of 1 to 1.3 thousand million light-years, and we can determine from the redshift in their spectra that they are receding at a speed of about 21,000 km/s, which is about $1/14$ the speed of light. The cluster remains together and recedes as a unit, which is not itself expanding.

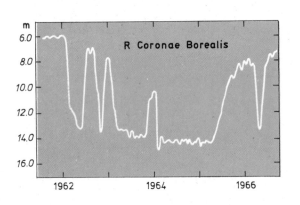

The irregular variable star **R Coronae Borealis** varies in brightness in a totally unpredictable manner from 6^m to 15^m. The diagram shows the light-curve during the long minimum in the 1960s. Spectroscopic methods showed that the atmosphere of the star contains 67 per cent carbon. R CrB is therefore a 'heavy smoker', which occasionally shrouds itself in clouds of 'soot' that absorb its light. When the carbon cloud disperses the star shines again with undiminished brightness, attaining its maximum of 6^m.

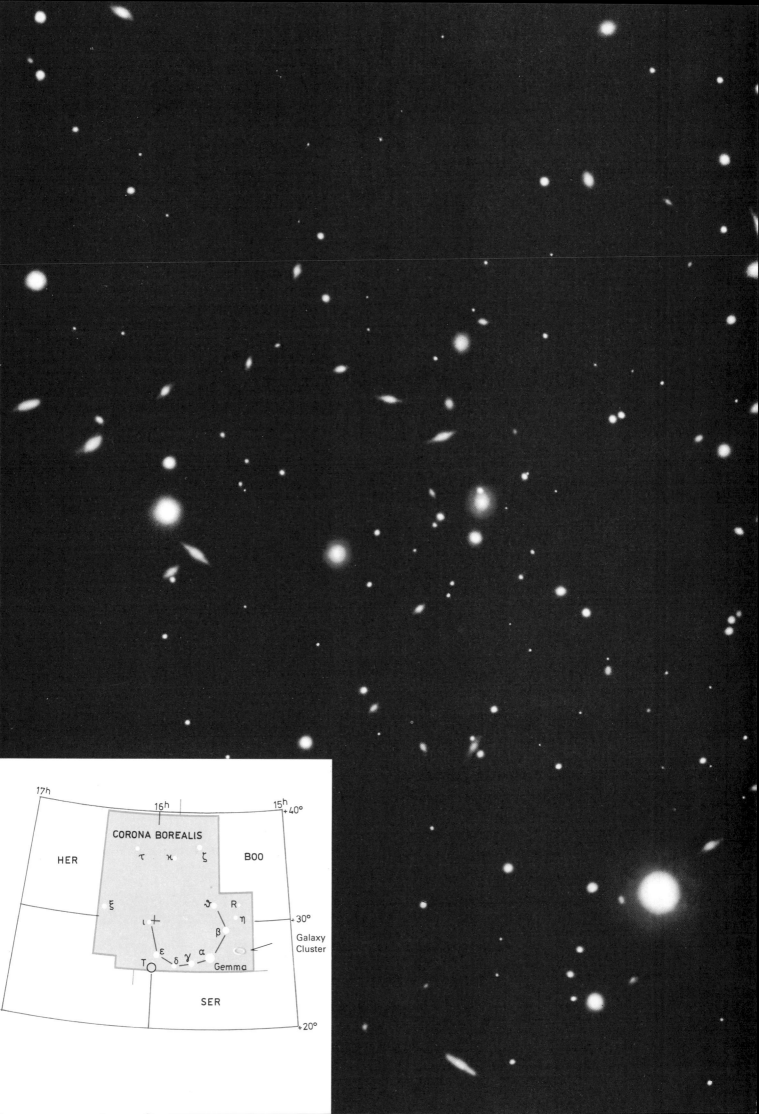

CORONA BOREALIS

HER

BOO

τ κ ζ

ξ

ι ϑ R

η

β

ε δ γ α

T Gemma

Galaxy Cluster

SER

17ʰ 16ʰ 15ʰ +40°

+30°

+20°

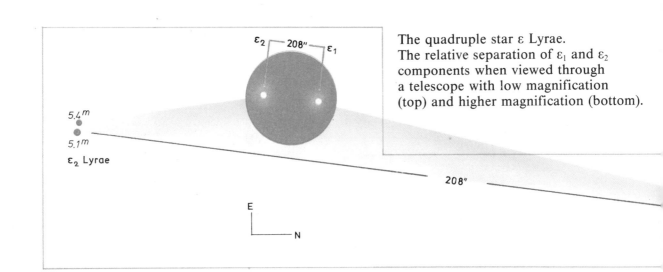

The globular cluster M13.
Littrow, *Himmelsatlas*, 1854.

α Lyrae—Vega. The brightest star in the Summer Triangle (see p. 168); fifth brightest star in the sky, mag. 0.04. Distance about 27 light-years; diameter 3.2 times that of the Sun, i. e. about 4.5 million km. Luminosity 58 times that of the Sun, surface temperature 9,200 K, spectrum A0, colour blue-white. In 1983 infra-red detectors on the IRAS satellite recorded a dust ring around Vega that might perhaps be an embryonic planetary system.

ε Lyrae. One of the most famous multiple systems, known as the 'Double-double'. A person with excellent eyesight can resolve the two components ε_1 and ε_2 (with a separation of about 3.5'), even without a telescope. With a telescope we can see that both components are close doubles (bottom picture). The whole system is about 180 light-years distant. The true distance between components ε_1 and ε_2 is nearly 13,000 astronomical units and their orbital motion is indiscernibly slow. The distance between the components of both close double stars averages about 160 astronomical units.

M13—NGC 6205 (top right). The most familiar globular cluster in the northern sky. Even with the naked eye it is visible as a small hazy patch and it is one of the favourite objects for observation with a telescope. Its total brightness is 5.7^m; apparent diameter 23' (only 10' in a small telescope). True diameter about 160 light-years, its distance being estimated as lying between 21 000 and 25 000 light-years. The cluster contains about 1 million stars and it is estimated to be some 10 thousand million years old.

M92—NGC 6341 (not illustrated). A bright, readily observed, globular cluster. Total brightness 6.5^m; apparent diameter 8'; distance 35,000 light-years.

The quadruple star ε Lyrae.
The relative separation of ε_1 and ε_2 components when viewed through a telescope with low magnification (top) and higher magnification (bottom).

The globular cluster M13. The stars only appear to be tightly clustered together. In reality the average distribution in the cluster is one star per cubic light-year. Even in the centre of the cluster the distance between neighbouring stars is more than one hundred thousand million times the diameter of a star.

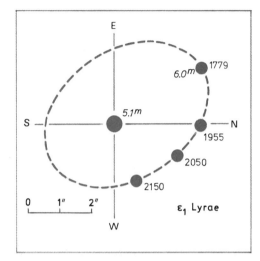

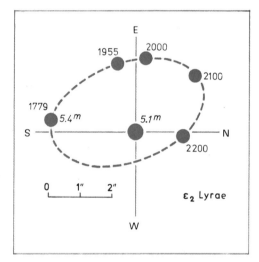

The apparent orbits of the components of the double stars ε₁ Lyrae and ε₂ Lyrae.

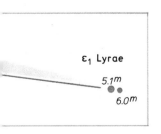

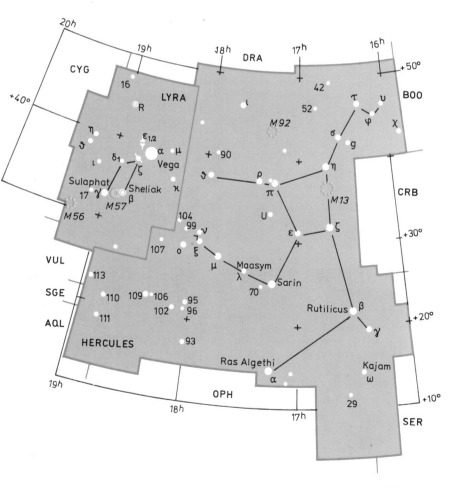

The Ring Nebula in Lyra

Lyra (the Lyre).
P. Apianus, *Quadrans*, 1532.

β Lyrae—Sheliak. A prominent eclipsing binary, chief representative of an important group of eclipsing binaries (the β Lyrae class). In this class both stars have the shape of spheroids with unequal axes. The light-curve is like a sinewave. β Lyrae has a mag. of 3.4 at maximum and 3.8 to 4.1 at minimum. The period is 12.9 days and the variations in brightness can be readily observed with the naked eye or binoculars by comparing it with the nearby star γ Lyrae, which has a mag. of 3.25; every 13 days the brightness of β decreases to half of the brightness of γ. Although β Lyrae is probably the most thoroughly studied star after the Sun, no satisfactory explanation has yet been found for many peculiarities in its spectrum. Both stars are very elongated as a result of their mutual gravitational attraction and rapid rotation. They are so close to one another that their atmospheres intermingle and matter flows from the larger star to the smaller. At the same time some of the gas probably escapes in a spiralling stream into surrounding space. β Lyrae is about 860 light-years distant.

M57—NGC 6720. The Ring Nebula in Lyra is probably the most familiar planetary nebula. Its total brightness is 9^m; angular dimensions about $80'' \times 60''$; true diameter about 0.5 light-years. One can visualize the nebula as looking like a bubble of gas, though in reality it may be toroidal (doughnut-shaped). In the centre of the nebula is a faint star of about 16^m, which can be observed visually only with a large telescope. It is a very hot blue dwarf with a surface temperature of about 100,000 K. The intense ultraviolet radiation from this star is absorbed by the nebula and re-emitted in the visible region. For information about the characteristics of planetary nebulae see p. 12.

A probable model of β Lyrae (the Sun's disc 'S' is shown for comparison purposes).

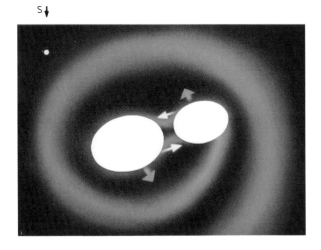

The light-curve of β Lyrae.

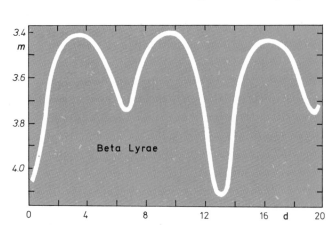

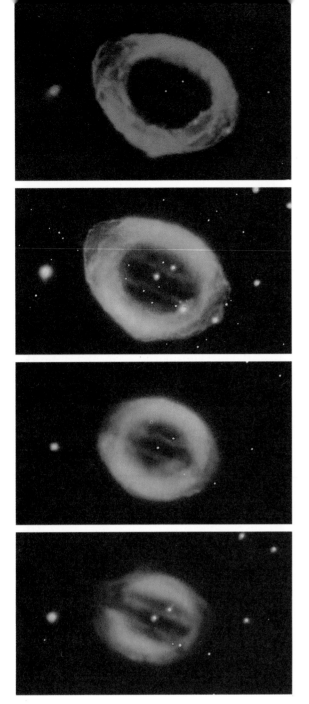

Left, from top to bottom: How M57 looks in photographs in red, yellow, green and blue light.

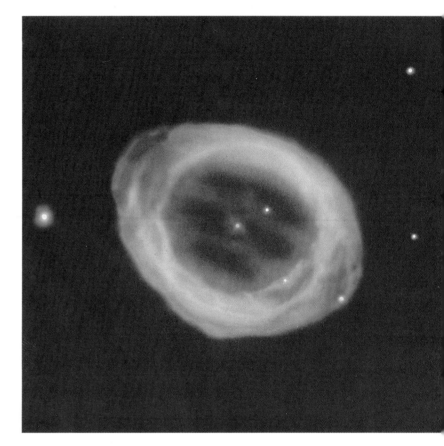

The delicate shades of colour of the Ring Nebula can be recorded only by means of photography. During visual observation we see only a faint blue-green tint.

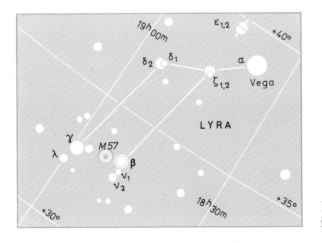

Left: A chart of the constellation of Lyra indicating the positions of the objects described.

Cygnus
Cygni—Cyg—The Swan

Vulpecula
Vulpeculae—Vul—The Fox

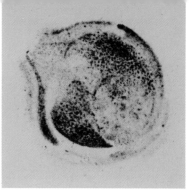

The Dumbbell Nebula according to Lord Rosse, 1840.

α Cyggni—Deneb. The bright star in the 'tail' of the Swan, one of the corners of the Summer Triangle (see p. 172). Mag. 1.3; distance about 1,600 light-years. One of the largest and most luminous of supergiants known, with a diameter about 60 times that of the Sun; mass of about 25 solar masses, luminosity equal to 60,000 Suns (!); spectrum A2, surface temperature 9,700 K.

Cygnus X-1. One of the most powerful sources of X-ray radiation in the Galaxy and the earliest to be discovered (1962). The source was identified in visible light as a 9th magnitude binary, one of whose components is invisible and has a mass of about 6 solar masses; this is most probably a *black hole* surrounded by a rapidly rotating disc of hot plasma which produces the X-ray emission.

M27—NGC 6853 (opposite, right). A bright planetary nebula known as **the Dumbbell Nebula.** Readily observed with a small telescope. A hazy 8ᵐ object, apparent dimensions about $8' \times 5'$. It is one of the closest planetary nebulae, its distance being estimated by various authorities as lying between 490 and 980 light-years. The central 13.5ᵐ star is an exceptionally hot dwarf with a surface temperature of about 85,000 K. The nebula is expanding at a speed of about 27 km/s and from this it may be estimated that it is about 48,000 years old.

β Cygni-Albireo. One of the most beautiful coloured double stars for observation with small telescopes. Distance 410 light-years.

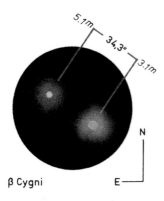

β Cygni

The light-curve of the long-period variable χ **Cygni**, with a period of 470 days. When close to maximum it is often visible to the naked eye.

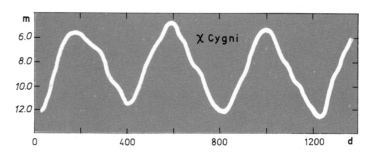

χ Cygni

The open cluster M39—NGC 7092 in Cygnus. It contains about 30 stars, and has an apparent diameter of 0.5°. Its distance is about 800 light-years.

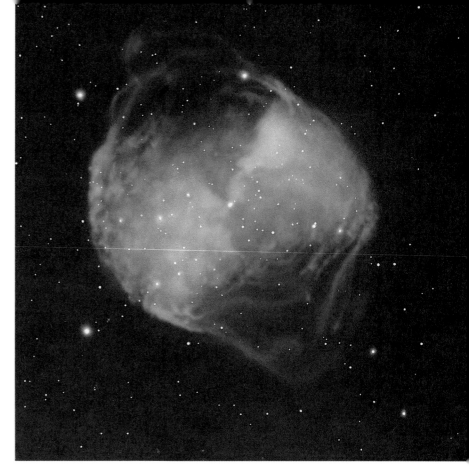

M 27—NGC 6853

The sparse open cluster C 399 in Vulpecula, readily resolved with binoculars. The outline of a coathanger is formed by the 5ᵐ—7ᵐ stars.

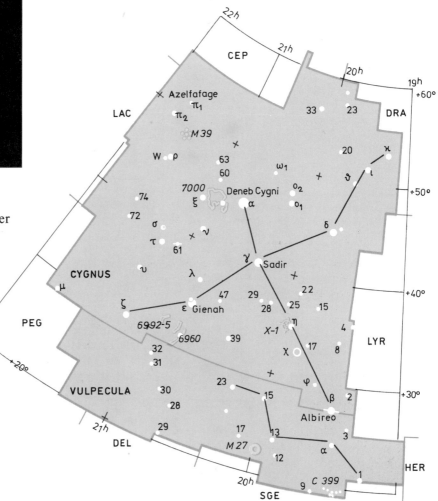

181

Nebulae in Cygnus

Cygnus (the Swan).
14th century
astronomical codex.

NGC 7000—The North America Nebula (Top right). A diffuse nebula which, when observed with the naked eye or binoculars, appears as a small, relatively bright, hazy spot more than 1.5° in diameter, situated in the Milky Way about 3° east of Deneb. In photographs one sees a remarkable resemblance to the outline of the North American continent. West of the 'Gulf of Mexico' is the small nebula IC 5067, known as the Pelican Nebula. NGC 7000 is about 1,600 light-years away and has a diameter of about 45 light-years. The main source of this nebula's radiation (apart from other, fainter stars) is Deneb, which is the same distance from the Solar System.

NGC 6960 and **NGC 6992—The Veil (or Cirrus) Nebula** in Cygnus. A beautiful complex of nebulae, whose extraordinarily delicate structure is discernible only in photographs made with large telescopes. On the opposite page at bottom left, NGC 6992 can be seen as a bright arc on the left-hand side of the picture; at the right-hand edge is NGC 6960 near the bright star 52 Cygni. The structure of NGC 6992 is clearly visible in the detailed view shown at bottom right. It seems that the whole complex of nebulae is part of an expanding cloud which has an apparent diameter of 2.6°, corresponding to a true diameter of about 70 light-years. Its distance is estimated to be 1,500 light-years. The Veil Nebula is apparently a remnant of an ancient supernova explosion, whose outburst occurred some 30,000 to 40,000 years ago. So far no one has had any success in reliably identifying a possible stellar remnant, i. e. the source of radiation for the Veil Nebula.

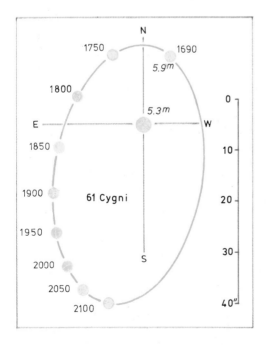

The apparent orbit of the double star **61 Cygni.** The separation of the components changes from 11″ to 34″ with a period of 653 years. A historically important object, because this was the first star to have its parallax successfully determined by trigonometry, so for the first time it was possible to determine a star's distance from the Sun (F. W. Bessel, 1838). The distance of 61 Cygni is 11.1 light-years. The system also includes a third, invisible object of exceedingly low mass, a mere 0.008 solar mass, which is eight times the mass of Jupiter. It may be a planetary-type object.

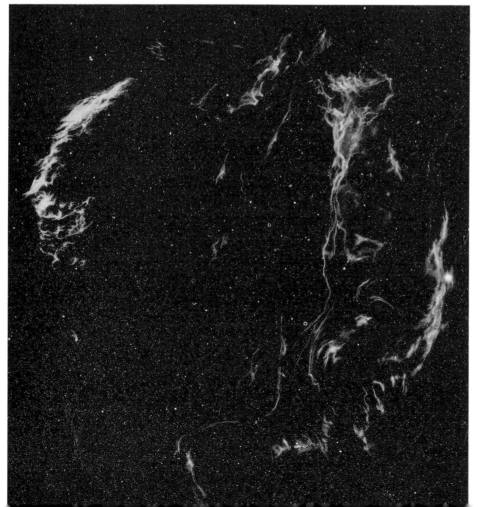

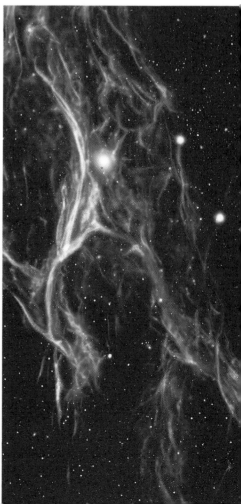

Ophiuchus
Ophiuchi—Oph—The Serpent Bearer

Ophiuchus
(the Serpent Bearer).
14th century
astronomical codex.

Barnard's Star (Barnard's 'Runaway Star'). This tiny, faint, 9.5^m star is a great favourite. Of all the stars it has the largest proper motion yet discovered — 10.29″ in one year. (The star shifts across the background of more distant stars by a distance equivalent to the apparent diameter of the Moon in a period of about 175 years). It is the second closest star to the Earth (only α Centauri is closer), being only 6.0 light-years distant. Barnard's Star is a red dwarf, spectrum M5, luminosity 1/2,500 of that of the Sun, surface temperature 3,200 K; mass only 0.16 solar mass; diameter about 225,000 km. The star travels through space at a speed of about 165 km/s. Periodic changes in the star's motion testify to the existence of at least one very small companion — perhaps a planet.

M10—NGC 6254 (opposite, bottom left). A bright globular cluster easily visible even in binoculars, total magnitude 7.0; apparent diameter about 12′. Estimates as to the distance of M10 range between 16,000 and 22,000 light-years. Close to M10 — about 3.5° northwest — lies another bright globular star cluster, M12.

The star clouds and dark nebulae in the southern part of Ophiuchus are among the loveliest parts of the Milky Way. Close to the star ϑ Ophiuchi it is possible to see with the naked eye a large dark cloud the shape of a tobacco pipe, about 7° long and with a 'bowl' 2° high; the true size of the Pipe Nebula is several hundred light-years. When we observe this region and the neighbouring part of the Milky Way in Sagittarius we are looking towards the centre of our Galaxy.

The proper motion
of Barnard's Star over
the period 1900 to 2020 A. D.

The apparent orbit of the double star **70 Ophiuchi**. The components are 4.2^m and 5.9^m, their separation changes from 1.7″ to 6.7″ with a period of 87.85 years. Distance 16.5 light-years.

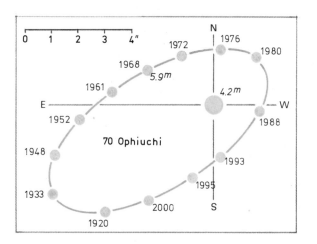

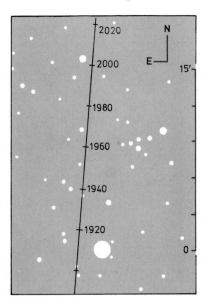

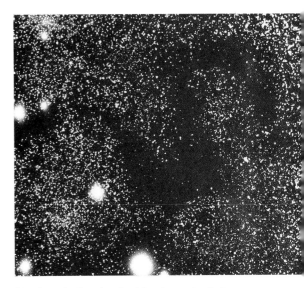

Dark nebulae in Ophiuchus. At left is the large Pipe Nebula and close by Barnard's Star the small 'S-Nebula' (top).

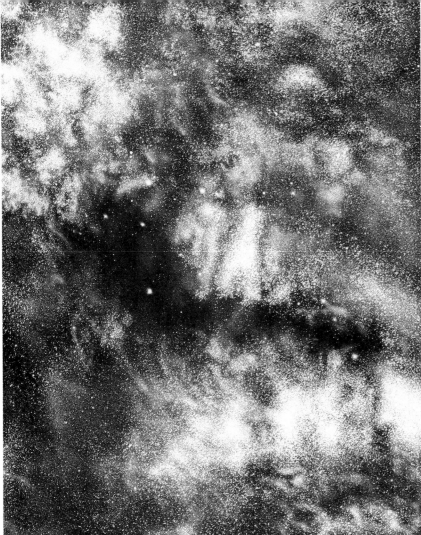

M10— NGC 6254

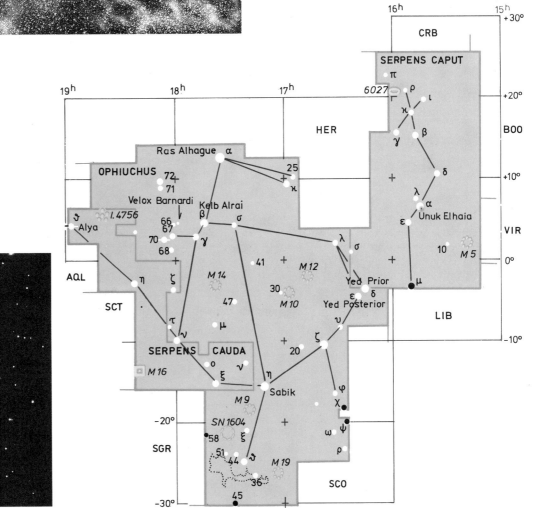

Serpens
Serpentis—Ser—The Serpent

Serpens Caput
(Head of the Serpent).
14th century astronomical codex.

The constellation of Serpens is split into two parts (see chart on p. 185): Serpens Caput (Head of the Serpent) and Serpens Cauda (Tail of the Serpent).

M16—NGC 6611 (top right). A large open cluster surrounded by a diffuse nebula, one of the loveliest objects of its kind. In the literature it is often called **The Eagle Nebula**. R. Burnham introduced the romantic name **The Star-Queen Nebula** from the dark silhouette in the middle of the nebula, resembling a queen seated on a throne. The cluster chiefly consists of hot, high-luminosity giants spectral classes O and B. The mean age of the star cluster is estimated to be 800,000 years, but the formation of new stars within the nebula is still continuing. The glowing nebula is an H II region of ionized hydrogen; in the foreground are regions of cold and dark interstellar matter forming bizarre shapes. The nebula's mass is equivalent to about 12,500 solar masses. Determining the distance of M16 is very difficult and estimates range from 4,200 to 11,000 light-years, the average estimate being 8,000 light-years; the corresponding true diameter of the nebula would then be 70 light-years. In photographs made with efficient telescopes, M16 covers an area equal to that of the Full Moon; however its glow is very faint and it is difficult to observe even with large telescopes.

M5—NGC 5904. A bright, conspicuous globular cluster. Distance about 27,000 light-years; it contains more than half a million stars.

ϑ **Serpentis.** One of the prettiest double stars for observation with small telescopes. Distance 130 light-years.

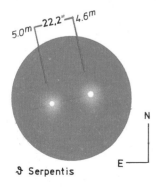

Above: The open cluster M16, surrounded
by a nebula with the same designation.

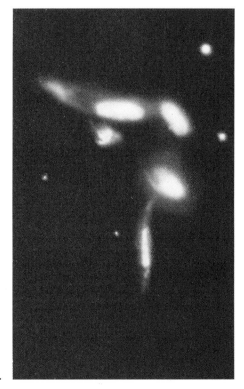

NGC 6027.
An unusual group
of galaxies in Serpens.

AQL
DEL
SCT
SGE

Aquila
Aquilae—Aql—The Eagle

Delphinus
Delphini—Del—The Dolphin

Scutum
Scuti—Sct—The Shield

Sagitta
Sagittae—Sge—The Arrow

Aquila (the Eagle).
P. Apianus, *Quadrans*, 1532.

The constellation of Aquila with the bright star Altair is surrounded by a group of constellations that are among the smallest in the heavens: Delphinus, Sagitta and Scutum.

α Aquilae—Altair. The southern apex of the Summer Triangle, magnitude 0.77; spectrum A7; distance 16 light-years. Diameter 1.5 times that of the Sun, luminosity 9 times greater. The star has an extraordinarily rapid rotation; it rotates round its axis once in just 6.5 hours, which is evidently the reason it has the shape of a greatly flattened ellipsoid.

M11—NGC 6705. One of the loveliest and most richly star-studded open clusters. It is visible on the northern edge of the Scutum Star Cloud, which is part of the Milky Way and is of course much farther away than M11. The cluster is visible as a small hazy object even with binoculars, but resolution of the individual stars is possible only with a larger telescope. The apparent diameter of M11 is 12′; it contains about 500 stars brighter than 14^m and many fainter ones; the total mass of the star cluster is about 2,900 solar masses and the total luminosity is about 10,000 times that of the Sun. The distance of M11 is 5,500 light-years.

M71—NGC 6838. An unusual star cluster in the constellation of Sagitta possessing characteristics of both open and globular clusters. Its distance is probably 18,000 light-years, its apparent diameter is 6′; true diameter about 30 light-years.

γ **Delphini.** A pretty double star for observation with small telescopes. Distance about 100 light-years.

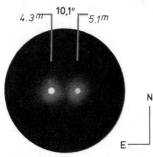

The light-curve of the variable star η **Aquilae.** It is a cepheid, ranging in brightness from 4.5^m to 3.7^m; period of 7.2 days. Distance 1,300 light-years.

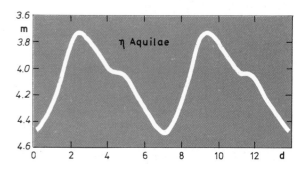

188

Above, left to right: Open star cluster NGC 6709 in Aquila; planetary nebula NGC 6781 in Aquila; galaxy NGC 6814, type Sb, in Aquila; star cluster M71—NGC 6838 in Sagitta.

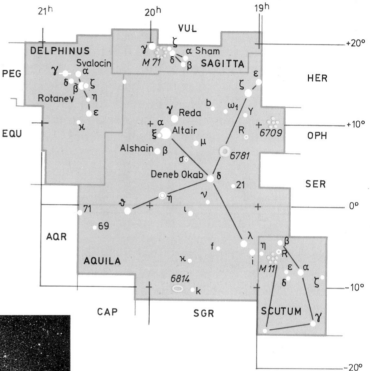

Scutum Star Cloud.

The open cluster M11.

189

Libra
Librae—Lib—The Scales

Scorpius
Scorpii—Sco—The Scorpion

Scorpius (the Scorpion)
(detail). 14th century
astronomical codex.

α Scorpii—Antares. Magnitude 0,92, a red supergiant of spectral class M1. The diameter of the star is about 950 million km — about 700 times the diameter of the Sun. Its distance is 520 light-years; luminosity 9,000 times that of the Sun; surface temperature 3,100 K. Antares is a variable star (irregularly changing in brightness from 0.89^m to 1.06^m) and is also a double star: its 6.5^m companion is separated from it by 3.0″. Antares is embedded in a nebula about 5 light-years in diameter.

ν Scorpii. A very good example of a quadruple star, resembling the familiar ε Lyrae system (see p. 176). With a small telescope it is visible as a double star; with a larger instrument components C and D are readily resolved, whereas the resolution of components A and B is more difficult. The distance of the system is 400 light-years.

M6—NGC 6405 (opposite, bottom left). One of the loveliest open clusters visible in a small telescope. Apparent diameter 25′; it contains about 50 stars ranging from 7^m to 10^m. Its true diameter is about 20 light-years; distance about 1,300 light-years. Close to M6 is another rich cluster **M7** (**NGC 6475**), which can be resolved even with binoculars; it has an apparent diameter of more than 30′ and is about 800 light-years distant.

M4—NGC 6121. One of the brightest, largest and closest globular clusters readily visible even with binoculars. Distance 6,000—7,000 light-years.

Scorpius X-1. The strongest source of X-ray emission in the sky. The object is a close binary, one component being apparently a rapidly rotating neutron star. X-ray radiation occurs during mass transfer (the transfer of extremely hot plasma) from the normal star to the neutron component.

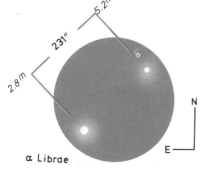

α Librae

Left: **α Librae—Zuben el Genubi.** A double star visible with binoculars. Distance 65 light-years. The brighter component is a spectroscopic binary.

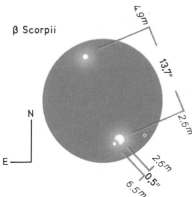

β Scorpii

Left: **β Scorpii—Acrab.** A quintuple system. Components A and C form a very nice double star for observation with small telescopes. Component B is visible only with a large telescope. Components A and C are spectroscopic binaries. The distance of the system is about 600 light-years.

Right: The quadruple star ν Scorpii.

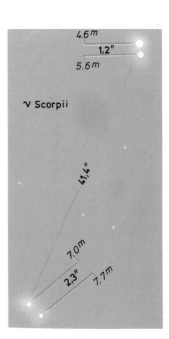

ν Scorpii

NGC 6231 — a very pretty open cluster in Scorpius. The apparent diameter of the central condensation is 15′, and the true diameter is 8 light-years. Distance 5,700 light-years.

The region around Antares contains numerous dark clouds. The globular cluster to the right of α Scorpii is M4. The bright star near the right edge of the picture is σ Scorpii. The bluish nebula at the top surrounds the double star ρ Ophiuchi.

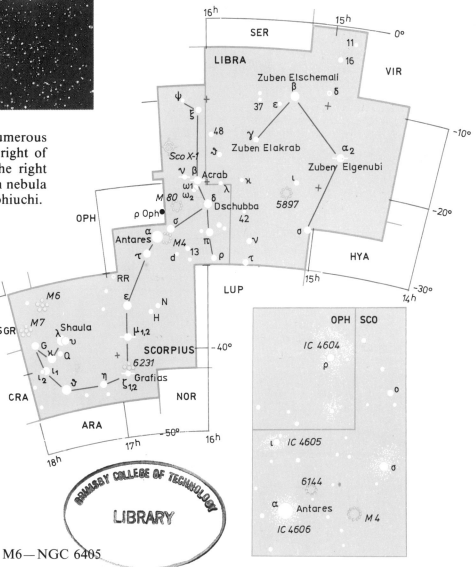

M6 — NGC 6405

Sagittarius
Sagittarii—Sgr—The Archer

Sagittarius (the Archer) (detail). 14th century astronomical codex.

When we look at the constellation of Sagittarius we are looking straight towards the centre of our Galaxy, about 30,000 light-years distant and obscured by clouds of stars and interstellar material. It is possible to observe the nucleus of the Galaxy, however, for example at infrared or radio wavelengths (bottom picture). The nucleus of the Galaxy contains a strong source of radio emission designated 'Sagittarius A'. The constellation of Sagittarius contains many star clusters and nebulae that are among the loveliest objects of their kind.

M24—A star cloud in the Milky Way which can be observed with the naked eye. Its apparent dimensions are about 2° × 1°. Located about 3° to the east is the bright open cluster M25 (IC 4725). Another, the very pretty open cluster M23 (NGC 6494) is located about 5.5° west of M24.

M22—NGC 6656—one of the brightest globular clusters in the whole sky, brighter than the familiar M13 in Hercules. The apparent diameter of M22 is 18'; the true diameter of the central brightest region is about 50 light-years. Its distance is about 9,600 light-years (this is one of the closest globular clusters).

NGC 6822—Barnard's Galaxy — an irregular dwarf galaxy discovered by E. E. Barnard in 1884. Angular dimensions 20' × 11'. A member of the Local Group of galaxies; distance about 1.7 million light-years; true dimensions about 10,000 × 5,000 light-years.

A radio 'picture' of the nucleus of the Galaxy at a wavelength λ = 3.75 cm (left), and a detail of the nucleus as seen at wavelenght λ = 6 cm (right). A mass about 10 million times the mass of the Sun is concentrated in the nucleus.

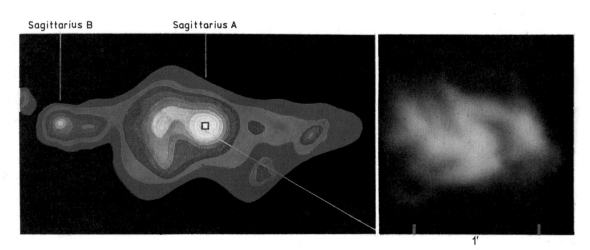

Sagittarius B Sagittarius A

1'

M17—NGC 6618. A diffuse nebula in Sagittarius called the Omega or Swan Nebula. Apparent dimensions 45′ × 35′; true diameter about 40 light-years; distance about 5,700 light-years.

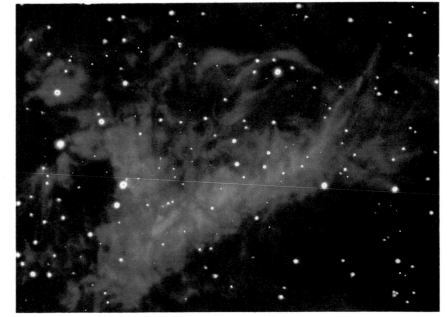

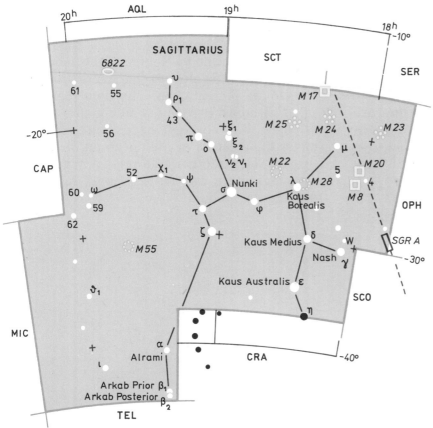

The rectangle (SgrA) on the adjacent chart marks the position of the centre of the Galaxy and corresponds in format to the radio image.

Below from left to right:

M24 — star cloud in the Milky Way

M22 — globular cluster

NGC 6822 — irregular galaxy

Nebulae in Sagittarius

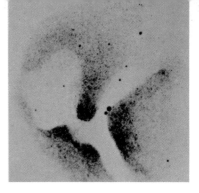

The Trifid Nebula.
Littrow, *Himmelsatlas*, 1854.

M8—NGC 6523 (bottom right). A diffuse nebula called **The Lagoon Nebula**. A very bright object, easily visible even with binoculars. With a telescope, and especially in pohotographs, we can see the complex structure of this H II region. The nebula surround the sparse cluster NGC 6530, which consists entirely of very hot, young stars of spectral classes O and B. The two objects are closely connected: the nebula is the place where new stars are formed. This is shown by the presence of small circular dark nebulae — or globules — that we see as black spots against the background of luminous gas (see also the Rosette Nebula on p.153). The brightest detail in the nebula is the formation approximately 30″ in size, called the Hourglass because of its shape. The true diameter of M8 is probably more than 100 light-years and its distance is more than 5,000 light-years.

M20—NGC 6514 (top right). A diffuse nebula called **The Trifid Nebula** after the characteristic division of the brightest parts by three dark bands. M20 is fainter and more difficult to observe visually than neighbouring M8. Photographs of the Trifid Nebula are among the most admired and most frequently published pictures of celestial objects. The central region of the nebula, from which the dark dividing bands extend, is a sextuple star whose brightest component (7^m), a hot giant of spectral class O7, is probably the principal source of the nebula's radiation. The red colour is characteristic of glowing clouds of hydrogen. The blue regions are filled with dust particles, which scatter the light of young, very hot stars. According to some estimates the distance of M20 is about the same as that of M8, but other, and relatively numerous, estimates place the Trifid Nebula far beyond the Lagoon Nebula.

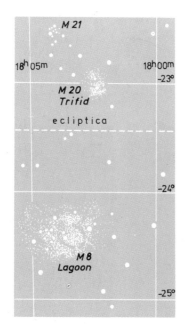

The diffuse nebulae M8 and M20 in the constellation of Sagittarius lie close to the ecliptic (dashed line on the chart), so we can occasionally observe planets or the Moon in their vicinity. Compare the angular dimensions of the nebulae with the disc of the Moon, which has an apparent diameter of 30′.

Constellations in the region of the south celestial pole

The ship Argo. Cellarius, *Harmonia macrocosmica*, 1763.

Finding our way in this part of the sky is somewhat more difficult than in the north polar region. The constellations around the south pole generally consist of faint stars, and they are not particularly conspicuous in the sky.

The simplest place to start is in the band of the Milky Way. Here the Southern Cross (*Crux*) lies near the dark area in the Milky way called the Coalsack. The line joining the brightest stars in *Centaurus* (the Centaur) points toward this cross, thus helping to distinguish it from the so-called 'false cross' on the boundaries of *Vela* (the Sail) and *Carina* (the Keel). In Centaurus we find the brightest globular cluster ω Centauri, visible even with the naked eye.

In the immediate vicinity of the south pole there is no bright star that indicates the position of the pole as Polaris does in the north. Here, there is only the very faint constellation of *Oc-*

tans (the Octant), and the role of Polaris is filled by the faint 5th-magnitude star σ Octantis. The position of the pole can be roughly estimated with the help of the Southern Cross (whose longer arm points to it), or else with the help of the Magellanic Clouds, which form a more or less right-angled triangle with the pole. Both Magellanic Clouds (the Small Magellanic Cloud — SMC — and the Large Magellanic Cloud — LMC) are easily visible even when the Moon is shining.

A useful guide in the southern skies is the line joining the three bright stars Canopus, Achernar and Fomalhaut. On this line we can find the faint constellations of *Pictor* (the Painter's Easel), *Dorado* (the Dorado — a type of fish), *Reticulum* (the Net), *Horologium* (the Pendulum Clock), and *Phoenix* (the Phoenix).

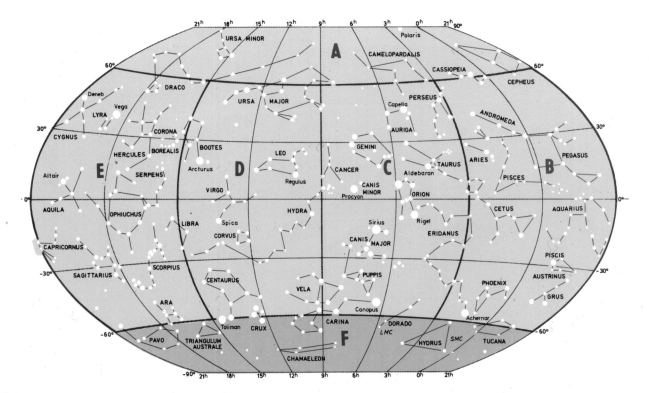

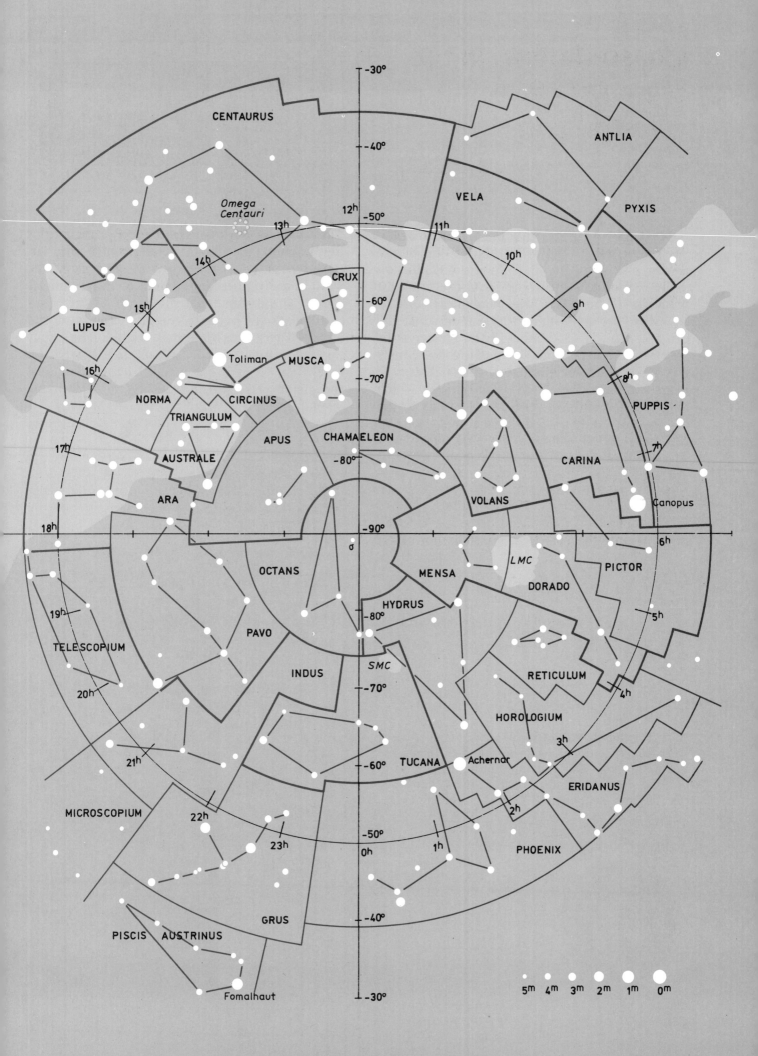

Crux

Crucis—Cru—The Cross,
The Southern Cross

CRU

The Southern Cross. Cellarius,
Harmonia macrocosmica, 1763.

NGC 4755 (top right). An open cluster called **The Jewel Box**. A beautiful object, one of the richest objects of its kind. Spread out over an area 10′ in radius are about 50 of the brightest members of the cluster with magnitudes of 6 to 10. Most are high-luminosity supergiants, for example, the brightest star in the cluster is of spectral class B9 and its luminosity equals 80,000 Suns. The occurrence of stars of this type bears witness to the 'youth' of the cluster, which is only a few million years old. Data as to the distance of NGC 4755 differ markedly; one of the more recent estimates is 7,700 light-years. The diameter of the cluster is about 50 light-years.

The Coalsack dark nebula. This is probably the best known dark nebula, readily visible with the naked eye. It looks like a 'hole' in the Milky Way in the immediate vicinity of the Southern Cross. The dark nebula shows up all the more distinctly here because the star clouds of the Milky Way are exceptionally bright. The angular dimensions of the Coalsack are 7° × 5°; its true diameter is more than 60 light-years, and the distance is estimated to be 500—600 light-years.

Left: The double star **α Crucis—Acrux.** One of the most beautiful double stars in the sky. Distance 370 light-years. The orbital motion of the components is very slow and the period is not known. The brighter component is a spectroscopic binary.

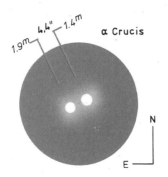

α Crucis

198

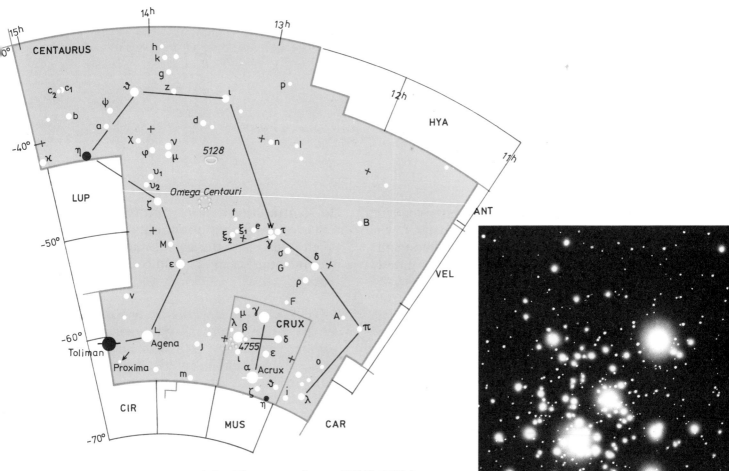

Right: The open cluster NGC 4755 known as the Jewel Box in the Southern Cross.

The Coalsack ↑

Centaurus
Centauri—Cen—The Centaur

Centaurus (the Centaur)
and Lupus (the Wolf).
14th century astronomical codex.

α Centauri—Toliman. The third brightest star in the sky, ma. —0.27. It is the closest star to the Sun. A triple star: bright components A (—0.04^m) and B (1.17^m) form a pretty double star (bottom). The third component is a red dwarf, magnitude 10.7, more than 2° away from the bright pair. It is called Proxima Centauri ('closest in Centaurus') because, of the three components, it is closest to the Earth: 4.28 light-years, i. e. about 270,000 astronomical units.

ω Centauri—NGC 5139 (opposite, bottom). The brightest and largest globular cluster in the sky. It is visible to the naked eye as a hazy spot of 4^m. (That is why, in the 17th century, Bayer designated it as a star, giving it the letter ω.) It is one of the closest globular clusters, being about 17,000 light-years distant. Visually the cluster appears to be the same size as the Moon in the sky. The true diameter of the densest, central region is about 100 light-years. In the centre of the cluster the density of the stars is about 25,000 times greater than in the neighbourhood of the Sun, and the average distance between the individual stars is about one-tenth of a light-year.

NGC 5128 — Centaurus A (opposite, top). An extraordinary, giant galaxy; an extremely strong source of radiation, which is emitted at visual, radio, X-ray, and infrared frequencies. It contains three times as many stars as our Galaxy and is about 12 million light-years distant. In all probability this object was formed when two galaxies combined following their collision. The large elliptical galaxy, consisting of old stars, appears to be divided into two parts by a dark ring of dust, which is the remnant of the second, younger galaxy. A large number of young, blue stars that were perhaps formed as a result of the collision can be seen shining in the dust ring.

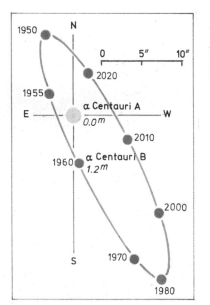

Left: The apparent orbit of the two brightest components (A and B) of the triple star α Centauri. The separation of the components ranges between 2″ and 22″, with a period of 80 years.

Right: Comparison of the size of components A, B and C of α Centauri with the Sun (top).

Carina
Carinae—Car—The Keel

Vela
Velorum—Vel—The Sail

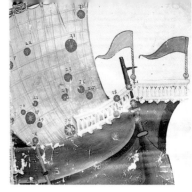

The ship Argo (detail).
14th century
astronomical codex.

α Carinae—Canopus. The second brightest star in the sky, magnitude −0.72. Its distance is about 100 to 120 light-years; diameter 30 times that of the Sun, 1,400 times the Sun's luminosity. Canopus is used for the navigation of most interplanetary probes: the great distance of this star from the ecliptic prevents it from being accidentally mistaken for a bright planet by a probe's navigational sensor.

NGC 2516. A conspicuous, bright open cluster visible with the naked eye. With a telescope we see more than 100 stars within an area 1° in radius. The true diameter of the cluster is about 20 light-years, and its distance is 1,200 light-years.

NGC 3532. One of the richest open clusters in the sky. It is elongated in shape and has a considerable angular size: 60′ × 30′. It contains about 400 stars, of which 150 have a magnitude less than 12. The true diameter of the cluster is 25 light-years; its distance is 1,300 light-years.

NGC 3132. A planetary nebula with a very bright central star of 10^m. The star has a 16^m companion, 1,65″ distant — a dwarf with the exceedingly high surface temperature of 100,000 K, which is the source of the nebula's radiation. The true diameter of the nebula is 0.5 light-years, and its distance is 2,000 to 2,800 light-years.

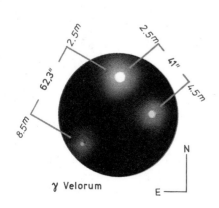

γ Velorum

γ Velorum. A multiple system with a conspicuous bright double star having components of 2.5^m and 4.5^m, which can be resolved even with binoculars. The primary component is a typical example of a 'Wolf-Rayet' star, i. e. an exceptionally luminous, hot giant with a surface temperature of more than 50,000 K and a rapidly expanding atmosphere. Its distance is about 800 light-years.

NGC 3132. (The Eight-Burst Nebula) a planetary nebula on the boundaries of Vela and Antlia. Apparent dimensions 84″ × 52″.

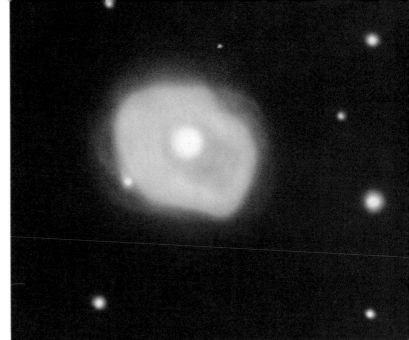

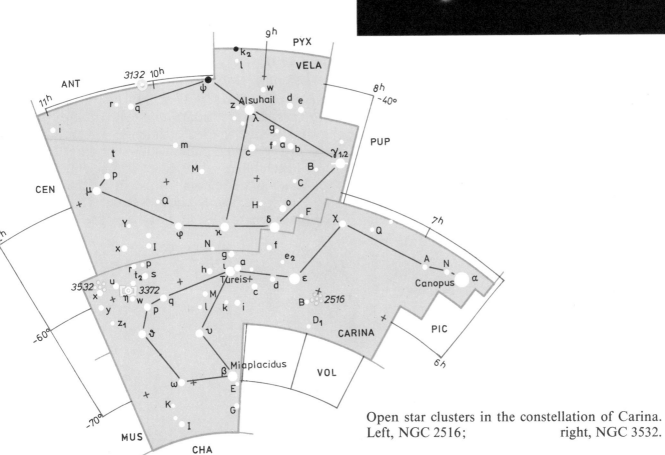

Open star clusters in the constellation of Carina. Left, NGC 2516; right, NGC 3532.

η Carinae Nebula

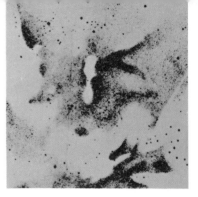

The η Carinae Nebula
according to Herschel.
Littrow, *Himmelsatlas*, 1854.

η Carinae. An irregular, nova-like variable star, which is a very remarkable object. Variations in its brightness have been observed since the second half of the 17th century, when it appeared as a star of 4^m. The fluctuations in brightness were irregular; in 1730 it reached 2^m and continued to vary between 2^m and 4^m until 1820, when it began to increase systematically as shown by the light-curve below. η Carinae attained its maximum brightness of −0.8^m in April 1843, when it became the second brightest star in the sky. Then came a decline in brightness below the limit of visibility with the naked eye. During the course of the 20th century the star's brightness has been round 7^m to 8^m. The star is surrounded by an expanding gaseous envelope with an apparent diameter of about 20″. This apparently separated from the star following its

outburst in 1843. The distance of η Carinae is almost 3,900 light-years. This means that in 1843 the star's luminosity was more than a million times the luminosity of the Sun and that at present the star is more than 1,000 times as bright as the Sun.

NGC 3372—η Carinae Nebula. A large, glowing H II region, covering an area larger than one square degree on the sky. It has a complex structure, bands of dark matter dividing it into several wedge-shaped segments. The brightest part of the nebula contains a small dark formation resembling a keyhole, from which the whole nebula sometimes takes its name — being known as **The Keyhole Nebula.** This is also the place where we will find the star η Carinae.

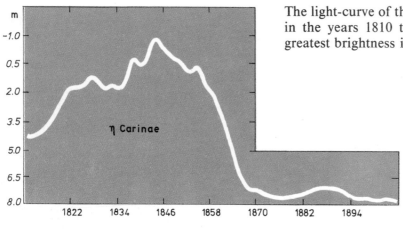

The light-curve of the irregular variable η Carinae in the years 1810 to 1906. The star attained its greatest brightness in 1843.

Dorado
Doradus—Dor—The Dorado

Mensa
Mensae—Men—The Table Mountain

Pictor
Pictoris—Pic—The Painter's Easel

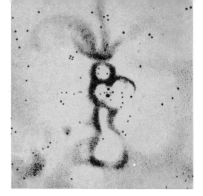

The nebula in the Large
Magellanic Cloud.
Littrow, *Himmelsatlas*, 1854.

Magellanic Clouds. These are two small hazy clouds which look like detached fragments of the Milky Way, and form a more or less right-angled triangle with the south celestial pole. They were first described in detail by the Portuguese navigator Ferdinand Magellan in the early 16th century. Not until the 1920s, however, did astronomers determine that the Magellanic clouds are small, nearby, irregular galaxies. **The Large Magellanic Cloud** has a diameter of about 26,000 light-years and is 170,000 light-years distant. **The Small Magellanic Cloud** has a diameter of 16,000 light-years and is about 205,000 light-years away. At such a small distance (small as far as galaxies are concerned) — merely one tenth of the distance to M31 in Andromeda — individual stars can be observed in the Magellanic Clouds and not only giants, but also fainter stars like our Sun. Thus, for instance, it is possible to make direct comparisons between the luminosities of various types of stars, more readily than in our Galaxy, because they are all at practically the same distance from Earth. The laborious determination of distances of individual stars that is essential here 'at home' in the Milky Way if we want to convert actual stellar distances to a single standard distance in order to determine star's luminosities, therefore becomes completely unnecessary.

Comparison of the luminosity of the stars in the Magellanic Clouds led, for example, to the extremely important discovery of the correlation between the period of variation in magnitude and the luminosity of a certain type of variable star — the cepheids. Cepheids may be found in even more remote galaxies, and serve as reliable lighthouses of known luminosity, from which the distance of the star, and of the system in which it is found, can then be readily determined.

The Magellanic Clouds are linked to our Galaxy not only by the force of gravity, but also by a gigantic bridge of cold, neutral hydrogen. This enormous trail of gas, called the Magellanic Stream, may perhaps extend from the Small Magellanic Cloud as far as the plane of our Galaxy. It is probably mater 'pulled out' by the small galaxy during its passage through the galactic plane. The two Magellanic Clouds are also linked together by hydrogen clouds.

The bluish glow of the Magellanic Clouds reveals the presence of a large number of young, hot, and very luminous giant stars.

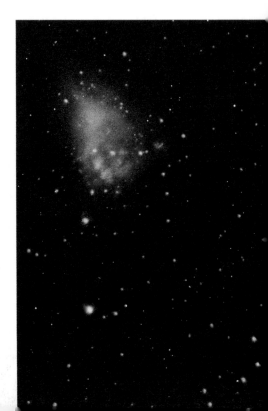

Both Magellanic Clouds (right) can be readily seen at one time. Their separation is 20° and together they occupy about as large a part of the sky as the familiar seven stars of the Plough in Ursa Major. On the left side of the picture is the Small Magellanic Cloud with an apparent diameter of 2.5° (i. e. 5 times the apparent diameter of the Moon), on the right side is the Large Magellanic Cloud with a diameter of about 6°. The gaseous (hydrogen) envelope that surrounds both, and joins the two small galaxies together, is invisible to the naked eye.

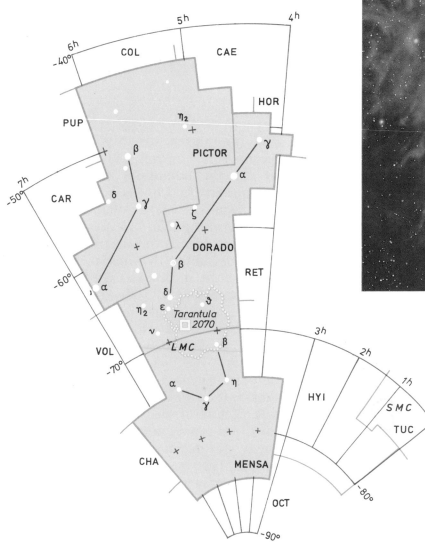

Above: The giant diffuse nebula, called **The Tarantula Nebula**, in the Large Magellanic Cloud is the largest object of its kind known in the Universe. If it occupied the place of the familiar Great Nebula in Orion it would be about three times brighter than Venus and would cover the whole constellation of Orion. (Further details about the Tarantula Nebula are given on the following page.)

Large Magellanic Cloud

Dorado (the Dorado).
Cellarius, *Harmonia macrocosmica*, 1763.

If we were able to see our Galaxy from outside we would see three nearby small satellites—the Magellanic Clouds. A similar system is the Andromeda Galaxy, where we also observe various small satellite galaxies.

The Large Magellanic Cloud is 170,000 light-years distant. It has a diameter of about 26,000 light-years and a mass of about 10 thousand million solar masses, which is about one-thirtieth the mass of our Galaxy. On charts and in the literature it is usually abbreviated to LMC (Large Magellanic Cloud). Originally the Large Magellanic Cloud was classified as an irregular galaxy. It was discovered later that there were signs of spiral structure and some relationship to barred spirals, i. e. to type SB galaxies. The 'bar' is the most conspicuous part of of the LMC and looks like a bright elongated stellar cloud about 20,000 light-years long. Along the length of the 'bar' there are numerous reddish nebulae of ionized hydrogen, excited into radiation by hot, young stars. These are regions where stars are being formed at the present time.

The LMC contains a great many exceptionally bright supergiants reaching luminosities as much as a million times that of the Sun. The most luminous super-supergiant was long believed to be the unusual variable star, S Doradus. In recent years, however, its luminosity has decreased and the luminosity record is now held by the star HD 33579, which has a mass of 50—100 solar masses and a diameter about 4,000 times that of the Sun.

The gigantic diffuse nebula NGC 2070, known as the **Tarantula Nebula**, surpasses all records. It can be seen with the naked eye as the brightest object in the LMC, located to the side of the 'bar) (see also the picture on p. 207). This object, the largest diffuse nebula known, has a diameter of about 800 light-years and, if its outer filaments are included, more than 1,700 light-years. The total mass of the nebula is probably more than 400,000 solar masses. Concealed in the centre of the Tarantula Nebula is the source of its radiation, the dazzling object R 136, which has three components. The brightest component, designated R 136a, has a diameter of 3 light-years and seems to be a single 'superstar' that is quite unique in its dimesions. It has a surface temperature of 60,000 K, a luminosity 30 million times that of the Sun, and totals 2,500 to 4,400 solar masses. Such a gigantic object would be about 10 to 20 times as massive as the most massive stars otherwise known.

Supernova 1987 A, recorded in February 1987 in the neighbourhood of the Tarantula Nebula (compare with the opposite picture). This was the first supernova visible with the naked eye since the times of Kepler's Star of 1604, and the first object of its kind sufficiently bright to be observed by all types of modern astronomical equipment and, for the first time, also by the neutrino detectors (neutrinos are particles released during the gravitational collapse of the nucleus of a star which became a supernova in the final stage of its development). Astrophysics was thus enriched by extremely important new pieces of information.

Tucan
Tucanae—Tuc—The Toucan

The Small Magellanic Cloud

Tucana (the Toucan). Cellarius, *Harmonia macrocosmica*, 1763.

The Small Magellanic Cloud (SMC) is a nearby irregular galaxy about 16,000 light-years in diameter and with a mass of about two thousand million solar masses. It is 205,000 light-years distant, and together with the Large Magellanic Cloud (p. 208) it orbits our Galaxy like a satellite. A large part of the mass of the SMC consists of interstellar clouds of hydrogen, the basic building material for stellar formation, which takes place here on a large scale. Proof of this is the large number of young, hot stars — blue giants — that give the SMC its blue coloration.

In 1984, Australian radio astronomers discovered that the SMC in reality consists of two separate galaxies, one behind the other, one being hidden, so we see only a single object in the sky. The more distant galaxy was named the Mini Magellanic Cloud (MMC); it is about 32,000 light-years from the SMC. Both 'clouds' (SMC and MMC) are receding from each other at a speed of about 40 km/s and it was the difference in the velocities of the two objects that revealed the double nature of the Small Magellanic Cloud.

NGC 104—47 Tucanae. A very bright globular cluster, seen even with the naked eye as a small hazy 4.5^m spot about 2.5° west of the SMC. NGC 104 ranks immediately after ω Centauri (p. 200) as the second-loveliest and second-richest globular cluster. The beauty of the cluster is heightened by the conspicuous central condensation where the stars appear to be crowded one upon the other. A large telescope is necessary to resolve the object visually because the brightest stars have an apparent magnitude of only 11.5.

The distance of NGC 104 is between 15,000 and 20,000 light-years, according to various measurements. The true diameter of the cluster is more than 200 light-years.

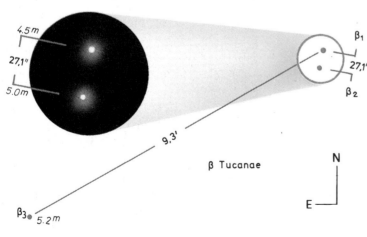

β Tucanae

β Tucanae—a sextuple system. With a small telescope we can see the pretty double star β₁ and β₂, with component β₃ 10′ away. All three components are close doubles.

210

Above: In the Small Magellanic Cloud we see objects similar to those in our Milky Way system: individual stars — amongst them luminous blue giants — open, as well as globular clusters, and the reddish clouds of diffuse nebulae.

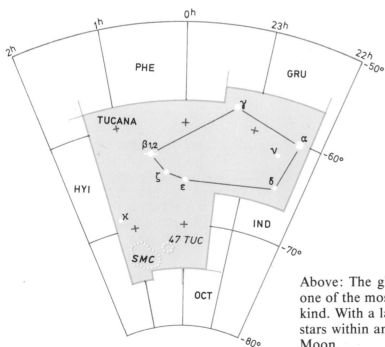

Above: The globular star cluster NGC 104 (47 Tucanae) is one of the most beautiful, brightest, and closest objects of its kind. With a large telescope we can see tens of thousands of stars within an area larger than the apparent diameter of the Moon.

211

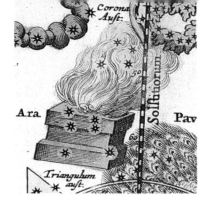

ARA	# Ara
	Arae—Ara—The Altar
OCT	# Octans
	Octantis—Oct—The Octant
PAV	# Pavo
	Pavonis—Pav—The Peacock

Ara (the Altar).
Cellarius, *Harmonia macrocosmica*, 1763.

NGC 6397 (top right). A globular cluster in Ara considered to be the closest objects of this kind. It is about 8,200 light-years distant from the Earth. The apparent diameter of NGC 6397 is 20′, i. e. about two-thirds of the diameter of the Moon's disc. The brightest stars in the cluster have an apparent magnitude of 10 to 12; they are red giants about 500 times as luminous as the Sun. The total luminosity of the star cluster is about 8,000 times that of the Sun, which is a relatively low value when compared with the brightest globular clusters.

NGC 6752 (opposite, bottom left) in Pavo, is one of the brightest and largest globular clusters in the heavens. Its apparent magnitude is 7.2 and according to photographs it has an angular diameter of 42′, i. e. it is larger than the disc of the Moon. The total luminosity of the cluster is almost 100,000 times that of the Sun and its distance is about 20,000 light-years.

NGC 6188 (bottom right). A diffuse nebula in Ara where there is a dramatic contrast between light and dark nebulosity. The nebula surrounds the open cluster NGC 6193, whose hot giant stars excite the clouds of interstellar hydrogen to radiation. The most remarkable part of this complex is the glowing border outlining the dark dust clouds, slightly reminiscent of the Horsehead Nebula in Orion. Here the absorption of the star-light by clouds of interstellar dust is dramatically illustrated. We see that on one side of the boundary there are a great many more stars than on the other side (bottom half of the picture), where only individual stars are scattered here and there. It is this that reveals the presence of an invisible (non-luminous) dust cloud, which like an impenetrable shroud conceals the stars in the background permitting us to see only those that are in the foreground, between the dark nebula and ourselves.

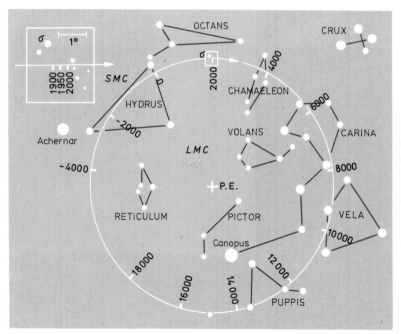

Due to the Earth's precession the celestial poles are not fixed but move amidst the stars. The picture shows the path of the south celestial pole in 1 platonic year (25,800 years). At present the role of Polaris in the north is played in the southern sky by the faint (5.5^m) star **σ Octantis**, located about 1° from the south pole.

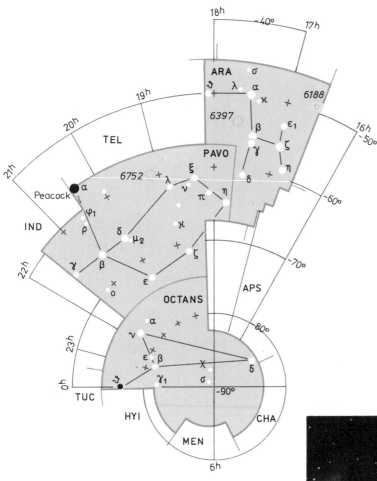

Above: NGC 6397 — a globular star cluster in Ara. It is probably the closest of all globular clusters.

Right: NGC 6188 — a magnificent group of bright and dark nebulae in Ara. The contours of the dark clouds of dust and gas give an inkling of the immense volume of the material that fills the seemingly empty interstellar space.

Below: NGC 6752 — a globular cluster in Pavo. One of the richest globular clusters in the sky.

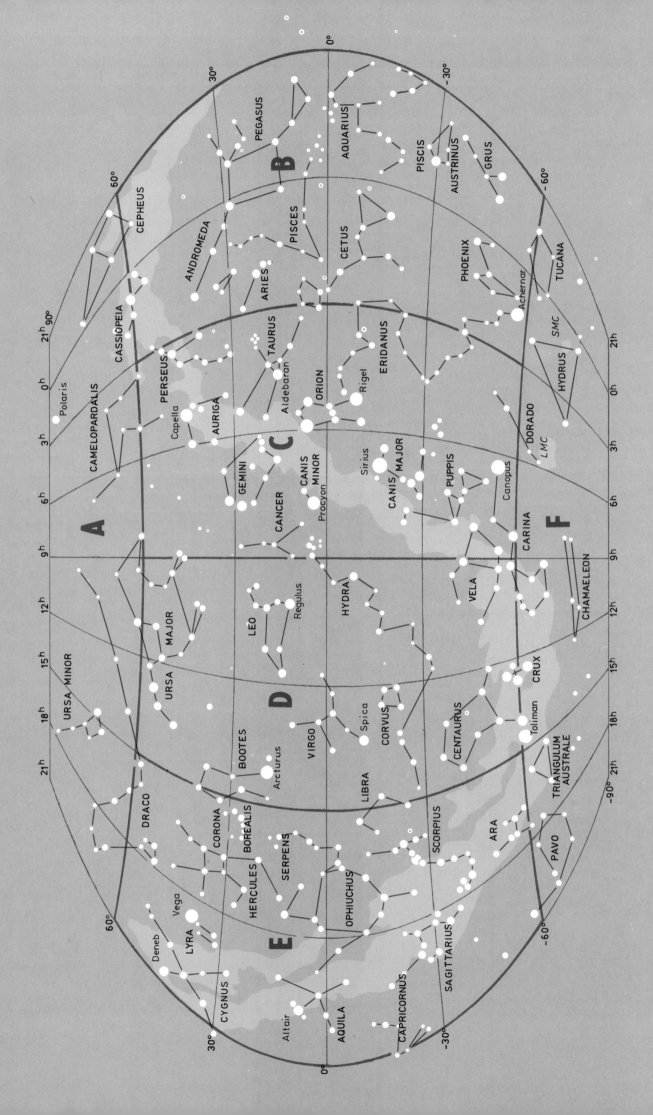

Constellation Index

Numbers in semi-bold type indicate the page with detailed map and description of the constellation.

How to find and observe celestial objects

Those who are interested in nature are generally not content with merely looking at pictures, but wish to see and observe what they can with their own eyes. The simplest astronomical observations are made casually when we explore the realm of nature with 'seeing' eyes. We admire the ruddy disc of the setting Sun and notice the dark spots on the silvery disc of the Moon. On a clear, moonless night, when we are on holiday far from the city, we are filled with awe at the sight of millions of stars in the heavens. Occasionally we may glimpse a shooting star — a meteor.

However, the first time we stand beneath the night sky with the intention of finding a specific object we are faced with difficulties. Where do we begin? What should we use as a starting point? First of all it is necessary to put aside the impression that the night sky is merely a chaotic jumble of stars. Long before the beginning of the 20th century, Man introduced order to the seeming chaos of stars.

The imagination of our ancestors saw groups of bright stars as representing the figures of mythological beings, animals and objects. This is how the constellations came into being. Their number and outline evolved over a period of thousands of years, until the year 1930, when the International Astronomical Union determined that the whole sky would be divided into 88 constellations. Each of these were given definitive boundaries, running along lines of celestial latitude and longitude. Constellations, then, are not just figures outlined by stars, they are distinct areas in the sky and only their irregular boundaries and exotic names remind us of their pictorial origin.

We can get to know the boundaries of the constellations by studying star charts, but they won't remain fixed in our memory. A much better method of locating objects in the heavens is to bear in mind the imaginary lines joining the bright stars in a constellation. In place of the complex mythological figures of old we thus get simple configurations such as triangles, polygons, letters, etc., which can be remembered readily and can then be found in the sky with the aid of a star chart. In getting to know the constellations we generally begin with Ursa Major, the most familiar constellation in the northern hemisphere. With a star chart in hand we can then proceed outwards from Ursa Major in various directions — first of all timidly in the immediate vicinity, where we find Polaris and Ursa Minor, then farther out past Polaris to the constellation of Cassiopeia, etc. — working from the known to the unknown.

A source of difficulty for beginners is the constant change in the visibility of the constellations, caused by the apparent daily rotation of the sky. The constellations rise and set, and the novice helplessly turns the chart this way and that, trying to find which constellations are above the horizon at that particular time and where they are. The problem is excellently solved by a planisphere (a revolving star chart) or by a series of small maps depicting the constellations above the horizon for specific dates and times. Many similar aids are available to the amateur, and any society or planetarium will gladly advise him which to choose. As a matter of fact, a planetarium is the best place to start in getting to know the constellations. The planetarium's projector creates a faithful picture of the night sky, on which the lecturer's light pointer easily leads the gaze of the viewer from one constellation to another.

Throughout the course of the year we will gradually acquire a series of 'landmarks' covering the whole sky. Apart from the three just mentioned — Ursa Major, Polaris and Cassiopeia, they may be the following groups of stars: the Spring Triangle — Regulus, Arcturus and Spica (see p. 160); the Summer Triangle — Vega, Deneb and Altair (see p. 172); the Square of Pegasus (see p. 118); and the winter polygon around the constellation of Orion (see p. 134). If we are observing the southern sky then the starting points are the Southern Cross and the Magellanic Clouds.

As we gradually become acquainted with the constellations and bright stars, the night sky becomes a place where we are able to find our way around, just as we can in a well-known landscape. We can now take a further step and look for interesting celestial objects in the constellations. Which ones? To begin with, the brightest and most interesting which are given in the list on p. 220.

In most cases it cannot be done without a chart. Comparing a chart with the sky is not difficult if we already know several guiding points, such as bright stars and constellations. The object we are seeking can then be found by following suitably selected lines joining the stars. As an example, let us try finding the globular cluster M13 in Hercules. A great help in locating the indistinct constellation of Hercules is the Summer Triangle, particularly the bright star Vega located alongside Hercules — see chart on p. 173 or on p. 177. In the centre of the constellation of Hercules is a quadrangle made up of the stars π, ε, ζ, and η. The star cluster we are looking for is located on the line joining the stars ζ and η, about one-third of the way from η. Under ideal conditions the star cluster may be seen with the naked eye as a faint hazy star. With binoculars, however, M13 is clearly visible as a hazy patch and greater magnification with a larger telescope resolves the cloud into a myriad stars.

The problem is more difficult when the object cannot be seen at all with the naked eye or binoculars, and is so small and faint that it can only be detected with a telescope. In such a case we must use a more detailed star atlas (see the list of recommended books on p. 228) which includes fainter stars that will lead us to our goal. Pointing the telescope at the nearest bright star visible with the naked eye, we can continue from there by successively 'hopping' from star to star until we come to the desired object. When doing so, we must, of course, jump small distances only so as to keep abreast of the position on the chart and sky, because in the field of view of a telescope we are usually only able to see a very small part of the sky, probably no larger than that covered by the disc of the Moon. There are also other methods of finding celestial objects: if the telescope is on an equatorial mounting with setting circles it can be pointed rapidly and precisely by using celestial coordinates, but that is more suitable for the experienced amateur.

Up to this point, we have discussed finding objects that are distant in space. The situation is different for objects in the Solar System. We would seek them in vain on star charts because they are continually changing their position. Our principal interests will be in the planets, their paths among the stars, their conjunctions — when they appear close together — and also their appearance when viewed through a telescope. Five of them can be seen with the naked eye, the other three (Uranus, Neptune, Pluto), only with a telescope. They are always found near the ecliptic and if we know the zodiacal constellations we shall immediately notice any

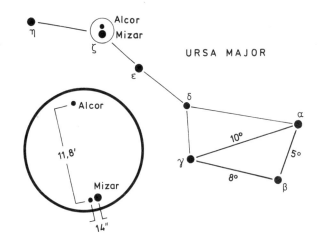

Fig. 5 — Angular distances in the sky

planet that appears as a stranger, and changes the shape of the constellation. We can then identify the planet according to its known brightness and colour. Any doubts can be resolved by an astronomical year book where we can find the equatorial coordinates (right ascension and declination) of the planets for any given date, and then, by using a chart, determine exactly where the planets are at the given time. Year books also include charts for finding Uranus and Neptune. Pluto can be detected only with a large telescope.

It is very important for the beginner to become familiar with estimating the apparent size of celestial objects in terms of angles, or degrees of arc. Metres, feet, inches and other linear measurements are of no use here. The Moon's disc, which has an angular diameter of approximately 0.5° (half a degree), or 30′ (30 minutes of arc), is a good standard for comparison. Other things — ones that are always present in the night sky — can also serve as a scale, for example the angular separation of certain pairs of stars in Ursa Major (fig. 5). The triangle formed by the stars α, β, and γ provides a good idea of larger angular distances that are expressed in degrees. A scale for the measurement of degrees is actually found on all the constellation maps in this book, because they are marked with a network of coordinates, showing parallels of declination spaced 10° apart. The pair of stars Alcor and Mizar, with a separation of 11′, i. e. about one-third the angular diameter of the Moon, serves as a scale for the measurement of minutes. Alcor and Mizar can be resolved with the naked eye without any problem. If we have a telescope, then Mizar can also serve as a scale for the measurement of seconds, because it is a double star in which the separation between the two components is 14.5″. The angular separation of the components of double stars, as well as the angular diameters of planetary discs, are generally expressed in seconds of arc.

Under ideal conditions a person with very good eyesight is able to see stars of 5th to 6th magnitude, and to resolve double stars with a separation of several minutes of arc. If we wish to observe fainter objects and see in greater detail we must use a telescope. What type shall we choose? We shall certainly not go wrong if we start out with good, medium-size, prismatic binoculars, say 7 × 50 (7-fold magnification, diameter of the objective 50 mm). Besides, these can also be used for other subjects, not just for astronomical observations. With such binoculars we will be able to see craters on the Moon, the satellites of Jupiter, certain double stars, clusters and nebulae (see the list on p. 220). They will provide us with a magnificent view when pointed towards the centre of the Milky Way, where we will be able to identify the large M8 (Lagoon) nebula, the richly-studded open cluster M7, and other objects. Binoculars are also very good for observing eclipses of the Moon, brighter comets, finding the planet Mercury, and whenever it is desirable to have a large field of view.

During such observations the binoculars should be provided with a steady support, for example by placing them against a windowsill, fence, tree trunk, or the like. Still better is to attach them to a tripod so as not to touch them at all during observation. Only then can we fully utilize the optical quality of prismatic binoculars, particularly their resolving power. Compare, for example, how the Moon looks through hand-held binoculars and then through the same binoculars provided with a steady support or attached to a tripod.

If we want to see more, better, and in greater detail, then we will have to have a telescope. The selection of telescopes available in shops is very large and the prices vary widely so it is best for amateurs to seek the advice of someone who has experience with such equipment. One way or the other, we must first of all decide what we want from such a telescope, and for what purpose we intend to use it. Do we want to observe celestial objects only occasionally for our own pleasure and the delight of discovering the hidden beauty of the night sky? Or has astronomy become our hobby, and do we therefore intend to probe more deeply, and to make systematic observations of a specialized nature? It is also possible for the amateur to make a telescope himself — popular astronomical magazines contain numerous examples of excellent amateur telescopes constructed at lower cost than factory-made instruments with the same specification.

More detailed information on types of telescopes — such as refractors and reflectors — their optical characteristics and auxiliary equipment, how to use a telescope, etc., may be found in the recommended literature. Here we will limit ourselves to advice for those who plan to buy their first 'family telescope' merely for occasional observation of the sky for their own pleasure, and to enlarge their horizons. For this purpose a small refractor (in which the principal optical element is an achromatic lens) with an objective 4 to 7 cm in diameter is very suitable. The focal lengths of such objectives are between 50 and 100 cm and allow for magnifications of 50 to 100, depending on the eyepiece (the magnification of a telescope can be calculated by dividing the focal length of the objective by the focal length of the eyepiece). With such high magnifications, of course, observation is hampered by the slightest vibration of the telescope and therefore its mounting must be sufficiently steady. A small refractor is light, readily carried, and also a good companion on a holiday. It will even show us deep-sky objects that are fainter than those listed on p. 220. The faintest stellar magnitude that is detectable with our telescope can be checked by observing the faint stars in the vicinity of the north pole — see map on p. 108.

The telescope's power to resolve details may be checked by the amateur by observing double stars with close components. Theoretically a good quality objective with diameter D (in mm) should resolve two stars with a separation of $r'' = 120''/D$. For example: a 60-mm objective should have a resolving power of approximately 2″, which suffices for the resolution of all four components of the 'double double', ε Lyrae (p. 176).

With a telescope of the size and type mentioned we can observe numerous details on the surface of the Moon under changing illumination. We can distinguish the phases of Venus, the most prominent albedo formations on Mars, the belts on Jupiter, and Saturn's rings. Equally interesting is observation of the Sun with the continually changing number and arrangement of dark sunspots. But here we must give an important WARNING: Never look at the Sun directly, either with a telescope or with the naked eye! You may seriously damage, or even lose your eyesight! The Sun can be observed, safely and comfortably, by projection. Hold a sheet of white paper about 30 cm beyond the eyepiece and, using the shadow of the telescope as a guide, point the instrument so that a clear picture of the Sun appears on the paper. Then sharpen the image by focussing the eyepiece. The same method may be used with binoculars to observe the Sun safely.

Astronomical observations require patience and perseverance in order to gradually acquire the necessary experience. The untrained eye sees little even with a large and expensive telescope. In general, it is only after many evenings of practical observation that the beginner is able to fully utilize the potential of any given telescope and to see very faint details. Try drawing a certain object in the minutest detail a number of times — a crater on the Moon, the belts on the disc of Jupiter, or nebula M42 in Orion. This is a very good practice, and during it you will become aware of details that would otherwise escape your notice.

The modern observational equipment available to scientific institutions provides astronomers with very effective methods of research. Visual observation has been replaced by much more effective, and precise, detectors of radiation, and not only does the modern astronomer no longer look through a telescope, but often he is not even present during telescopic observations, because everything takes place automatically. Nevertheless, or perhaps because of this very fact, there still remain fields in which amateur astronomers can make scientifically valuable observations. Some of the societies that organize observations by amateurs are listed on p. 228. Contact with similar organizations would be beneficial for anyone interested in astronomy. There one will meet people who have the same hobby and will get valuable advice, suggestions and information about the latest findings in this field. The regular perusal of one of the magazines for amateur astronomers is equally useful.

New, inimitable views of space are revealed to our gaze every day and every hour. All that's needed is to know how to look and to see . . .

A selection of the most interesting objects
for observation with the naked eye, binoculars or small telescopes

Bright stars and their colours

Designation	Name	Magnitude	Colour	Page
α CMa	Sirius	−1.4	white	158
α Boo	Arcturus	−0.06	orange	162
α Lyr	Vega	0.04	white	176
α Aur	Capella	0.06	yellow	138
α Tau	Aldebaran	0.86	orange	142
α Sco	Antares	0.92	yellow-red	190
α Ori	Betelgeuse	0.2—1.2	yellow-red	148

Variable stars and eclipsing binaries whose variability can be observed with the naked eye or binoculars

Designation	Name	Magnitude variations[1]	Period (days)	Page
δ Cep		3.6—4.3	5.4	110
μ Cep	Garnet	3.7—5.0	irregular	110
β Lyr	Sheliak	3.4—4.1	12.9	178
β Per	Algol	2.1—3.4	2.9	136
o Cet	Mira	3—9	231	130

Double stars and multiple stars

Designation	Name	Colour and magnitude of components	Angular separation	Resolution[2]	Page
ζ UMa + 80 UMa	Mizar and Alcor	both white 2.4 + 4.0	11.8′	E	112
ζ UMa	Mizar	both white 2.4 + 4.0	14.4″	T	112
αCap	Algiedi	both white 3.8 + 4.5	6.4′	E	128
ε Lyr		all white 4.5 + 4.7	3.5′	E	176
β Cyg	Albireo	orange and blue 3.1 + 5.1	34.3″	B	180
α Cen	Toliman	both white 0.0 + 1.2	20″	T	200
α CVn	Cor Caroli	both white 2.9 + 5.6	19.6″	T	116
ϑ Ori	Trapezium	all white 5.4 + 6.8 + 8.0 + 6.3	19″ to 9″	T	150
γ And	Alamak	orange and blue-green 2.1 + 5.1	10″	T	120
γ Ari	Mesarthim	both white 4.8 + 4.8	7.8″	T	126
γ Leo	Algieba	orange and yellow 2.1 + 3.4	4.7″	T	164
α Cru	Acrux	both white 1.4 + 1.9	4.4″	T	198

Globular clusters

Designation	Constellation	Magnitude	Angular diameter	Visibility[3]	Page
M13	Hercules	5.7	23′	B	176
M5	Serpens	6.2	13′	B	186
M15	Pegasus	6.5	12′	B	124
ω Centauri	Centaurus	4	30′	E	200

Open clusters

Designation	Name	Constellation	Characteristic	Angular dimensions	Visibility[3]	Page
M45	Pleiades	Taurus	large, very bright	100′	E	144
χ, h	Double Cluster	Perseus	very bright	35′ + 35′	E	136
M44	Praesepe (Beehive)	Cancer	total brightness 4.5m	80′	E	140
M35		Gemini	total brightness 5.5m	30′	B	138
M7		Scorpius	50 stars 7—11m	60′	B	190
NGC 4755		Crux	50 stars 6—10m	10′	B	198
M11	Wild Duck	Scutum	200 stars 11—14m	12′	B	188

Planetary nebulae

Designation	Name	Constellation	Magnitude	Angular diameter	Visibility[3]	Page
M27	Dumbbell	Vulpecula	8	8′ × 5′	B	180
M57	Ring Nebula	Lyra	9	80″ × 60″	T	178
NGC 3132		Vela	8	84″ × 52″	T	202

Diffuse nebulae

Designation	Name	Constellation	Magnitude	Angular diameter	Visibility	Page
M42	Orion Nebula	Orion	5	65′	E	150
M8	Lagoon	Sagittarius	5	80′ × 40′	B	194
M17	Omega	Sagittarius	6	45′ × 35′	B	193
M1	Crab Nebula[4]	Taurus	9	5′ × 3′	T	146
NGC 2070	Tarantula[5]	Dorado	5	20′	E	207, 208

Galaxies

Designation	Name	Constellation	Magnitude	Angular diameter	Visibility	Page
M31	Andromeda Galaxy	Andromeda	5	160′ × 40′	E	122
M51	Whirlpool Galaxy	Canes Venatici	8	10′	T	116
M81		Ursa Major	8	18′ × 10′	T	114
M83		Hydra	8	10′ × 8′	T	170
LMC	Large Magellanic Cloud	Dorado	1	6°	E	206, 208
SMC	Small Magellanic Cloud	Tucana	1.5	3.5°	E	206, 210

Notes: 1 — dates of the maxima and minima are to be found in astronomical year books
2 — the components may be resolved: E — with the eye, B — with binoculars, T — with a telescope with 5-cm diameter objective
3 — visibility with the eye, binoculars, telescope
4 — a supernova remnant
5 — part of the LMC

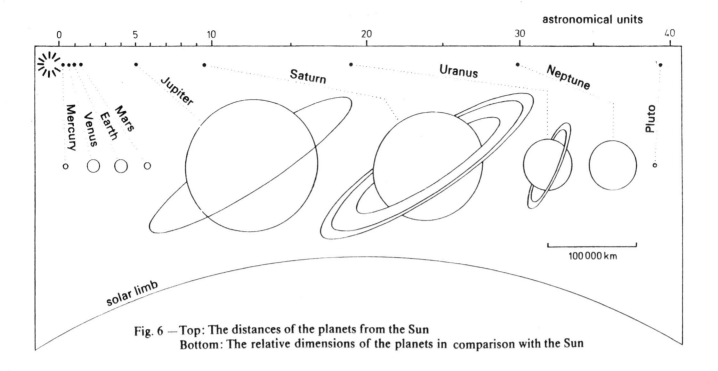

Fig. 6 —Top: The distances of the planets from the Sun
Bottom: The relative dimensions of the planets in comparison with the Sun

Numerical data on the planets

	average distance from the Sun		orbital period around the Sun	equatorial diameter		period of rotation at the equator	mean density	mass
	10^6 km	AU	years	km	Earth = 1	d = days h = hours	H_2O = 1	Earth = 1
Mercury	57.9	0.39	0.24	4 878	0.38	58.6 d	5.4	0.06
Venus	108.2	0.72	0.62	12 104	0.95	243.0 d	5.2	0.82
Earth	149.6	1.00	1.00	12 756	1.00	23.9 d	5.5	1.00
Mars	227.9	1.52	1.88	6 796	0.53	24.6 d	3.9	0.11
Jupiter	778.3	5.20	11.86	142 796	11.27	9.9 h	1.3	317.89
Saturn	1 429.4	9.55	29.46	120 660	9.44	10.7 h	0.7	95.15
Uranus	2 875.0	19.22	84.01	50 800	4.10	17.3 h	1.2	14.54
Neptune	4 504.3	30.11	164.79	48 600	3.88	18 h	1.7	17.23
Pluto	5 900.0	39.45	248.5	2 400	0.19	6.4 d	0.9	0.002

Numerical data on the planetary satellites

Name	average distance from the planet 10^3 km	orbital period around the planet days	diameter km	average density H_2O	magnitude	discovered by	year of discovery
Satellite of the Earth							
Moon	384.4	27.32	3 476	3.3	−12.7	—	—
Satellites of Mars							
Phobos	9.4	0.32	28 × 22 × 18	1.9	11.6	A. Hall	1877
Deimos	23.5	1.26	16 × 12 × 10	2.1	12.7	A. Hall	1877

Satellites of Jupiter

Name							
Metis	128.0	0.30	40		17.4	S. Synnott	1979—80
Adrastea	129.0	0.30	24 × 20 × 16		18.9	D. Jewitt, E. Danielson	1979
Amalthea	181.3	0.50	270 × 170 × 150		14.1	E. Barnard	1892
Thebe	221.9	0.68	110 × ? × 90		15.5	S. Synnott	1979—80
Io	421.6	1.77	3 630	3.6	5.0	S. Marius, G. Galilei	1610
Europa	670.9	3.55	3 138	3.0	5.3	S. Marius, G. Galilei	1610
Ganymede	1 070	7.16	5 262	1.9	4.6	S. Marius, G. Galilei	1610
Callisto	1 880	16.69	4 800	1.8	5.6	S. Marius, G. Galilei	1610
Leda	11 094	238.7	10		20.2	C. Kowal	1974
Himalia	11 480	250.6	180		14.8	C. D. Perrine	1904—5
Lysithea	11 720	259.2	20		18.4	S. B. Nicholson	1938
Elara	11 737	259.7	80		16.7	C. D. Perrine	1904—5
Ananke	21 200	631	20		18.9	S. B. Nicholson	1951
Carme	22 600	692	30		19.0	S. B. Nicholson	1938
Pasiphaë	23 500	735	40		17.7	P. Mellote	1908
Sinope	23 700	758	30		18.3	S. B. Nicholson	1914

Satellites of Saturn

Name							
1981 S13	in Encke division		20			M. Showalter	1990
Atlas	137.7	0.60	38 × ? × 26		18	Voyager 1	1980
Prometheus	139.4	0.61	140 × 100 × 74		16.5	Voyager 1	1980
Pandora	141.7	0.63	110 × 84 × 66		16	Voyager 1	1980
Janus	151.5	0.69	220 × 190 × 160		14.5	A. Dollfus	1966
Epimetheus	151.4	0.69	140 × 120 × 100		15.5	A. Dollfus	1966
Mimas	185.5	0.94	392	1.4	12.9	W. Herschel	1789
Enceladus	238.0	1.37	500	1.2	11.8	W. Herschel	1789
Tethys	294.7	1.89	1 060	1.2	10.3	G. D. Cassini	1684
Telesto	294.7	1.89	? × 24 × 22		19	B. Smith et al.	1980
Calypso	294.7	1.89	30 × 24 × 16		18.5	B. Smith et al.	1980
Dione	377.4	2.74	1 120	1.4	10.4	G. D. Cassini	1684
Helene	377.4	2.74	36 × 32 × 30		18	Voyager 1	1980
Rhea	527.0	4.52	1 530	1.3	9.7	G. D. Cassini	1672
Titan	1 221.9	15.94	5 150	1.9	8.4	C. Huygens	1655
Hyperion	1 481.1	21.28	350 × 234 × 200		14.2	W. Bond	1848
Iapetus	3 561.3	79.33	1 460	1.2	10.2—11.9	G. D. Cassini	1671
Phoebe	12 954	550.4	220		16.5	W. Pickering	1898

Satellites of Uranus

Name							
Cordelia	49.8	0.34	50			(Voyager 2)	1986
Ophelia	53.8	0.38	50			(Voyager 2)	1986
Bianca	59.2	0.43	50			(Voyager 2)	1986
Cressida	61.8	0.46	60			(Voyager 2)	1986
Desdemona	62.7	0.48	60			(Voyager 2)	1986
Juliet	64.4	0.49	80			(Voyager 2)	1986
Portia	66.1	0.51	80			(Voyager 2)	1986
Rosalind	69.9	0.56	60			(Voyager 2)	1986
Belinda	75.3	0.62	60			(Voyager 2)	1986
Puck	86.0	0.76	170			(Voyager 2)	1985
Miranda	129.4	1.41	562	1.3	16.5	G. Kuiper	1948
Ariel	191.0	2.52	1 158	1.6	14.4	W. Lassell	1851
Umbriel	266.0	4.14	1 172	1.4	15.3	W. Lassell	1851
Titania	435.9	8.71	1 580	1.6	14.0	W. Herschel	1787
Oberon	583.5	13.46	1 524	1.5	14.2	W. Herschel	1787

Satellites of Neptune

Name							
Naiad	48.2	0.30	50			(Voyager 2)	1989
Thalassa	50.0	0.31	90			(Voyager 2)	1989
Despina	52.5	0.33	140			(Voyager 2)	1989
Galatea	62.0	0.40	160			(Voyager 2)	1989
Larissa	73.6	0.55	210 × 190			(Voyager 2)	1989
Proteus	117.6	1.12	400			(Voyager 2)	1989
Triton	354.6	5.88	2 720	2.0	13.6	W. Lassel	1846
Nereid	5 510.7	359.40	340	2.0	18.7	G. Kuiper	1949

Satellites of Pluto

Name							
Charon	19.7	6.39	1 200	0.9	17	J. Christy	1978

Note: The table includes data known up to the end of the year 1990. It does not include data on moons that were observed only once and whose existence has not been confirmed.

Glossary

Absorption (of radiation) The absorption of radiation by atoms or molecules of gas. In the broader sense, the term implies loss in radiation along the path of a ray from the source to the surface of the Earth.

Albedo The reflecting power of the surface of an object. The ratio of reflected radiation to the total amount falling on the surface. Highly reflecting bodies have high albedoes (chalk 0.85; clouds 0.70); poorly reflecting bodies have low albedoes (granite 0.31; the Moon 0.12; lava 0.04). The so-called Bond, or spherical, albedo of planets, is the ratio of the amount of radiation scattered in all directions by the surface of a sphere, to the total amount in a parallel beam of radiation falling on the surface of the sphere.

Algol The most famous eclipsing binary. The brightness of Algol changes regularly in a period of 68.8 hours between a maximum of 2.1^m and minimum of 3.4^m by the mutual eclipsing of the two components.

Angular Measure Measurement in terms of angles or degrees of arc. An entire circle is divided into 360° (degrees), each degree into 60' (minutes), and each minute into 60" (seconds). This scale is used to denote, among other things, the apparent size of celestial bodies, their separation on the celestial sphere, etc. One example is the diameter of the Moon's disc, which measures approximately $0.5° = 30'$.

Aphelion The point farthest from the Sun in the orbit of a planet or comet, or of an artificial satellite orbiting the Sun.

Apogee The point in the elliptical orbit of a satellite round the Earth that is farthest from the Earth.

Apollo (programme) Manned flights orbiting and landing on the Moon in the years 1968—72. First men on the Moon on 20th July, 1969 (Apollo 11). Devoted to direct exploration of the Moon, the collection of rock samples, and installation of scientific instruments on the lunar surface.

Apparent Diameter (of an object) The diameter of a celestial object expressed in angular measure. E.g. the apparent diameter of the Moon is approximately 30'.

Asteroid (also minor planet, small planet, planetoid) A small object orbiting Sun, mainly between the orbits of Mars and Jupiter. A typical asteroid measures several kilometres in diameter. It is a 'dead' body exhibiting no activity.

Astronomical Unit (AU) A unit of length equal to the average radius of the Earth's orbit (i. e. 149.6 million kilometres), used in measuring distances in the Solar System. *One light year* = 63,300 AU.

Atmosphere The gaseous envelope surrounding a celestial object.

Basalt An extrusive volcanic rock, crystallized from lava, usually very dark, greyish black or dark grey. Various types of basalts are found in large amounts on the terrestrial planets and on the Moon.

Big Bang The term applied to the instant the Universe came into being as an extraordinarily dense and hot primaeval atom. The Big Bang marked the beginning of the *expansion of the Universe*.

Black Hole A collapsed star with a mass greater than that of two Suns. The hole is black because it emits no radiation. It does possess an external gravitational field.

Bolide (or Fireball) A brilliant meteor, brighter than Venus.

Caldera A large volcanic crater formed by the collapse of the surface into an underground cavity produced by the rapid eruption of large quantities of magma.

Captured Rotation Most satellites revolve about their planets in such a manner that one hemisphere of the satellite remains permanently turned towards the planet, the other hemisphere being permanently turned away from the planet. Captured rotation is the result of the action of the tidal forces between the planet and the satellite. Captured rotation also occurs in some double stars.

Celestial Equator The great circle on the celestial sphere defined by the projection of the plane of the Earth's equator. It divides the celestial sphere into the northern and southern hemisphere. The celestial equator has a declination of 0°.

Celestial Sphere An imaginary sphere of infinite radius, in the centre of which the observer is located, and against which all celestial bodies appear to be projected.

Cepheids Pulsating variable stars. The star Delta Cephei is a typical example. Cepheids are very luminous supergiants. Their diameter and temperature change regularly with periods of 1 to 60 days. The period of magnitude variation is in proportion to a cepheid's luminosity, and if we know its luminosity then the distance of such a star, or of the cluster or galaxy of which the cepheid is a part, can be determined from the period-luminosity relation.

Constellation A precisely defined part of the celestial sphere. In the older, narrower meaning of the term, it is a group of fixed stars forming a characteristic pattern. The names and boundaries of the constellations are mostly derived from ancient mythology. The heavens are divided into 88 constellations.

Coordinates (celestial, or planetary) A pair of spherical coordinates (angles) defining the position of a point on the celestial sphere, on a planet, or on a satellite. They are expressed in degrees, minutes, seconds (°, ', "), or in hours, minutes, seconds (h, m, s). In every instance they are analogous to the geographical coordinates latitude and longitude. They differ in their definition of a fundamental reference plane (e. g. the equator), of a fundamental direction (e. g. the prime meridian) and designation (for example, on Mars areographic latitude and longitude are used).

Cosmogony The branch of science that deals with the study of the origin and evolution of celestial objects.

Cosmology The branch of science that deals with the study of the Universe as a whole.

Crater A bowl-shaped cavity, usually with a raised rim. A very common formation on celestial objects with a solid surface. Impact or meteoritic crater — a crater produced by the impact of a meteorite or of ejected matter (secondary craters). Volcanic crater — a crater produced by volcanic activity, i. e. by the internal activity of the celestial body.

Declination Analogous to geographical latitude. The angular distance of a celestial body from the celestial equator. It is measured along the celestial meridian that passes through the celestial body and is at right angles to the equator.

Doppler Effect If the source of radiation (star, galaxy, etc.) is receding then the spectral lines shift towards the red end of the spectrum. If the source of radiation is approaching, the spectral lines in the source's spectrum shift towards the violet end of the spectrum. The speed of the source's motion can then be determined by the extent of the measured shift.

Double Star

Optical Double — two stars that appear to be very close to each other in the heavens but which, in reality, are not. They do not form a physical system.

Physical Double — a system of two stars mutually bound by gravitational force, orbiting a common centre of gravity.

Spectroscopic Binary — two very close components that cannot be resolved with a telescope; the presence of the second component is revealed by the doubling of the spectral lines.

Coloured Binary — differences in the temperature and brightness of the two components, together with effects of colour vision, produce a colour contrast between the components (e. g. β Cygni—Albireo).

Visual Double — a pair where the two components may be resolved with a telescope.

Eclipsing Binary (Eclipsing Variable) — the two components cannot be resolved with a telescope

but their regular mutual eclipses are indicated by periodic variations in brightness (e. g. β Persei—Algol).

The components of double stars are generally designated A and B (additionally, in multiple systems, C, D, etc.).

Double Star, Apparent Orbit of If the brighter of the two components of a double star is regarded as fixed, the positions of the fainter component (i. e. position angles and angular distances) may be measured in relation to the brighter one. We thus obtain the apparent orbit of the double star.

Ecliptic
1. The apparent annual path of the Sun on the celestial sphere. The Sun traverses the whole ecliptic in a year.
2. The path of the Earth's orbit round the Sun.

Erosion (of a planet's surface) Degradation of the surface by the action of water, wind, and other natural factors. Objects that have no atmosphere are subject to erosion by micrometeorites — microscopic meteorites with a diameter measured in hundredths and thousandths of a millimetre.

Expansion of the Universe The more distant a galaxy is from the Earth, the greater is the speed with which it is receding. This does not mean that our Galaxy is at the centre of an expanding universe, because the same phenomenon would be observed from any other galaxy. The velocity of expansion is conveniently described by what is known as 'Hubble's constant', whose numerical value is not known precisely, but which is probably approximately 55 km/sec per 1 Mps (1 million parsecs).

Fluorescence The property of a substance to produce visible radiation as a result of the so-called photo-excitation process. Fluorescence is produced, for example, by irradiation of gas in a planetary nebula by the invisible ultraviolet radiation from the hot central star.

Galaxy
1. Our Galaxy — the stellar system of which the Sun is a member. The surrounding parts of our Galaxy are seen in the sky as the Milky Way.
2. External galaxies — stellar systems similar to our Galaxy.

Galaxies, Cluster of A large system consisting of hundreds or thousands of galaxies. Several thousand such clusters are known to astronomers. Example: cluster of glaxies in Coma Berenices (p. 163).

Giant and Supergiant (star) A star with a very high luminosity and

a much larger diameter (10 to 1,000 times) than that of the Sun.

Greek Alphabet Small letters are used for denoting bright stars in constellations (this practice was introduced by J. Bayer in his *Uranometria* in 1603).

α	alpha	ι	iota	ρ	rhó
β	béta	κ	kappa	σ	sìgma
γ	gamma	λ	lambda	τ	tau
δ	delta	μ	mu	υ	ypsilon
ε	epsilon	ν	nu	φ	phi
ζ	zéta	ξ	xi	χ	chi
η	eta	o	omicron	ψ	psi
ϑ	theta	π	pi	ω	omega

H-R Diagram Hertzsprung-Russell diagram, also HRD. A diagram showing the temperature-luminosity (or spectrum-luminosity) relationship of stars. This diagram is of basic importance and shows the relation between the main stellar characteristics at a glance. See also p. 10 and 104.

Infrared Radiation Invisible electromagnetic waves that are longer than those at the red end of the visible spectrum.

Interstellar Gas The gaseous component of interstellar matter, consisting of electrons, ions, atoms and molecules. About 99 per cent of interstellar gas consists of hydrogen and helium. The basic forms of interstellar gas clouds are the H-I and H-II regions (H—hydrogen).

H-I regions contain cold, non-luminous clouds of neutral hydrogen. They are invisible, but produce radio emission at a wavelength of 21 cm, and can therefore be observed by radiotelescopes.

H-II regions are clouds of ionized hydrogen in the vicinity of very hot, type O and B stars. If the gas is sufficiently dense they are seen as bright nebulae.

Ionization The change from an electrically neutral particle (an atom or molecule) into a particle that carries an electric charge (into an ion).

Libration (of the Moon) The apparent side-to-side oscillation makes it possible for terrestrial observers to see approximately 59 per cent of the Moon's surface over a period.

Light Visible electromagnetic radiation. In a vacuum it travels in a straight line from the source with a speed of about 300,000 km/s.

Light-curve A diagram showing the course of changes in the brightness of a celestial object (e. g. a variable star).

Light Year A unit of length, used in popular literature, equal to the distance traversed by light in the course of one year. As the velocity of light is 300,000 km/sec it follows that:

1 light year = 9,460,000,000,000 km = 9.46×10^{12} = 9.5 million million km

1 light year = 63,300 AU = 0.307 pc

Local Group of Galaxies A group of galaxies that includes our Galaxy, the Magellanic Clouds, M31 in Adromeda, M33 in Triangulum and many other dwarf galaxies. The Local Group has a minimum of 24 members and a true diameter of more than 6 million light-years.

Luminosity The total energy radiated from the surface of a star (or stellar system) for a given unit of time. It is often stated in relation to the luminosity of the Sun = 1 (e. g. a star is of 50 solar luminosities, i. e. is 50 times as luminous as the Sun). Instead of luminosity, the *absolute magnitude* of the star is frequently given.

Luna The Luna (USSR) lunar probes and automatic station explored the Moon in the years 1959—76:

L 2—first probe to reach the Moon, 12 September 1959

L 3—first photographs of the far side of the Moon, 10 October 1959

L 9—first soft landing on the Moon, 3 February 1966

L 10—first artificial lunar satellite, 3 April 1966

L 16, L 20, L 24—automatic collection of lunar rock samples brought back to Earth, 1970—76

L 17 and L 21—automatic mobile laboratories Lunokhod 1 and 2, 1970 and 1973.

Lunar Orbiter The artificial satellites Lunar Orbiter 1-5 (USA) mapped practically the whole of the Moon's surface in detail in the years 1966—67.

Magellan Artificial satellite of Venus equipped with a radar system for detailed mapping of the entire planet with a resolution of detail down to 120 m. It has been operating successfully since September 1990.

Magma Mass of molten rock beneath the Earth's surface, erupted by volcanic activity at the surface as lava.

Magnitude A number representing the brightness of a star. The faintest stars visible to the unaided eye are of approximately 6th magnitude—designated as 6^m or 6 mag. Very bright stars are of the 1st magnitude 1^m (Spica), ones that are still brighter have a magnitude of 0^m (Vega), and the brightest stars have a negative magnitude, e. g. -1.4^m (Sirius). A star of a given magnitude is 2.512 times as bright as a star one whole magnitude fainter. Thus a star of 1^m is 100 times as bright as a star of 6^m ($2.512^5 = 100$).

Unless stated otherwise the term magnitude always means the apparent magnitude, in other words the star's brightness as it appears to the terrestrial observer.

Magnitude, Absolute To compare the *luminosities* of stars, their *apparent magnitudes* are converted to a value corresponding to their brightness (magnitude) at a distance of 10 parsecs. This is the absolute magnitude. If we designate the absolute magnitude with the letter M, then M = m + 5 — 5 log r, where m is the apparent magnitude and r the star's distance in parsecs.

Mariner A type of interplanetary probe (USA) used in the years 1962—1964 to explore the terrestrial planets.

Mariner 2 was the first successful interplanetary probe in history; on 14th December 1962 it flew past Venus.

Mariner 9 in 1971—72 mapped the entire surface of Mars.

Mariner 10 in 1974—75 made a detailed exploration of Venus and Mercury, mapping half of the surface of Mercury for the first time.

Mars (probes) Automatic interplanetary probes (USSR) that explored the planet Mars in the years 1971—74.

M 3 — first landing on Mars, 2 December 1971.

M 6 — first measurements in Mars' atmosphere, 12 March 1974

Messier Number—M The number of an object (cluster, nebula or galaxy) in the catalogue made by the French astronomer C. Messier (1730—1817). The catalogue contains 103 objects, all bright and readily seen with an amateur telescope (e. g. M42—the Orion Nebula).

Nebula, Galactic A mass of gas or dust (or a mixture of both) in interstellar space.

Emission nebula — the gas is made luminous by the radiation of hot nearby stars (*H—II region*).

Planetary nebula — the large luminous envelope surrounding hot star. It appears in a telescope as a disc like a planet — hence the name.

Dark nebula — a cloud of dust, which may be seen against the background of luminous nebulae and star fields

Reflection nebula — clouds of dust made visible by the scattered light from nearby stars.

Neutron Star The final stage in the evolution of a star, whose original mass was equal to 1.4 to 2.5 times that of the Sun. Gravitational collapse caused the star to contract to a sphere with radius of 10 to 20 km, consisting mainly of free neutrons. The density of a neutron star is a hundred million million times (10^{14}) greater than the density of water. Some rotating neutron stars give rise to *pulsars*.

Nomenclature of Formations on Planets and Moons

Internationally valid Latin terms, approved by the International Astronomical Union (I. A. U.). The following are the most common terms (the plural is given in parentheses).

Catena
(Catenae) — a chain of craters
Chasma
(Chasmata) — a deep valley with steep sides, canyon
Dorsum (Dorsa) — a ridge
Fossa (Fossae) — a long, narrow, shallow depression
Lacus (Lacus) — 'lake', a small, relatively smooth, dark area
Mare (Maria) — 'sea', a large, relatively smooth, dark area
Mons (Montes) — mountain
Palus (Paludes) — 'marsh', a mixed smooth and rough dark area
Patera (Paterae) — an irregular crater, scalloped edges
Planitia
(Planitiae) — a plain
Planum (Plana) — a plateau
Promontorium
(Promontoria) — a cape
Regio
(Regiones) — a large area distinguished by its shading or colour
Rima (Rimae) — fissure
Rupes (Rupes) — scarp
Sinus (Sinus) — bay
Tholus (Tholi) — hill or dome
Vallis (Valles) — valley

Nova A star that suddenly increases in brightness by 7—16 magnitudes and then declines to its original magnitude. This happens in the case of old stars (white dwarfs) that form close binaries with Main Sequence stars. The increase in the nova's brightness is the result of the sudden explosive ignition of hydrogen gas that has streamed from the other component onto the white dwarf.

Parallax, Annual The annual parallax of a star is the angle subtended at the star by the radius of the Earth's orbit. The inverse value of parallax π'' is the distance **d** in parsecs:

$$d(pc) = \frac{1}{\pi''}.$$

Parsec (pc) The basic unit of measurement of astronomical distances. It corresponds to the distance at which one astronomical unit (the mean radius of the Earth's orbit) would appear to have a parallax of 1 second of arc.

1 parsec = 206,265 astronomical units
= 3.26 light years
1,000 pc = 1 kpc = 1 kiloparsec
1,000,000 pc = 1 Mpc = 1 megaparsec

Phase (of the Moon, planets) The Sun illuminates one hemisphere of any object that emits no light of its own. The terrestrial observer generally sees only part of the illuminated hemisphere. The apparent shape of the illuminated part of the object (the Moon or a planet) is called its phase. The main phases of the Moon are: New Moon, first quarter, Full Moon, and last quarter.

Photon A quantum of radiant energy (the smallest indivisible part). It carries energy at the speed of light.

Pioneer and Pioneer-Venus The interplanetary probes Pioneer 10 and 11 (USA) made the first preliminary explorations of Jupiter and Saturn in 1973—1979. The probes Pioneer-Venus 1 and Pioneer-Venus 2 explored Venus from orbit and by dropping probes to the surface in 1978 and 1980 producing the first general map of the surface of Venus based on radar measurements.

Planet A celestial body that emits no light of its own, but is only visible by the light it reflects and which originates from the central star about which it revolves.

Plasma A gaseous mixture of freely moving electrons and ionized atoms (ions). It is produced at high temperatures. Most of the gas in the Universe exists as plasma.

Poles, Celestial Points at which the extensions of the Earth's axis cut the celestial sphere. The north celestial pole has a declination of $+90°$, the south pole $-90°$. The celestial sphere appears to revolve around the poles.

Position Angle (of double stars) The angle between a line connecting the brighter component of a double star with the fainter component, and a line pointing due north. It is measured from the north ($0°$) through the east ($90°$), i. e. anticlockwise.

Proper Motion The shift in the position of a star in the sky caused by the actual motion of the star in space. Barnard's Star has the greatest proper motion of all the stars ($10.34''$ in 1 year).

Precession The conical motion of the Earth's axis of rotation about the axis of the ecliptic describes a cone with its apex at the Earth's centre of gravity. Because of the Earth's precession the celestial poles move round the poles of the ecliptic with a period of about 26,000 years. At the same time the vernal equinox moves along the ecliptic, producing a change in the right ascensions and declination of all stars and other celestial objects. For this reason the position of the *vernal equinox* or the date for which it holds good must be indicated on every chart of the sky. All the charts in this book are valid for the beginning of the year 2000.

Pulsar A rapidly pulsating source of radio (and occasionally visible light or X-ray) radiation. Pulsars are rapidly rotating *neutron stars* emitting radiation in a narrow beam like a lighthouse. Every time the rotating beam sweeps past the Earth it is observed as a short pulse. Example: the pulsar in the Crab Nebula (p. 146).

Quasar A celestial object that resembles a star (quasi-stellar object) but with an extraordinarily large redshift in its spectrum, indicating that it is situated in an extremely remote region of the Universe. Quasars are probably the extremely intensive nuclei of young galaxies.

Radio Astronomy The branch of astrophysics that uses radio waves to obtain data and information about particular regions in the Universe.

Radiotelescope An instrument designed to intercept and record radio waves from celestial sources. Astronomy's most important instrument after the optical telescope.

Radio Source An object emitting strong radio radiation (a star, planet, galaxy, etc.). Some objects emit more radiation at radio frequencies than in the region of visible light.

Ranger The lunar probes Ranger 7, 8 and 9 (USA) in 1964—65 made close-up photographs of the Moon showing details smaller than 1 metre.

Red Dwarf A small star with a low surface temperature, of spectral class M or K. Such stars have the faintest luminosity of all the *Main Sequence* stars.

Redshift A shift of spectral lines emitted by a radiant body (a star or galaxy) towards the longer wavelengths at the red end of the spectrum, and caused by the body's recession from the Earth (see Doppler Effect).

Regolith The fragmented stony layer covering the surface of the Moon, due to cosmic erosion (impact of meteoritic bodies over a long period of time). The regolith of the Moon is 10 to 100 metres deep. Regolith also forms the surface layer on other bodies unprotected by an atmosphere.

Right Ascension An equatorial coordinate, which, together with *declination*, gives the position of a point on the celestial sphere. Right ascension is analogous to geographical longitude. It is the arc, measured along the celestial equator, between the *vernal equinox* and the celestial meridian passing through the given point. It is generally expressed in hours (from 0 to 24), minutes, and seconds.

Shield Volcano A broad, convex-shaped volcano with gentle slopes built up, layer by layer, by the repeated, long-terms effusion of basaltic lava from a central source. Examples are Mauna Loa in Hawaii and Olympus Mons on Mars.

Signs of the Zodiac Sections, or signs, each of $30°$, dividing the *ecliptic* into 12 equal parts, beginning at the *vernal equinox* and named after the constellations in which they lay about 2000 years ago, when the division was established by ancient astrologers. Because of the *precession* of the Earth's axis, however, the signs are at the present time shifted by $30°$ (one constellation behind) relative to the constellation of the same name.

Symbols of the zodiacal constellations (signs of the zodiac):

♈ Aries (the Ram)
♉ Taurus (the Bull)
♊ Gemini (the Twins)
♋ Cancer (the Crab)
♌ Leo (the Lion)
♍ Virgo (the Virgin)
♎ Libra (the Scales)
♏ Scorpius (the Scorpion)
♐ Sagittarius (the Archer)
♑ Capricornus (the Goat)
♒ Aquarius (the Water Carrier)
♓ Pisces (the Fishes)

Spectral Classification The classification of stars into spectral classes according to the presence and intensity of certain lines in their spectra. The main spectral classes are designated by the letters O, B, A, F, G, K, M, the surface temperatures of the stars diminish with this sequence from 30,000 K to 2,000 K. Their colours also change from blue through white and yellow to red. Each class is divided into 10 subclasses (e. g. G0, G1 . . . to G9—a type very close to type K0).

Spectrum (visible light)

Continuous spectrum: a continuous colour band stretching over a range of wavelengths. Although the colours in any source grade imperceptibly into one another, they are conventionally described in the following order: violet, indigo, blue, green, yellow, orange, red. A spectrum is obtained by the dispersion of light through a prism or a diffraction grating. Radiant, solid or liquid bodies, and greatly compressed gases, have a continuous spectrum.

Line spectrum: a spectrum showing distinct, relatively narrow lines, and which may be either an emission or absorption spectrum.

Emission spectrum: a spectrum which consists of individual coloured lines — emission lines — which correspond to particular wavelengths of radiation emitted by specific processes occurring in atoms of gas.

Absorption spectrum: a spectrum that shows dark spectral lines on a light (i. e. continuous) background. It is produced when radiation passes through a transparent medium (e. g. cooler gas in the atmosphere of a star) that absorbs the emission at certain wave lengths. Absorption lines are the 'signature' of chemical components of the absorbing medium. Elements also emit radiation at the same wavelengths at which they absorb.

Star A celestial body which is self-luminous as a result of thermonuclear reactions in the stellar interior. A star generally consists of plasma.

Star Cluster A system of stars of common origin bound to each other by the force of gravity.

Open Cluster (also galactic cluster) — a cluster of irregular shape containing a smaller number of stars, all young (hundreds of millions of years)

Globular Cluster — a cluster of spherical shape, with stars concentrated towards the centre, and which may contain several million stars; globular clusters may sometimes exceed 10 thousand million years of age.

Sun (as a unit) As a well-known star of average properties, the Sun serves as a standard of comparison. The mass, diameter, luminosity, and density of stars are therefore often given in 'solar' units (e. g. 30 solar diameters = a diameter 30 times the diameter of the Sun).

Supernova An explosion of a star during which its luminosity increases up to 10 thousand million times. The explosion occurs during the gravitational collapse of a star of above-average mass, which eventually becomes a neutron star (and possibly a pulsar). The cast-off material, the supernova remnant, remains in the sky in the form of an expanding nebula (see the Crab Nebula, p. 146).

Surveyor The soft-landing lunar probes Surveyor 1, 3, 5, 6 and 7 (USA) made a detailed exploration of the

Moon's surface at the points where they landed.

Temperature, Absolute This is measured as a positive number from absolute zero — i. e. from the lowest possible temperature — and is given in Kelvin (K).
Absolute zero = 0 K = −273.16 °C
Freezing point of water: = 273.16 K = = 0 °C

Temperature Scale In astronomy temperature is generally given in Kelvin (K), in normal everyday life in degrees Celsius (°C), or degrees Fahrenheit (°F). The lowest possible temperature is 0 K = −273.16 °C.

Freezing point of water

Celsius	Fahrenheit	Kelvin
0 °C	32 °F	273.16 K

Boiling point of water

Celsius	Fahrenheit	Kelvin
100 °C	212 °F	373.16 K

Terminator The line dividing the illuminated and dark parts, and therefore separating the day and night sides, of a non-luminous body (such as a planet or satellite).

Tides and Tidal Forces The mutual gravitational action of two close celestial bodies also causes their deformation (change of shape), and, in extreme cases, even their partial or complete disintegration. Examples are the flood and ebb tides on Earth, the volcanic activity on Io caused by the tidal forces of Jupiter, and changes in the shape of galaxies because of their close approach.

Ultraviolet Radiation Electromagnetic waves having a wavelength shorter than the wavelengths of visible light — situated beyond the visible spectrum at its violet end.

Variable Star A star whose magnitude varies. The main types of variable stars are pulsating variables, whose radius becomes larger and smaller at regular intervals, and eruptive or cataclysmic variables, whose brightness increases suddenly, sometimes to an extraordinary degree (novae, supernovae), and generally quite irregularly. A special group are eclipsing variables or eclipsing binaries whose variation in brightness is caused by the periodic eclipse of one component by the other.

Vega (probe) The interplanetary probes Vega 1 and 2 (USSR and other countries) were launched in 1984 to explore the planet Venus and Halley's Comet.
Vega 1 — first measurements from a balloon in the atmosphere of Venus, June 1985. Both probes explored the

region of the comet's nucleus in March 1986.

Venera The automatic interplanetary probes Venera (USSR) have been exploring Venus since 1967.
V 4 — first direct exploration of the atmosphere of Venus, 18 October 1967
V 7 — first measurements on the surface of Venus, 15 December 1970
V 9, V 10 — first photographs of the surface of Venus, first artificial satellite of Venus, October 1975

Vernal Equinox One of the two points on the celestial sphere where the celestial equator intersects the ecliptic. The Sun is at the vernal equinox in spring when day and night are of equal length (about March 21). The vernal equinox serves as the zero-point for the system of equatorial coordinates (*right ascension* and *declination*).

Viking The interplanetary probes Viking 1 and 2 (USA) explored the planet Mars in great detail from orbit, as well as with the aid of 2 landing modules, in the years 1976—1982. They transmitted more than 40,000 photographs to Earth.

Voyager The interplanetary probes Voyager 1 and 2 (USA) made detailed explorations of Jupiter and its moons (1979) and Saturn with its rings and moons (1980—81). Important discoveries (volcanic activity on Io), first maps of the moons of major planets. Voyager 2 for the first time explored the Uranus system (1986) and the Neptune system (1989). Both probes are now on the way out of the solar system.

White Dwarf A collapsed star in the final stage of evolution. It consists of degenerate gas — i. e. greatly compressed atoms whose nuclei have been forced into close proximity thereby greatly increasing the star's density. White dwarfs are the size of planets but weigh as much as the Sun. Their density may be as much as $1\,000$ kg/cm^3.

X-ray Radiation Electromagnetic radiation of extremely short wavelength — 10 nm to 0.001 nm. The primary source of X-ray radiation in the sky is the Sun; other sources are the remnants of supernovae, certain stellar systems and quasars.

Zodiac An imaginary belt in the heavens, centred on the ecliptic and which encompasses the apparent paths of the Sun, the Moon and the planets. It is divided into 12 zodiacal signs.

Recommended reading

American Association of Variable Star Observers, **AAVSO Variable Star Atlas**, Sky Publishing, Cambridge, Mass., 1980

British Astronomical Association, **Guide to Observing the Moon**, Enslow, Hillside N.J., 1986

— —, **Handbook**, London, annually

— —, **Satellite Observers' Manual**, London, 1974

— —, **Star Charts**, London, 1981

Burnham, R., **Burnham's Celestial Handbook**, (3 vols.), Dover, New York, 1978

Covington, M., **Astrography for the Amateur**, Cambridge University Press, 1985

Dunlop, S., **Astronomy: A step by step guide to the night sky**, Hamlyn, London, 1985

Dunlop, S. & Tirion, W., **Atlas of the Night Sky**, Hamlyn, London, 1984

Duffett-Smith, P., **Practical Astronomy with your Calculator**, 2nd edn, Cambridge University Press, 1981

Duffett-Smith, P., **Astronomy with your personal computer**, Cambridge University press, 1985

Eastman Kodak Co., **Astrophotography Basics**, Publication AC-48, Rochester, N.Y., 1980

King-Hele, D., **Observing Earth Satellites**, Macmillan, 1983

Moore, P., ed., **Practical Amateur Astronomy**, Lutterworth Press, Guildford, 1975

Norton, A. P., **Norton's Star Atlas**, 17th edn, Longman, London, 1986

Ronan, C. A. & Dunlop, S. R., (eds), **Amateur Astronomy**, Newnes, London, 1984

Royal Astronomical Society of Canada, **Observer's Handbook**, Toronto, annually

Sidgwick, J. B., **Observational Astronomy for Amateurs**, (4th edn, ed. Muirden, J.), Pelham, London, 1982

Tirion, W., **Sky Atlas 2000.0**, Sky Publishing, Cambridge, Mass., 1981

JOURNALS AND MAGAZINES

Astronomy, AstroMedia Corp., P.O. Box 92788, Milwaukee (monthly)

Journal, British Astronomical Association, Burlington House, Piccadilly, London W1V 0NL (bimonthly)

New Scientist, London (frequent astronomical articles, weekly)

Popular Astronomy, Junior Astronomical Society, 10 Swanwick Walk, Tadley, Basingstoke, Hants. RG26 6JZ (quarterly)

Quarterly Journal, Royal Astronomical Society, Burlington House, Piccadilly, London WIV 0NL (quarterly)

Science News, Science Service Inc., Washington, D.C. (frequent astronomical items and articles, weekly)

Scientific American, New York (frequent astronomical articles, monthly)

Sky & Telescope, Sky Publishing, 49 Bay State Road, Cambridge, Mass. 02138 (monthly)

The Astronomer, 177 Thunder Lane, Thorpe St. Andrew, Norwich NR7 0JF (amateur observations, monthly)

ORGANIZATIONS

United Kingdom

British Astronomical Association, Burlington House, Piccadilly, London W1V 0NL

British Interplanetary Society, 27-29 South Lambeth Road, London SW8 1SZ

Junior Astronomical Society, 10 Swanwick Walk, Tadley, Basingstoke, Hants. RG26 6JZ36

Royal Astronomical Society, Burlington House, Piccadilly, London W1V 0NL

North America

American Association of Variable Star Observers, 25 Birch Street, Cambridge, Mass. 02138

American Meteor Society, Dept. of Physics and Astronomy, State University College, Genesco, N.Y. 14454

Association of Lunar & Planetary Observers, P.O. Box 16131, San Francisco, California 94116

Astronomical League, P.O. Box 12821, Tucson, Arizona 85732 (for addresses of local societies)

Astronomical Society of the Pacific, 1290 24th Avenue, San Francisco, California 94122

Royal Astronomical Society of Canada, 136 Dupont Street, Toronto, Ontario M5T 1V2

Western Amateur Astronomers, P.O. Box 2316, Palm Deser, California 92261 (for addresses of local societies)

Other countries

Astronomical Society of New South Wales. P.O. Box 208, Eastwood, N.S.W. 2122, Australia

Astronomical Society of South Australia, P.O. Box 199, Adelaide, South Australia 501, Australia

Astronomical Society of Southern Africa, c/o South African Astronomical Observatory, P.O. Box 9, Observatory, 7935, Cape, Republic of South Africa

Astronomical Society of Victoria, P.O. Box 1059J, Melbourne, Victoria 3001, Australia

British Astronomical Association, (New South Wales Branch), Sydney Observatory, Sydney, N.S.W. 2001, Australia

Royal Astronomical Society of New Zealand, P.O. Box 3181, Wellington C1, New Zealand

INDEX OF DEEP-SPACE OBJECTS

Page numbers printed in bold refer to pages with detailed illustrations.

STARS

type: **d** — interesting double and multiple stars
     v — interesting variable stars and eclipsing binaries
     G — red giant, supergiant

R — red dwarf (one of the components of a double or multiple star)
W — white dwarf (one of the components of a double or multiple star)

Named stars

229

type	name	designation (abbreviation)	page
	Phekda	γ UMa	113
	Pherkad	γ UMi	109
	Pleione	28 Tau	144
	Polaris	α UMi	107, 108, 109
	Pollux	β Gem	135, 139
d	Porrima	γ Vir	166, 167
d W	Procyon	α CMi	135, **152**, 153
R	Proxima Centauri	(Cen)	199, **200**
	Rana	β Eri	157
	Ras Algethi	α Her	177
	Ras Alhague	α Oph	185
	Ras Elased Australis	ε Leo	165
	Ras Elased Borealis	μ Leo	165
	Reda	γ Aql	189
	Regulus	α Leo	161, 164, 165
	Rigel	β Ori	135, 148, 149
	Rotanev	β Del	189
	Rutilicus	β Her	177
	Sabik	η Oph	185
	Sadalachbia	γ Aqr	129
	Sadalmelek	α Aqr	129
	Sadalsud	β Aqr	129
	Sadir	γ Cyg	181
	Saiph	κ Ori	149
	Sarin	δ Her	177
	Sceptrum	53 Eri	157
v G	Scheat	β Peg	124, 125
	Schedir	α Cas	111
	Segin	ε Cas	111
	Sham	α Sge	189
	Shaula	λ Sco	191
v	Sheliak	β Lyr	177, **178**, 179
	Sheratan	β Ari	127
d W	Sirius	α CMa	135, **158**, 159
	Sirrah	α And	119, 121, 125
	Skat	δ Aqr	129
	Spica	α Vir	161, 166, 167
	Subra	o Leo	165
	Sulaphat	γ Lyr	177
	Svalocin	α Del	189
	Tabit	π₃ Ori	149
	Taygeta	19 Tau	144
	Theemin	v₂ Eri	157
	Thuban	α Dra	108, 109
d	Toliman	α Cen	161, 197, 199, **200**
d	Trapez	ϑ Ori	**150**, **151**
	Tureis	ι Car	203
	Unuk Elhaia	α Ser	185
W	Van Maanen's Star	(Psc)	126, 127
	Vega	α Lyr	173, 176, 177
	Vindemiatrix	ε Vir	161, 167
	Wezen	δ CMa	159
	Yed Posterior	ε Oph	185
	Yed Prior	δ Oph	185
	Zaurak	γ Eri	157
	Zavijah	β Vir	167
	Zibal	ζ Eri	157
	Zosma	δ Leo	165
	Zuben el Akrab	γ Lib	191
d	Zuben el Genubi	α Lib	**190**, 191
	Zuben el Schemali	β Lib	191

Stars denoted only by letters or numbers

type	designation	abbreviation	page
d	Beta Monocerotis	β Mon	153, **154**
d	Beta Tucanae	β Tuc	**210**, 211
d	Gamma Delphini	γ Del	**188**, 189
d	Gamma Velorum	γ Vel	**202**, 203
v G	Delta Cephei	δ Cep	110, 111
v G	Epsilon Aurigae	ε Aur	138, 139
	Epsilon Eridani	ε Eri	156
d	Epsilon Lyrae	ε Lyr	176, **177**
d	Zeta Aquarii	ζ Aqr	**128**, 129
d	Zeta Cancri	ζ Cnc	**140**, 141
d	Zeta Piscium	ζ Psc	126, 127
v	Eta Aquilae	η Aql	**188**, 189
v	Eta Carinae	η Car	**204**, 205

type	designation	abbreviation	page
d	Iota Triaguli	ι Tri	**120**
v	Lambda Tauri	λ Tau	**142**, 143
d W R	Omicron 2 Eridani	o₂ Eri	**156**, **157**
v	Rho Cassiopeiae	ρ Cas	110, 111
	Sigma Octantis	σ Oct	212, 213
	Tau Ceti	τ Cet	131
v	Chi Cygni	χ Cyg	**180**, 181
	AE Aurigae	AE Aur	**139**
v G	L₂ Puppis	L₂ Pup	158, **159**
	NP 0532 (pulsar in M 1)	(Tau)	146
v G	R Aquarii	R Aqr	128, **129**
	R Coronae Borealis	R CrB	**174**, 175
v G	R Hydrae	R Hya	170
v G	VV Cephei	VV Cep	110, 111
d	61 Cygni	61 Cyg	**182**
d	70 Ophiuchi	70 Oph	**184**

NOVAE, REMNANTS OF SUPERNOVAE

designation (year of outburst)	name	constellation	page
N 1901	Nova Persei	Per	**136**
SN 1054	Crab Nebula NGC 1952 — M1	Tau	143, 146, **147**
SN 1572	Tycho's Star	Cas	110, 111
SN 1604	Kepler's Star	Oph	185
SN 1680 ?	Cassiopeia A	Cas	**111**
SN 1987 A	(in LMC)	Dor	**208**

OPEN CLUSTERS

designation in NGC or IC catalogues	designation in Messier's catalogue, name	constellation	page
NGC 869	h Persei	Per	119, 136, **137**
NGC 884	Chi Persei	Per	119, 136, **137**
NGC 1039	M34	Per	136, **137**
NGC 1912	M38	Aur	138, 139
NGC 1960	M36	Aur	138, 139
NGC 2099	M37	Aur	138, **139**
NGC 2158		Gem	**139**
NGC 2168	M35	Gem	135, 138, **139**
NGC 2244		Mon	152, 153
NGC 2264	(the Christmas Tree)	Mon	154, **155**
NGC 2287	M41	CMa	158, **159**
NGC 2323	M50	Mon	153
NGC 2362		CMa	158, **159**
NGC 2422	M47	Pup	159
NGC 2437	M46	Pup	159
NGC 2447	M93	Pup	159
NGC 2477		Pup	158, **159**
NGC 2516		Car	202, **203**
NGC 2548	M48	Hya	168, **169**
NGC 2632	M44 Praesepe	Cnc	135, 140, **141**
NGC 2682	M67	Cnc	140, 141
NGC 3532		Car	202, **203**
IC 4725	M25	Sgr	192, 193
NGC 4755	(the Jewel Box)	Cru	198, **199**
IC 4756		Oph	185
NGC 6231		Sco	**191**
NGC 6405	M6	Sco	**191**
NGC 6475	M7	Sco	**191**
NGC 6494	M23	Sgr	192, 193
NGC 6530		Sgr	194, **195**
NGC 6531	M21	Sgr	194
NGC 6611	M16	Ser	185, 186, **187**
NGC 6705	M11	Sct	188, **189**
NGC 6709		Aql	**189**
NGC 7092	M39	Cyg	**181**
NGC 7654	M52	Cas	110, **111**
	Alpha Persei	Per	136, 137
	Hyades	Tau	135, 142, **143**
	M24	Sgr	192, **193**
	M45—the Pleiades	Tau	135, **144**, **145**
Collinder 399	(the Coathanger)	Vul	**181**

GLOBULAR CLUSTERS

designation in NGC catalogue	designation in Messier's catalogue, name	constellation	page
NGC 104	47 Tucanae	Tuc	210, **211**
NGC 2419		Lyn	140, **141**
NGC 5199	(Omega Centauri)	Cen	161, 197, 199, 200, **201**
NGC 5272	M3	CVn	116, **117**
NGC 5897		Sco	191
NGC 5904	M5	Ser	185, **186**
NGC 6093	M80	Sco	191
NGC 6121	M4	Sco	190, **191**
NGC 6144		Sco	**191**
NGC 6205	M13	Her	173, 176, **177**
NGC 6218	M12	Oph	185
NGC 6254	M10	Oph	184, **185**
NGC 6273	M19	Oph	185
NGC 6333	M9	Oph	185
NGC 6341	M92	Her	176, 177
NGC 6397		Ara	212, **213**
NGC 6402	M14	Oph	185
NGC 6626	M28	Sgr	193
NGC 6656	M22	Sgr	192, **193**
NGC 6752		Pav	212, **213**
NGC 6779	M56	Lyr	177
NGC 6809	M55	Sgr	193
NGC 6838	M71	Sge	188, **189**
NGC 6981	M72	Aqr	129
NGC 7078	M15	Peg	124, 125
NGC 7089	M2	Aqr	128, 129
NGC 7099	M30	Cap	129

PLANETARY NEBULAE

designation in NGC catalogue	designation in Messier's catalogue, name	constellation	page
NGC 650	M76	Per	136, **137**
NGC 2392	(the Eskimo)	Gem	138, **139**
NGC 3132		Ant, Vel	202, **203**
NGC 3242		Hya	168, **169**
NGC 3587	M97 (the Owl Nebula)	UMa	**113**
NGC 6543		Dra	108, **109**
NGC 6720	M57 (the Ring Nebula)	Lyr	177, 178, **179**
NGC 6781		Aql	**189**
NGC 6853	M27 (the Dumbbell Nebula)	Vul	180, **181**
NGC 7009	(Saturn)	Aqr	128, **129**
NGC 7293	(Helix)	Aqr	128, **129**
NGC 7662		And	120, **121**

DIFFUSE AND DARK NEBULAE

designation in NGC or IC catalogues	designation in Messier's catalogue, name	constellation	page
IC 405		Aur	**139**
IC 434		Ori	148, **149**
NGC 1499	(California)	Per	136, **137**
NGC 1976	M42 (Great Nebula in Orion)	Ori	149, 150, **151**
NGC 1977		Ori	150, **151**
NGC 1982	M43	Ori	150, **151**
NGC 2023		Ori	149
NGC 2024		Ori	148, **149**
NGC 2070	(the Tarantula Nebula)	Dor	207, **208, 209**
NGC 2237	(the Rosette Nebula)	Mon	152, **153**
NGC 2261	(Hubble's Variable Nebula)	Mon	153, 154, **155**
NGC 2264	(the Cone Nebula)	Mon	153, 154, **155**
NGC 3372	(η Carinae Nebula)	Car	203, 204, **205**
IC 4604	(ρ Ophiuchi Nebula)	Oph	**191**
IC 4605		Sco	**191**
IC 4606		Sco	**191**
IC 5067	(the Pelican Nebula)	Cyg	182, **183**
NGC 6188		Ara	212, **213**
NGC 6514	M20 (the Trifid Nebula)	Sgr	193, 194, **195**
NGC 6523	M8 (the Lagoon Nebula)	Sgr	193, 194, **195**
NGC 6611	M16 (the Eagle Nebula) (the Star-Queen Nebula)	Ser	185, 186, **187**
NGC 6618	M17 (the Omega or Swan Nebula)	Sgr	**193**
NGC 6960	Veil (Cirrus) Nebulae	Cyg	181, 182, **183**
NGC 6992—5	Veil (Cirrus) Nebulae	Cyg	181, 182, **183**
NGC 7000	(the North America Nebula)	Cyg	181, 182, **183**
NGC 7635	(the Bubble Nebula)	Cas	110, **111**
B 33	dark nebula (the Horsehead Nebula)	Ori	148, **149**
	dark nebulae in Ophiuchus	Oph	**185**
	the Coalsack dark nebula	Cen, Cru	197, 198, **199**

GALAXIES

L — member of the Local Group of Galaxies

designation in NGC or IC catalogues	designation in Messier's catalogue, name	constellation	page
NGC 55		Scl	130, **131**
L NGC 147		Cas	110, 111, 121, 122, **123**
L NGC 185		Cas	110, 111, 121, **122**
L NGC 205		And	122, **123**
L NGC 221	M32	And	122, **123**
L NGC 224	M31 (the Andromeda Galaxy)	And	119, 121, 122, **123**
NGC 253		Scl	130, **131**
NGC 520		Psc	127
L NGC 598	M33	Tri	120, **121**
NGC 628	M74	Psc	127
NGC 891		And	120, **121**
NGC 1068	M77	Cet	130, **131**
NGC 1232		Eri	156, **157**
NGC 1275	(Perseus A)	Per	136, **137**
NGC 1300		Eri	156, **157**
NGC 1365		For	132, **133**
NGC 1398		For	132, **133**
NGC 2403		Cam	108, **109**
NGC 2523		Cam	108, **109**
IC 2574		UMa	114
NGC 2623		Cnc	**141**
NGC 2976		UMa	114
NGC 3031	M81	UMa	113, 114, **115**
NGC 3034	M82	UMa	113, 114, **115**
NGC 3077		UMa	114
NGC 3081		Hya	169
NGC 3115		Sex	164, **165**
NGC 3351	M95	Leo	164, **165**
NGC 3368	M96	Leo	164, **165**
NGC 3623	M65	Leo	164, **165**
NGC 3627	M66	Leo	164, **165**
NGC 4038/39		Crv	168, **169**
NGC 4374	M84	Vir	166, **167**
NGC 4406	M86	Vir	166, **167**
NGC 4486	M87	Vir	166, **167**
NGC 4565		Com	162, **163**
NGC 4594	M104 (the Sombrero Galaxy)	Vir	166, **167**
NGC 4736	M94	CVn	116, **117**
NGC 4826	M64	Com	162, **163**
NGC 4889		Com	162, **163**
NGC 5128	(Centaurus A)	Cen	199, 200, **201**
NGC 5194	M51 (the Whirlpool Galaxy)	CVn	116, **117**

231

CLUSTERS OF GALAXIES

RADIO SOURCES

X-RAY SOURCES

GENERAL INDEX